BLIGHTY OR BUST

BLIGHTY OR BUST

The daring 2,000-mile escape of WWII prisoner of war, Raymond Bailey, in his own words

Raymond Bailey

Edited by David Wilkins

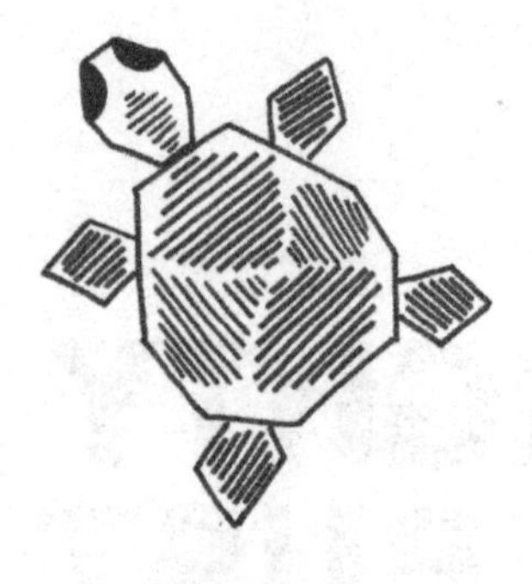

First published 2024

Tartaruga Books
tartaruga.books@icloud.com

British Library Cataloguing in Publication Data.
A catalogue record for this book is available from the British Library.
ISBN 978-1-83952-793-7

Design, typesetting and origination by Tartaruga Books
Cover design by Jim Pollard
Published by Tartaruga Books and under licence by Brown Dog Books

Printed and bound in the UK.

This book is printed on FSC® certified paper

feedback@blightyorbust.com

The publisher and editor of Blighty or Bust are extremely grateful to Raymond Bailey's closest living relative, Pamela Roy, for granting permission to reproduce Raymond's original manuscript in full.
Pamela recognises that Raymond's lengthy account of his experiences, written when he was such a young man, was a rare achievement. She shares our belief that the work deserves the widest possible audience.

BLIGHTY OR BUST: a true story of the Second World War

Preliminary Note for Readers

In the autumn of 2018, a cardboard box containing around twenty old notebooks, plus various assorted photos, newspaper cuttings, maps and letters was sold to a private buyer at a rural auction saleroom in north west England.

A year later, the box and its contents had been put up for auction twice more and by a slice of luck had come into the possession of David Wilkins, editor of this book. The notebooks turned out to contain an 80,000 word, hand-written account by a British soldier of his escape from a prisoner-of-war column in northern France in 1940. The 21 year-old soldier had been captured alongside 25,000 other British and French troops at the militarily disastrous Battle of St. Valery.

After his escape the soldier made a perilous journey through France and Spain, ending eventually at the British territory of Gibraltar, 2,000 miles from his starting point. From Gibraltar he was able to travel home by sea. The soldier's several months on the road, mostly spent travelling alone, required tremendous courage and physical endurance. Arguably though, his most important inherent asset was his unshakeable belief that eventually, somehow, some way or other, everything would turn out alright

Very soon after his arrival back in Britain, the young soldier began writing an account of his epic experience. The exact date he started writing is unknown but it appears to have been early in 1941. The task seems to have been completed sometime in 1942, when he was 23 years old. Research suggests that this may make the author the youngest British soldier of the Second World War to have written a book-length memoir of his experiences – and now of course, the youngest to have his memoir published. It is probable too that his memoir is also the earliest to have been written by any British soldier at all. For these reasons it is a unique and important document.

The section, The Story Behind The Book, on page 261 explores the history of the original manuscript in more detail and seeks to understand how such an engaging and lucid narrative could have been written by so young and inexperienced a writer, especially given the difficult circumstances under which he was forced to write. This same section also includes a description of the editing process. This description explains the changes that were necessary to make the original manuscript accessible to a modern readership without interfering with the soldier's original words.

Around half of the chapters in the book are preceded by introductory notes. These notes provide a simplified outline of the military, political and social background to the writer's experiences in the chapter that follows. The aim is to enable even those who know little about World War II to better understand the events that are being described. These introductory notes can easily be skipped by readers who are already knowledgeable about the period and the circumstances. Further interesting background information is included in the editor's endnotes to the book, as are the sources for the factual content and the quotations. These endnotes are indicated by superscript numerals in the text.

Everything else is the soldier's own story.

Contents

The Story behind the Book

APPENDICES

Dunstable Borough Gazette and Luton Journal

FRIDAY, DECEMBER 13, 1940

No. 3043

Glass & China and Xmas Gifts
SEE OUR WINDOWS
FOR
SPECIAL DISPLAY
DURRANT'S
48, HIGH ST. NORTH

CHRISTMAS PRESENTS
AN EXCELLENT CHOICE AT KEENEST PRICES
F. MONK & SON

DUNSTABLE SOLDIER'S ESCAPE FROM NAZIS

FREEDOM AFTER MONTHS OF PRIVATION

Quick Wits Overcame "Spots Of Bother"

MESSERSCHMITT HELP FOR SPITFIRE FUND

Enemy Plane On View In Grove House Gardens

DUNSTABLE HELP PLEDGED IN WAR WEAPONS WEEK

Local Total Passes £200,000 In Record Week

WOMAN "ALL IN FLAMES"

Dies In Hospital At Bedford

SAILOR HAD TO GIVE

He Saw Spitfire Down Bomber

HEAVIER FINES IN FUTURE

Dunstable Cyclists' Offences

WANTS TO HELP BRAVE SCOUT

Toddington Woman Sends Money

Prologue

On December 13th 1940, Private Raymond Bailey was headline news on the front page of his local newspaper, the *Dunstable Borough Gazette*:

> **DUNSTABLE SOLDIER'S ESCAPE FROM NAZIS**
>
> Quick Wits Overcame "Spots Of Bother"
>
> When the full story of a young Dunstable soldier's escape from his German guards can be told – and there are obvious reasons why his method of escape cannot be described in detail now – it will be a story of courage and determination, of the never-say-die spirit, which overcame apparently insuperable obstacles, of hunger and privations bravely borne, but rewarded at last by freedom...
>
> ...It was in June of this year that Pte. Bailey was taken prisoner but the thrilling story of his escape can only be told when those who aided him to regain his liberty are no longer within reach of Nazi vengeance. Details of his wanderings, of illness brought on by privations – there was one period when he had no food for five days – and of his own quick-wittedness in avoiding recapture on numerous occasions, must await happier times before they can be told with safety.

That long-ago local journalist could not have imagined that the wait would be more than eighty years – but here at last, in his own words, is Raymond Bailey's dramatic and engaging story. This book is offered as a tribute to Ray, and to the millions like him who did what needed to be done. We are still in their debt.

Who was Raymond Bailey?

Raymond Bailey, known to his family and friends as Ray, was born on January 26th 1919 in Chester-le-Street, County Durham. He was the elder of two sons born to Margaret and William Bailey. William was still on post-First World War service with the Royal Navy at the time of Ray's birth but before and after the war he worked as a miner. At some point in Ray's childhood, for unknown reasons, the Bailey family uprooted and moved almost 250 miles south to live in Dunstable in Bedfordshire. After the relocation William found employment as a labourer at the Vauxhall Motor Works in nearby Luton. In due course Ray also went to work at Vauxhall, in his case on an apprenticeship as a lathe operator. It is not possible to know for sure but the greatest likelihood is that, like almost all working class youngsters at that time, Ray left school and started work at the age of fourteen. If so, that would have been in 1934.[1]

Like the majority of other baby boys born in Britain at the end of the First World War, it was Ray's destiny to fight in the Second World War. Ray was among the first wave of men called up almost immediately after Britain declared war on Germany in September 1939. He undertook his initial basic training with the Middlesex Regiment, a machine gun regiment based at Mill Hill Barracks in north-west London. After around three months there, Ray and a group of other new recruits were chosen for transfer. They were sent off to boost the numbers of a small territorial (i.e. voluntary, part-time) regiment, Princess Louise's Kensington Regiment, for which the Middlesex Regiment was the "parent" regiment. The Kensingtons, as they were generally known, were also a machine gun regiment. They had recently been "embodied" [mobilised] and were preparing for a full-time role in the war.

In May 1940, not much more than eight months after Ray's call up, the 1st Battalion, Kensington Regiment was deployed to France as part of the British Expeditionary Force (BEF). The BEF's intended role was to bolster the defensive strength of the French army. It was fully understood throughout Europe that it was only a matter of time before the German army marched on France.

As it happened, the German offensive began less than four weeks after Ray's unit had arrived in France. In consequence, Ray and hundreds of thousands of other young, inexperienced soldiers, French and British, suddenly found themselves pitched into what was to be some of the bloodiest fighting of the entire war. It was a rearguard action from the start. Though they gave spirited and often heroic battle, the French and British armies in northern France were no real match for the marauding German forces who were greater in number, better trained, better equipped and using a terrifying new tactic, Blitzkrieg ("Lightning War"). For the French and British, it was a military calamity. Relentlessly, day after day, mile by mile, the Allied forces were driven backwards towards the Channel coast.

For the majority who survived this fighting retreat, the result was the greatest "disaster into triumph" episode in military history. In the space of just nine days, between May 26th and June 4th 1940, almost 350,000 British and Allied soldiers were successfully evacuated by sea from Dunkirk, many of them by the famous armada of "Little Ships". Most of the men who made it home by this route went on to fight another day. Unfortunately the men of the 51st Division – the division of which Ray's unit was a part – were not among that number. At the time of the Dunkirk evacuations, the 51st was still some way inland, offering stubborn resistance to the German invaders. Soon they also became cut off, not only from Dunkirk but also from Le Havre and Cherbourg where rescue by sea might still have been possible. The odds were stacked against them but the men of the 51st Division had no option. They had to fight on.

In the second week of June, harried by overwhelming German forces, the 51st found itself pinned down in the small, normally quiet and picturesque, fishing port of St Valery-en-Caux, situated between Dieppe and Le Havre. For these Allied soldiers, St Valery was quite literally the end of the road. They were soon almost completely surrounded by German troops who shelled and bombed the now-blazing town and the thousands of British and French soldiers trapped in its narrow streets. There was nowhere for the Allied troops to go in any direction on land – and German artillery, tanks and machine gunners held commanding positions on the cliffs overlooking the beach and the harbour. It was a perilous and desperate situation. An attempted "Dunkirk-style" evacuation by sea seemed initially to be a possibility but in the event only a handful of vessels made it anywhere near the shoreline in the vicinity of St Valery, and only a tiny fraction of the trapped men managed to board them.

The decision-making that underpinned the failure to mount an effective evacuation by sea remains contentious to the present day. Whatever was happening behind the scenes however, it gradually became clear to senior officers on the ground that there was to be no seaborne salvation for the men of the 51st Division. After that, the outcome was inevitable.

On June 12th, the day after most of the Allied troops had arrived at St Valery, first the French commanders and then the British realised they had no alternative but to surrender. It is estimated that between 25,000 and 46,000 Allied troops were forced to lay down their arms and give themselves up for capture.[2]

Estimates vary but it is generally accepted that around 10,000 of those taken prisoner were British. From the moment they first stood unarmed in front of their German captors, virtually all of those British soldiers, including around 270 men of the Kensington Regiment, were doomed to endure five, long, weary years in German prisoner of war camps, mostly in occupied Poland.[3] They would not be liberated until the fall of Germany in May 1945.

But this was not to be the fate of Pte Raymond Bailey. In early December 1940, not much more than a year after he left home to join the army and only six months since he had been captured at St Valery, Ray was to be found back home in Dunstable, sitting down to tea with his mum and dad.

Part One

CALLED UP!

Chapter 1: Becoming a soldier

INTRODUCTORY NOTE

There is no need to describe here the turbulent political events in Europe that led up to the Second World War. Suffice to say that by the time Germany invaded Poland on September 1st 1939, the second major war of the twentieth century had seemed all but inevitable for some time. On September 3rd, Great Britain and France, honouring treaty agreements with Poland, declared war on Germany.

On that same day, the National Service (Armed Forces) Act 1939 was rushed through Parliament. This legislation made all able-bodied men aged between 18 and 41 liable for conscription into the armed forces from October 21st onwards. An earlier, pre-emptive Act of Parliament passed in April 1939, had already made provision that men aged between 20 and 22 could be called up more quickly if necessary. Ray Bailey, who had turned twenty in January 1939, fell into this category. He was therefore among the earliest conscripts required to report for military service.

Immediately prior to the declaration of the war, the number of soldiers in the regular army was around 220,000. There were a further 175,000 men in the Army Reserve (former regular army personnel now back in civilian life). These reservists, as they were called, were already subject to call-up in the event of an emergency. A further 450,000 men served as volunteers in the Territorial Army and were also available for more or less immediate assimilation into the regular army. These three groups together gave the British Army a fighting strength of approximately 850,000 men.

By the end of 1939, the addition of conscripts and early volunteers had brought this number up to around 1.1 million. This means that, including returning reservists and Territorial Army men as well as conscripts and volunteers, around 900,000 new full-time soldiers reported to their regiments in the autumn and winter of 1939. Turning these men into an effective fighting force in a very short time was a huge challenge. This was most especially the case for conscripts like Ray of course. Few of these men would have thought of joining the army without conscription – and many would have thought themselves not cut out for the military life. Most would have had jobs and future plans that were now disrupted indefinitely. And of course, they were very young. Ray's youth and inexperience are both important factors in his story.

This opening chapter and the chapter that follows it, are noticeably more anecdotal than the rest of Ray Bailey's story. It is as if Ray originally conceived his memoir as a novice soldier's light-hearted reflection on his new life – but then realised as he wrote, that such a nonchalant standpoint could not be maintained once the war began in earnest. In Chapter 3, when the regiment is sent to France, Ray gradually shifts from being a semi-detached observer of the absurdities of military life to being a reporter of real events, emotions and experiences. Despite their rather flippant, juvenile tone however, these first two chapters are important in giving us a sense of Ray's personality and his attitude to life.

But these are early days. Ray's emergence as a brave and resourceful young man whose regiment should be proud of him lies some way in the future. On the opening day of his story we find Ray in civilian clothes, seated on a train. He is travelling to the base in North London, where his basic training will begin. He is nervous...

Becoming a soldier

The train to Mill Hill was a slow one, not that I really minded for it allowed me time to think. It was October 16th 1939 and I was going to join the army.[4] I had no idea of what the army was like and visualised the most dreadful ordeals ahead of me.

Outside the barrack gates at Mill Hill I met a regimental policeman who showed me into the barracks. He led me across the square to the gymnasium which was being used to receive recruits. Here I met more young men who had just been called up. We had a medical examination and went over to a table where a lance corporal wrote down a lot of particulars.

We were split into squads and marched to our barrack rooms. After dinner, which I thought was pretty foul, we went round to the quartermaster's store where we were issued with kit. For some reason or other we did not get our battledress until the next day so we had to stay in that night. When we did get it, I found mine had no buttons on the trousers. It took me a whole day to borrow enough buttons – and a whole evening to sew them on.

Our first few days of training consisted of foot-drill and of learning to march and salute. We were issued with rifles and had a lecture in the NAAFI[5] by Company Sergeant Major Stacey. He impressed upon us that although we were in uniform, we were only recruits and not soldiers. We were not to go around in battledress pretending we were heroes. "Because you're not!"

After the lecture, we were taught how to load and unload our rifles with dummy rounds. We were shown how to sight the rifle and the various positions to fire our rifles from. After this, our lives became one continuous programme of arms drill and physical training. Once we had mastered the rifle we were introduced to the Vickers machine gun. First we were acquainted with the names of the various parts and we learned to fire a few rounds on the thirty yard range. "To get the feel of the gun", as CSM Stacey would say, "and to prove the bullets come out of the muzzle end, where they can't hurt you – so no need to be afraid of it." After this came E.G.D. – elementary gun drill – which consisted of nothing but mounting and unmounting the gun on the barrack square, correctly and in the shortest possible time. This was the cause of much sweat, strained tempers and busted buttons.

Gas sentry duty was our chief bogey. The idea was to patrol the barracks observing the yellow gas detectors that were placed at intervals. In order to carry out these simple duties, we were harnessed in equipment: steel helmet, rifle and bayonet, a huge anti-gas cape, mittens, respirator, whistle, rattle and eye shields. Thus attired, a pair of us would perambulate round the barracks in the dead of night looking like a decontamination squad.

After the months in Recruit Company, we were transferred to No. 2 Machine Gun Company in order to complete our training.[6] Here I met Humphries. He came from Dagenham. The next time I met him was in a German prison camp, where he borrowed my razor.

Our training at Mill Hill was terminated by a trip to Bisley where we fired a course.[7] During the short time that followed we did many route marches. Even route marches in those days were rather happy affairs. We would swing along straining our lungs to see who could sing the loudest. Always we would sing our little ditty:[8]

"Why don't they send away the Old Diehards?
Why don't they send away the boys?
Every man in the regiment
Is willing to do or die – I don't think!
Why don't they send away the Old Diehards?
They're second to the navy on the sea
If it wasn't for the Old Diehards
Where would England be?"

...and that question was answered by a rude reply from the rear. But I often thought as I marched along, maybe one day they will send away the Old Diehards. And one day they did.

In late November, we were sent on a draft [permanently transferred] to the 1st Kensingtons.* There were about thirty of us. We had blanco-ed our equipment and cleaned the brasses as it was broadly hinted that this was customary in the regiment we were going to.[9] A train from Paddington took us to Taunton where we changed on to a local for Ilminster in Somerset. This train travelled very slowly and stopped at every station but it finally got us there. We were marched up the hill to the village and were taken to the HQ Company billet, the "Shirt Factory".[10] Everything seemed pretty well organised. Tea was ready when we arrived and all we had to do was sit down and eat it. During the meal we were issued with Kensington cap badges.[11]

We soon got down to the routine in the Kensingtons and gradually the draft that had arrived from Mill Hill was dispersed among the Machine Gun Company until only three or four of us remained in HQ. They were Carter, Francis, Elma and myself. We all slept on the top floor of the Shirt Factory, which was very convenient. It took the Orderly Sergeant some time to reach the top floor and I could always have an extra lie in bed at reveille. That was one of my weaknesses.

It was here I met John Suttle – "Gus" he was nicknamed – and we became great friends. Our favourite outing was a Saturday afternoon hitch-hike to Taunton. It was twelve miles away and out of bounds without a pass but little things like that did not worry us in the least. Besides this, the M.T. [motor transport unit] ran an unofficial taxi service to Taunton and you could be there in no time at all by the simple process of passing round the hat.

In HQ, we would start the day with a "gargle parade" before breakfast and woe betide anyone who tried to dodge it.[12] At eight

---

* This is an important moment for Ray. The "1st Kensingtons" are the 1st Battalion Princess Louise's Kensington Regiment. This regiment was a small territorial outfit, recently designated as a specialist machine gun regiment, for which the Middlesex Regiment was the "parent regiment". Ray would remain with the 1st Kensingtons for the duration of his service.

o'clock we would parade under Company Sergeant Major Butler. He would start with a rifle inspection. Sometimes I managed to scrape through this only to be hauled over the coals for some silly little mistake in arms drill. The result was that I would be sorted out along with a few others into what CSM Butler called his "awkward squad" because, he said, we spoiled his parade. This was generally followed by a few fatigues.[13] These were usually of the cookhouse variety – but we often skipped them and had a quite a long break during which we rushed across the square, crowding into Mary's Café for a cup of tea and a doughnut.

I was generally a "spare man". Probably they thought I wasn't capable of being anything else.[14] On December 11th, when we went on an exercise, Gus and I were turned overnight into stretcher bearers. We paraded outside the Medical Officer's office the night before to collect our stretcher and receive the usual detailed instructions. These were that we would go with "A" Company, joining them outside the Sergeant's Mess at 0530 hours.

Five thirty came and went, and we were still snoring loudly in bed. We awoke about ten past six. Rolling up our blankets and harnessing ourselves into battle order, we grabbed the stretcher and hurried off to the appointed meeting place, kidding ourselves it was 6:30 and not 5:30 we were supposed to meet them. Of course, there were no "A" Company trucks in sight when we got there. We returned to the billet where – after getting a piece of the Sergeant Major's mind – we went on the exercise with our own HQ Company.

It was still dark when we piled into the back of an overloaded 30 cwt lorry and headed off for Dorsetshire. We travelled for some time and the morning wore on. Convoy speeds are never fast at the best of times. We passed other troops and from the back of our truck, we laughed at the infantry who had to march. The company harboured at Melbury Deer Park and here we established our Regimental Aid Post. Being only a mock war though, we had no stretcher cases to deal with – not that we could have dealt with them if we had. We therefore had a lot of spare time. I'm quite unashamed to admit that we spent that time in making rabbit snares – but I am ashamed to admit we didn't catch a single rabbit.

We spent the night in the open. It was the first time that I had ever slept out at night. The majority of the men had booked up sleeping accommodation in the trucks but Gus and I being only spare men and returning late from a hunting expedition, had to do the best we could in the open. Using our stretchers as beds, we rigged up a bivouac affair with a tarpaulin sheet from one of the trucks. Of course, both ends of our tent were open but we succeeded in blocking one end with our packs and haversacks. The other end we left open. Our feet stuck out of it anyway. We had just nicely settled down for the night when we heard someone stumbling about outside in the darkness. It was the Medical Officer. "Do you want any beer?" he asked.

That shook us. It was an unusual question to be asked by an officer in the middle of the night. Not knowing what to say we simply answered, "Yes!"

"How many are there of you?"

"Two," answered Gus.

Two bottles of beer were shoved into the tent. We regarded this unexpected gift for a full minute then burst out laughing. What a lovely war it was!

Part Two

THREE BATTLES

The ruins of St Valery after the battle, June 1940.

Chapter 2: To France

INTRODUCTORY NOTE

In this coming chapter, the 1st Battalion Kensington Regiment is ordered to France. It is however impossible to make sense of what happens to them there, without some preliminary explanation here. The difficulty for readers is that, on its arrival, the 1st Kensington Battalion separates into two parts. The majority of the battalion – probably around three quarters or more of its strength (about 600-700 men) – heads off to join the British Expeditionary Force (BEF) on the Franco-Belgian border. Ray however, is allocated to the Kensingtons' reinforcement company which is left behind at a base camp in Rouen, not far inland from Le Havre where the battalion disembarked. Because of his separation from the main body of the battalion, Ray is not in a position to know what is happening in the situation as a whole. This introductory note draws on the Kensington Regiment's regimental history to put the pieces together.

The BEF and the "Phoney War"

After Britain and France declared war on Germany on September 3rd 1939, the British government immediately ordered that troops be sent to France. Britain's objective was to assist its ally in defending against the German invasion which was expected imminently. It was believed that the main thrust of the German attack on France would occur along that stretch of the Franco-Belgian border nearest the Channel coast. The great majority of the British Expeditionary Force was therefore stationed in that area.

As it happened, the German attack on France did not occur anything like as soon as was anticipated. For all sides, the declaration of war was followed by eight months of sitting tight and waiting for something to happen. This period of waiting soon became popularly known in Britain, as the "Phoney War". In fact, Germany had originally planned, as Britain and France expected, to invade in the autumn of 1939 but a long spell of poor weather caused delays and it gradually became clear to the German High Command that there was no alternative but to wait until the spring of 1940.

Deployment of the Kensingtons

As mentioned, on April 17th, a couple of days after its arrival in France, the main body of the 1st Kensingtons travelled to Armentières near the Belgian border. Their orders were to join the 5th Division of the BEF. Ray was not among this group. The First Line Reinforcement Company, the small unit of the Kensingtons to which he had been allocated, was not needed and had been left behind at Rouvrey Camp, a British base camp near Rouen. They would be called for as and when required.

On the day the main body of the Kensingtons arrived in Armentières, their commanding officer, Lt. Col. F. G. Parker, was informed that plans had already changed and his battalion was now to become part of the 51st (Highland) Division instead of the 5th Division. The 51st (Highland) Division had already been redeployed to the Saar region of France, on the border between France and Germany, over 250 miles south-east of Armentières.

Accordingly, a week later, the men of the 1st Kensingtons left Armentières and began their journey to the Saar region to meet up with their new comrades-in-arms. As the name implies, the nine infantry battalions that made up the bulk of the 51st (Highland) Division all came from the Scottish Highlands and Islands.[15] The Kensingtons were to be one of two machine gun battalions attached to the division. (The other was the 7th Battalion, Royal Northumberland Fusiliers). Their job in battle was to provide covering fire for the Scottish infantrymen who would help the French troops to patrol the German border.

The Kensingtons arrived in Metz, the principal city in the Saar region, in the early hours of April 28th. Back at the base camp in Rouen, Ray and the others in the reinforcement company had no way of knowing that their fellow Kensingtons had been relocated away from the Belgian border.

Why were these British troops sent to the Saar region?

In the years after the First World War, in north-eastern and eastern France, along its 280 mile border with Germany, the French government had built a formidable line of concrete fortifications known as the Maginot Line. The aim of the the fortifications, which lay between three and six miles (5 – 10 kilometres) inside France, was to provide a protective barrier for French forces defending French territory. It was hoped that this defensive line would make it permanently difficult, if not impossible, for Germany to invade along the Franco-German border.[16] One section of the Maginot Line passed through the Saar region, a coal mining area that was of historic dispute between France and Germany. In this small localised area, regular skirmishing had been going on between the two nations since the autumn of 1939.*

The troops positioned along the Maginot Line had been almost entirely French from the outset but the British High Command had decided that the small scale fighting there was an ideal setting to give British forces, particularly territorial forces, like the Highland and Islands men, a first taste of military action. Sending British soldiers to the Saar also actively demonstrated solidarity with the French, which was important politically. The 51st was the first full British division to be sent to the region. The 51st Division was deployed in one particular area between two forests, Heydwald and Forêt de Bouzonville, with French troops on either side. This deployment inevitably meant there would be direct engagement between the men of the 51st and the German forces raiding from over the border.

On their arrival in the Saar, the Kensingtons sent orders for a group

---

* Shortly after its declaration of war with Germany in September 1939, France had launched an unsuccessful offensive to try and take German territory in the Saar region. The French troops had been been forced to withdraw after five weeks of fighting that had resulted in hundreds of casualties on each side. The ongoing military activity in the area – although on a much smaller scale to that of the previous year – traced its roots back to that earlier action.

of men from the First Line Reinforcements to join them.[17] Among those called for is Ray Bailey. It is clear from Ray's manuscript that neither he nor any of the others in the group have any idea where the rest of the battalion is now located and, by extension, have no idea where they themselves are now being sent. Their expectation must have been that their fellow Kensingtons were still somewhere along the Belgian border. Once it becomes clear that this is not the case, the reinforcement men are baffled. It is probable that few, if any, of them would have known about the sporadic fighting between the French and Germans in the Saar – and even if they had known of it, they would certainly not have expected that British troops would have been deployed to fight there.

At this time (late April / early May 1940), this relatively small conflict in the Saar is the only direct military engagement taking place between the Allied and German forces anywhere in France. Despite the storm clouds of all-out war that are rapidly darkening overhead, the rest of France is still quiet. The 1st Kensingtons therefore suddenly find themselves among only a very small minority of British soldiers to see action prior to the German invasion.

To France

We soon began to witness our unit's preparations. The battalion was ready to move, France being the destination. Gus and I became separated. He went to "D" Company. I went to First Line Reinforcements[18] under Captain Williamson whom I remembered well, for he gave me my first seven days jankers.[19]

Our transport was the first to go. The rest of the battalion followed a few days later. I shall never forget April 13th 1940, the day we marched out of Ilminster on our way to France. How very different from the day we marched in. I think the whole village turned out to see us off – the Kensingtons were very well liked.[20] There were many waving hands and shouts of "Goodbye" and "Don't forget to write!" but only tender regrets and a few aching hearts were left to show that the Kensingtons had passed that way.

We went to Southampton by train where, after the usual wastes of time, we arrived at the docks. In one of the hangars, Sergeant Tobin gave us a demonstration on how to use the lifebelt. This put the wind up most of us. Each man was issued with a lifebelt as he went on board. Everyone claimed a cabin but we (the First Line Reinforcements) were shoved into the Ladies Saloon where we slept on the floor. It was an ex-LNER boat, the *Amsterdam*.[21]

Supper was Maconochie's, cold and straight from the tin.[22] I mean straight from the tin only in a sense for it was discovered that there were only two tin-openers! There were several hundred men at each meal – so there were two very hard-worked men on that boat. The convoy sailed about midnight but we were all snug down below – or as snug as we could be on the floor of the Ladies Saloon. We had just made ourselves comfortable when we were ordered on deck again to receive instructions on what we could and could not do.

I remember waking very early the next morning. The ship was rolling pretty badly. Looking out of a porthole I found that the wind had sprung up and the sea was rather rough. A long coastline lay ahead. Closing the porthole I concentrated on breakfast. It was Maconochie's again. I didn't eat all mine. Perhaps it was the excitement. Perhaps it was the boat. Or perhaps it was the Maconochie's itself. I don't know.

Soon we glided into the harbour at Le Havre. We were met by a tug manned by very noisy Frenchmen and tied up along the jetty. Clambering into full marching order we went on deck. Everywhere was a scene of activity. Hatches were opened and cargo was slung onshore. There was much hustle and bustle. But the troops onboard just waited and waited. I began to think we were forgotten.

After everything had quietened down and the jetty had assumed its normal appearance, a couple of Rail Transport Officers appeared. They had a conflab with our own officers and we were allowed to disembark. We fell in on the jetty and were marched down the road to a concrete hangar next to the railway station where we were allowed to take off our packs and rest. By now it was dinner time, so we had Maconochie's again. I was able to see Gus. We discussed France in particular, telling each other what we thought about it. We both thought the same.

I think this resting business lasted for a couple of hours during which we had our English money – those who had any – changed into French. How amazed we were to see the number of centime pieces we had to have to make a tanner[23] and the thick wad of notes we got for hardly anything at all. Eventually we were assembled and put into a very dilapidated train. Destination unknown. I did not think much of the French countryside. It seemed barren and was dotted with many tumbledown barns. We were to learn a lot more about these barns later on.

The train rattled on. Rumours went around – as rumours do – that we were going to the base at Rouen. Now Rouen, we knew, was by far the biggest town in that part of France, so we clapped our hands, thinking there would be no billeting on muddy farms for us. But our spirits fell when the train stopped at a tiny little station and we were told to get out. Thirty seconds later we were told to get back in. It was the wrong station…

Later we arrived at our destination but it was not Rouen. It was a small town, Yvetot. We thought ourselves lucky to have got a town at all but once more our jubilation was short-lived for our transport, which had come over a week before, collected us and dumped us at a miserable barn miles from anywhere. Our detachment was billeted by itself away from the rest of the battalion. HQ company was in a chateau a mile up the road – much to our regret, for we had to march there and back every meal-time.

I looked around our billet. It was a large barn, big enough to hold a regiment and had about two feet of straw on the floor. We stuffed up the holes in the walls for it was like a sieve. My comrades cursed their luck for they didn't like the place. I cursed mine for I was now separated from Gus. Then it rained for several days so we all cursed again. This barn was situated in the orchard of a little farm and to reach the main road it was necessary to wade through the muddiest farmyard it is possible to imagine.

Fortunately, we did not stay there for long as the main body of the battalion left Yvetot on April 17th and went to Armentières on the Belgian border to join up with the BEF. We (the First Line Reinforcements) left Yvetot soon after but ours was a destination unknown. The rumour again was that we were going to Rouen. Naturally, none of us believed it this time – until we saw Rouen out of the carriage windows. Very slowly the train entered Rouen Station but glided out the other end just as slowly. It finally stopped at Oissel about five miles further on. Here we got out and surveyed our dismal surroundings. It wasn't a station at all but a collection of railway sidings. There were detachments of troops everywhere of at least a dozen different regiments all lined up and ready to march off to the infantry base – which was back towards Rouen. This "going to Rouen" business was monotonous!

We marched off with them and that march proved to be one of the nastiest bits of exercise I'd had for some time. First the raucous voice of Sgt Jones started off with some crude barrack room song about four and twenty virgins who went to a ball at some place called Ballymore. We rattled along in our full marching order and "blanket rolled", breaking our necks to march faster than a famous regiment of light infantry who were just in front of us. The infantry seemed to know what was going on for they speeded up but we passed them on a hill where they all fell out for a five minute smoke rather than suffer the humiliation of being out-marched by a mechanised unit.[24]

We went over rough roads and moorland country until we arrived at a military camp only to discover that it was the wrong one. There appeared to be some misunderstanding so we sat down to rest while the officers fought it out among themselves. It had been a very hot day and, as if the gods had heard our cry for water, it began to rain – but they must have over-estimated our thirst for it began to rain harder and harder until it came down in a solid deluge. By the time we were nicely soaked to the skin a couple of trucks arrived and carted us off to the right camp. We were very hungry when we got there but enjoyed a supper of tea, corned beef and a packet of hard oatmeal biscuits.

Life at No. 1 Infantry Camp was tolerable and quite pleasant compared to the usual standard in France. I admit we were under canvas and it rained a good deal but we were quite comfortable. We did not stay long at Rouen. We never stayed long anywhere but I managed to have a good look round the town with Coombs and Gayler. On our way back to camp it was our habit to buy the *Paris Soir* from a woman who sold papers at the corner of the bridge and with the aid of a French/English dictionary, endeavour to translate it or at least, I did. Coombs could speak both French and German. Nor did I leave Rouen without doing seven days jankers.

So far the only guard we had ever done was the Motor Transport picket out in the middle of Watery Lane, Ilminster.[25] There, we had only Capt "Tubby" Milton to contend with and he always inspected the sentries in an umpteen horsepower Humber Snipe, which betrayed his presence whenever he was in it by the fact that it was always well down on the springs. Of a "pukka" guard, we had no idea, so we rehearsed it under Sgt Tobin who was to be guard commander.[26] The result was most amazing. The RSM, who I had had assumed would have a fit, actually proclaimed it was the best guard he had ever mounted. Of course, this went to our heads. We pranced up and down in front of the guard room like Grenadier Guards. I remember during the afternoon when I was doing my "two on", there seemed to be a million officers about. I was constantly marching up and down, stopping, turning to the front, saluting or presenting arms.

All this was very fatiguing so, in order to conserve my energy, I came up to the "present" and stayed there.[27] This proved very successful at first even with the subalterns who smiled to themselves – but suddenly a captain appeared. He saw the "present" and gave me a nasty look so I decided to discontinue the practice. I had been standing at ease for a few minutes when I realised that I had an audience. Several men in the detention room were crowded at the window, looking at me, mystified.

"Hey Joe!" I heard one shout to someone else in the room. "Have you seen this sentry outside? You should see him march up and down. When he turns he stamps his feet like a Prussian."

"Bet he's in a pukka mob," said another.

Somebody mentioned the Kensingtons. Then the owner of the loud voice shouted again, "Hey Joe! Do you know the Kensingtons?"

"Never 'eard of 'em," came the reply.

Once we had an air raid of the "tip-and-run" variety, a couple of bombs being dropped on the city. There was quite a lot of tracer about, plenty of "flaming onions" and a devil of a noise.[28] But that was all. It was nothing to write home about, even if you could.

At last the day arrived when the majority of us were sent to join the battalion which, to the best of our knowledge, was somewhere at the front.[29] Back we marched to Oissel where, to our disgust, we discovered we were to travel in horse boxes. We waited around the railway station for ages but were entertained by Pte King who made jokes and funny remarks from time to time. You could hear his cheery voice whenever anything went wrong, "You can't help laughing can yer?"

Finally we all clambered into the horseboxes. On the door it said "8 chevaux. 40 hommes." In our wagon there were thirty men but how the French could get forty in will forever be a mystery. As it was, we were overcrowded and sleeping was difficult. One would constantly hear groans as someone turned over and kicked someone else in the face. Once more Pte King came to the rescue and played us to sleep with *Jeepers, Creepers* on his trumpet.

When we awoke next morning the train had arrived at Arras. Alongside the railway were a number of large wooden tubs filled with water, so we were able to wash and shave. Breakfast was of corned beef and biscuits. This proved to be the usual menu for every meal during the journey, except of course when we had Maconochie's. The journey was dull and we had not the slightest idea where we were going. Our next stop was Lillers where the train was shoved into a siding. Here we stayed for a few hours at a "rest camp", an old warehouse where we had a hot meal. This time it was "soup" but made from Maconochie's.

Once back in our horseboxes there was much shunting about and we left the other troops who were travelling with us and evidently bound for the Belgian frontier and resumed our journey to some unknown destination. The train went back the way it had come then it turned south arousing our curiosity to a large degree. "Where are earth are we going?" everyone asked – but no-one seemed to know.

It was a monotonously slow train. It crawled along at such a speed that we could easily have got out and run along beside it. During the night it stopped at Laon where we got out to stretch our legs and in our best French, tried pumping the station staff as to where our train was going. An elderly guard drew a rough map of France on the ground with his stick and not only showed us where the train was going but where it had come from. He traced the entire journey with his stick and told us we were going to Metz.[30]

Chapter 3: Action on the Maginot Line and a withdrawal

INTRODUCTORY NOTE

German invasion of the Low Countries and France

Although Ray makes no reference to it, on May 10th 1940, the day after he and the other reinforcements arrived on the Saar Front to join the Kensingtons already there, the long-threatened German invasion of France finally began. Germany first attacked Holland, Belgium and Luxembourg, sweeping rapidly southwards toward Belgium's border with France. The main thrust of the German invasion reached the French border within a week by powering through the Ardennes region of Belgium, more than 100 miles (160 kilometres) east of where the BEF and the bulk of the French forces were concentrated.

This primary area of German attack was very thinly defended by comparison with the area where the Allies had expected the invasion to come. French military planners had believed that the steep hills and dense forest in the Ardennes made it more or less impossible that the Germans would attempt to enter France by that route. They had however, reckoned without the technical advances that Germany had made in respect of its tanks and armoured vehicles, not to mention the military superiority of its highly motivated and intensively trained soldiers.

Ray himself seems not to have grasped the full significance of what was happening in the wider situation. In the coming chapter, he describes German aircraft flying over the Saar in the early hours of May 10th as being on an "air-raid" and notes with relief that "the planes were not attacking us". The Kensington regimental history has no doubt what the planes were doing. It observes of this same incident, that this "large fleet of enemy bombers" was heading north-west to play its part in the invasion of Holland and Belgium.

Events on the Saar Front

It was never likely that Germany would make a serious attempt to invade over its own border with France because of the difficulties posed by the Maginot Line. Inevitably though, the events in northern France brought an escalation of activity on the Saar Front. On May 13th there was a noticeable increase in Germany artillery use[31] and on May 15th a full scale assault began. These happen to be the selfsame few days that Ray is pitched into active service for the first time. He is twenty one years-old and it is only a few months since he was an apprentice lathe operator at the Vauxhall Car Works in Luton. Like many of those around him, he is completely inexperienced as a soldier. He has a tough introduction and he needs to learn fast.

Action on the Maginot Line and a withdrawal

To cut a dreary journey short we did eventually arrive at Metz. Some trucks were awaiting our arrival and conveyed us to the other side of the town. Our barracks were once German cavalry barracks built when Metz was a German town. As it was, Metz still had quite a large German population and we were not allowed to go into the town itself without a special pass. This of course, was never granted. The boys were disappointed for they had seen some pretty girls on their way through.

We soon learned that the rest of our battalion was somewhere in front of the Maginot Line and on May 9th, about three days after our arrival in Metz a few of our trucks arrived to take us there. We chatted with the drivers, being quite pleased to meet comrades we had not seen since Ilminster – but they brought bad news. On May 5th, a German tommy gun had killed R.S.M. Frost. He was our first casualty.

We re-joined the battalion at Bibiche, which was then battalion headquarters. I shall never forget the ride there. We were crowded into 15 cwt trucks and taken over the worst, most bumpy, roads in the Moselle. Sometimes they took the wrong road and sometimes they very nearly left the road but somehow we arrived at Bibiche intact.

Bibiche was a hole. You must forgive me but that is the only way to describe it. It was a hole – a cesspool of mediaeval stink, consisting of broken down hovels and dung heaps. The billets had recently been occupied by French troops whose ideas were not very advanced in the way of sanitation. As soon as I arrived I started to look around for my pal, Gus. I found him busy at the back of his billet. It was washing day. He was boiling what appeared to be half his kit in a large iron pot. Greeting me, he proceeded to show me his billet – and the pigs in the sty next door.

Nearby a couple of men were burning some straw the French had left behind and which was full of live ammunition. The straw blazed furiously, the rounds exploded and bullets flew in all direction but the two men seemed to be enjoying it. I asked Gus what company he was in and he reminded me he was in D Company. On my return to where I had left the rest of the First Line Reinforcements, I found they were falling in prior to being detailed to various companies. Sergeant Major Butler was in charge and an officer from D Company stood by. He wanted men who had been in D Company before. C.S.M. Butler called for them and several men stepped forward. It was my chance to get back with Gus and I seized my opportunity.

"Have you been in D Company before?" asked the officer, knowing full well that I hadn't been.

"No sir," I replied, "but I'd like to."

"Alright," he said. "But you're the last."

And so I joined the ranks of D Company, thinking that even if Sergeant Major Butler had put me in his awkward squad, he was not such a bad fellow after all.*

That night I slept above the company office until I was awakened in the early hours by an air raid. The planes were not attacking us although they were twisting and turning upstairs while the ack-ack [anti-aircraft fire] thumped, making a devil of a noise.

The next day, strange to say, was set aside for gimping up.[32] It was pay-day so all the gimping up I did consisted of buying a couple of bottles of beer at the regimental canteen and departing with Gus for a little stroll to admire the scenery. We sat by a stream and discussed things in general. Gus, by the way, was in a different platoon. He explained that two companies would go up to the lines for five days and then return for five days rest, being relieved by another two companies and so on. When I asked him what conditions were like

---

* As will be seen, it is this apparently trivial incident makes Ray's eventual capture by the Germans inevitable. It is typical of his world view, that at no point in the memoir does he look back on this fateful moment and curse his luck.

up there he told me that they had had quite a lot of excitement during the last spell, mostly from enemy patrols creeping round the barbed wire in the dead of night. He then described our machine gun posts, which were in dugouts, each with two machine guns. Guarding the rear were grenade posts, for we were just as likely to be attacked from the rear as from the front. To get there he said, you had to go through Bouzonville Forest. You were liable to be attacked before you ever got there for Bouzonville Forest was notorious for its mud, its snipers – and its cuckoos. I had already heard about these "cuckoos" from one of the other fellows who was convinced that they were not real cuckoos at all but German snipers signalling to German patrols. I was much impressed by what Gus had to tell me. He concluded by saying all one would ever read about it in the papers was "Slight patrol activity in the Moselle" – and that would be that.

I understood D Company would not be going into action for at least three days – but that only proved how little I knew. My sense of security was rudely disturbed next morning, May 11th, when we received orders to pack up and get on trucks. We quickly loaded up, piled in and pushed off down narrow lanes and across rutted fields, stopping by the edge of a large wood. Gun kit was got out and made ready to be carried into position. I was detailed to carry a box of ammunition. This was no easy task for there were about nine inches of mud to wade through, nearly half a mile to hike and on top of that, the sun beat down pitilessly.

We skirted the wood for a good way, passing a stationary Bren Carrier which reminded me of a deadly spider lurking ready to pounce. We cut through the wood. It was my first experience of a French forest. Until then I had not realised how bad they could be. So dense were the trees overhead that despite the brilliant sunshine it was semi-dark. There was a lot of work to do when we got to our gun positions. It was like everything else the French had left behind. The gun pits were had to be rebuilt to suit our Vickers guns, the roofs had to be made higher and re-camouflaged, and the communication trench had to be bailed out. This, I was informed, was the "recoil line".[33]

That night, those who were not standing to[34] – including me – slept in a small mud hut we found a little further back in the forest. Our sleep however, was interrupted for no sooner had we settled down than an artillery battery opened up and continued firing at intervals, making the night sound horrible.

We stayed in the recoil line long enough for me to get lost in the forest. It happened on the second day when, with Simes and another chap, I went back to platoon HQ to collect the rations. Instead of following the usual roundabout path, we decided to take a short cut straight through the forest. We thought it would save us a good deal of time but we soon found out our mistake. We walked for some distance but not a sign of platoon HQ could we find – not even its approximate position at the edge of the forest. We halted and looked around hopelessly but all we could find were a dozen paths leading in a dozen different directions, while all around us was a blank wall of green.

Simes insisted on going one way while his pal was confident the other way was the right one. I, of course, believed them both wrong and was quite certain that a third path would take us to our destination. Needless to say, we were all wrong so I suggested we walk round in widening circles until one of us saw something he recognised. Simes was the first to spot it. He recognised a queer shaped tree at the bend of a path so we altered our course in that direction.

It was very nearly dark when we arrived at platoon HQ but it did not take us long to collect our rations and make a hurried retreat in order to get back before dark. We were not at all keen on getting lost again and staying out in the forest all night, with the probability of running into a German tommy gun patrol. Before we left however, Sgt Scott, platoon sergeant told us the password – "JACK123". On our way back we kept to the well-trodden path. We arrived intact with our rations.

The village of Colmen, at the front, had already been described to me by Gus when I first arrived at Bibiche but even so, I never expected to find it as I did. It was D Company's turn to go forward and we went straight from the recoil line. Our trucks took us as far as A Company HQ but beyond that the forest rendered transport by motor vehicles almost impossible. It was about three miles from here to Colmen, not as the crow flies but by the route we took. For those three miles we had to carry our guns, gun kit, ammunition and rations through the thick forest, notorious for being the happy hunting ground of Boche snipers.

The platoon moved off into the forest in single file. Of all the nasty places I know, Bouzonville Forest comes well nigh top of the list. The tracks through it were vague. We pushed our way through the bushes, climbed over fallen trees, tripped over roots and slid yards in the mud. Grumbles and curses were the order of the day for it was aggravating and exhausting work. We would step on ground which looked firm and solid only to sink down in mud halfway up to our knees. Before we reached Colmen the whole platoon got lost in the forest which shows that if the platoon sergeant could get lost, Simes and I had little to be ashamed of.

Colmen at last! It lay at the bottom of a valley and exactly opposite was the German village of Neunkirchen.[35] To the rear of Colmen and somewhat to the right was a neck of woods called the Tiergarten. The section I was in, under Sgt Pagan had its positions on the edge of the Tiergarten overlooking Neunkirchen. The other section of the platoon occupied a house in Colmen – the last house on the road to Germany. The two sections separated, one to take up position in the Tiergarten and the other under Sgt Wilmott in Colmen. I was in the Tiergarten section but was detailed to help the other section with their ammunition as they had much further to go.

We went down the hill into the village passing road barriers of farm machinery. The village seemed part of a dead world. It was so still, so silent and so utterly deserted. Through the village we went, making detours through houses, backyards, orchards and even the village school, to keep off the main street, which ran at right angles to the German lines. The whole length of it was under enemy observation. Blurred shapes seemed to lurk at odd corners and doorways. After staring at them for some time, I recognised them as Seaforth infantrymen. I was about the last man in our file. I was somewhat surprised when the men in front came to a halt by the side of a church and began peering around the corner before making a dash across the road one at a time into the house opposite. They had been in Colmen before. The road was scored with bullet marks.

Once in the house opposite we went up a narrow passage, out the back door, across a little yard and into the next house where we descended to the cellar. It was inky dark and like everything else in Colmen it was horribly filthy. We stamped and stumbled over strangely uneven ground which in the darkness gave me horrible suspicions about what I was walking on. Very closely, I followed the man in front, expecting any minute to step into some deep hole. We climbed through a hole in the wall into the next cellar and soon we had travelled halfway down the street. When we came up for air, we came up into a house full of Jocks. We were challenged and Sgt Wilmott gave the password, "Jack and Jill" and stated how many men he had with him – and on we went again.

We passed through a couple of bedrooms and went down some narrow, rickety steps into the cellars again. A glow of light filtered down from a small iron grating above and I could distinguish my surroundings more or less. This cellar was worse than the last one, refuse was piled up everywhere while a narrow gutter ran down the middle. It was bridged by duck-boards on which we stood precariously. The whole place stank to high heaven.

An N.C.O. stood by, directing operations. As I passed him, I happened to remark that this was a very dirty cellar.

"Cellar be damned," he cried. "This is a bloody sewer!"

I arrived at the gun position rather the worse for wear. It was in the very end house in the street. The advance party had already got the tea brewing. I was very grateful.

I returned to my own section at the edge of the Tiergarten and found that, unlike the boys in Colmen, we had no house to shelter us. Our gun positions were in dugouts that we had to rebuild. From these gun-pits I looked across the valley to Neunkirchen. In the sunshine it looked a peaceful little village with a tall church tower rising in the centre. This – strange to say – had a clock that chimed. I was curious about the clock but my comrades informed me that although it chimed it had never been known to strike the right time and was regarded as a German method of signalling.

"Post 74" as our position was called had two gun-pits, each housing a Vickers machine gun pointing towards Neunkirchen. Guarding the rear were four grenade posts – or shall I say three, as number two was empty. That one was too dilapidated to serve any practical purpose so we took the sandbags from it to reinforce the other three. Skirting the perimeter of the post were entanglements of barbed wire which was rusty, dangerous and ornamented with empty sardine tins that jangled at the slightest touch.

When the sun set and darkness began to fall over Colmen, I was detailed to spend the night in No. 1 grenade post with Lance Corporal Page and two other privates. The idea, I gathered, was to heave hand grenades at any enemy patrol which became too inquisitive. I had never thrown a live grenade before and did not feel too happy about it.

No sooner had darkness fallen than we could hear the barking of many dogs across the valley in Neunkirchen. They sounded far away and reminded me of hounds being un-kennelled for the chase. I looked enquiringly at L/Cpl Page. "German patrol dogs," he said. Then he turned back to peer through his loophole again. The night wore on but nothing happened. It was quiet apart from the numerous insect noises and the croaking of the frogs in the swampy forest. Contrary to our expectations, dawn came without any contact with the enemy. As the sky grew lighter I felt almost disappointed for I had spent my first night in the front line and nothing had happened.

That day dragged by slowly and monotonously, marked only by occasional bursts of enemy shell fire. Punctually, at every meal time, we would get a hail of shrapnel down through the tree tops, hacking off small branches and lacerating the tree trunks. Invariably, just when the stew was ready, we would have to take cover. Things reached a climax when Sgt Pagan was giving the stew an expert stir just before dishing it out. He had made this stew himself and was proud of it. Suddenly the Germans began sending over their shrapnel again. "Bang!" went an enemy gun and a shell whistled overhead to explode in the forest behind, sending a blast of shrapnel over us. Thereupon, Sgt Pagan thrust the ladle back into the stewpot with an air of finality. "That settles it," he declared. "If they upset my stew again, I'll go out there personally with a fixed bayonet!"

The infantry in the Tiergarten told us the most fantastic tales. The strangest was the one about the sniper in the green cage. A patrol of Jocks, I gathered, had discovered a German sniper. They had been after him for some time but at last they had unearthed him. Well, "unearthed" is an awkward word to use for they found him in a tree top. They emptied their rifles at him but without any effect. They tried their Bren Guns with no better result. In the end they discovered he was housed in a steel bullet-proof cage camouflaged in the tree tops.

I thought this all very fantastic when I was told. How could the Germans get a steel cage hung up and camouflaged behind our lines? The Jocks however, surrounded the area and sent a runner back to the Tiergarten – and it was from him that we heard the story.

"...and how are you going to get him out?" asked someone.

"With an anti-tank rifle!" was the reply.

I took it all with a pinch of salt until a few minutes later I saw a couple of Jocks lugging an anti-tank rifle through the forest. I felt the whole place was a gigantic madhouse.

On the third night we were dropped a hint that we might move out before schedule. It meant nothing to me, I had heard so many rumours. Another two days and we were due to move out in any case. Darkness fell once more over the forest and I took up my position in the grenade post again. All was quiet. It seemed as if the German artillery had packed up and gone home. That was a bad sign I was told for, when the guns stopped firing early in the evening, it was a sign of coming trouble. They never sent out shells and patrols at the same time. This night there were no shells.

The dogs barked again at Neunkirchen. The insects and the frogs made noises. But after a while, even these became quiet and all was still. The night dragged on, marked only by sporadic bursts of rifle fire from the direction of Colmen. I was standing by my loophole[36] when I thought I heard a whistle. I listened again and the second time, it seemed much nearer. It started very low, rising and dying away again. Page heard it too and we peered through our loopholes into the inky blackness of the forest. But we could see nothing. Time passed and nothing happened.

We began to relax. I thought it might have been a German patrol whistling their dogs and that they had gone straight past. But on this latter point I was mistaken. Page heard it first. The soft crunch of a boot a few yards away. They were very cunning for we never heard another sound for a good ten minutes. Then sound came again. A sharp "snip, snip" from the barbed wire. Page drew his pistol and levelled it through his loophole. He said something about seeing somebody. Then, "Get some grenades ready!"

I felt quite nervous. It's no good saying anything other. I wasn't quite used to this sort of thing yet. Page pulled the trigger three times in succession. I decided it was time for action. Pulling the pin from the grenade I was holding in readiness, I heaved it in the direction he had fired. Things quietened down a bit then until Page heard the sound again.

"Give 'em another just to make sure."

I did. But Jerry sent one back. Luckily it fell short, striking the sandbags in front and sending a shower of earth and stones over us. That was a parting gift though. He never bothered us again that night.

Late the next afternoon, on May 15th, we received the order to withdraw.[37] Three men were away at Company HQ at the time so we were short. It was almost dark by the time we got away and trekking through the forest was terrible at night when silence was essential. After a while we rested in the forest. Without a doubt everyone was all-in but the Indian Army Service Corps arrived with their pack mules and helped to get our guns out of action. We met the other platoons on their way out and forming a long column, emerged from that awful forest.

We marched for the greater part of the night, over bleak and desolate country until we came to the village of Dalstein. It was a tiring march, the column began to get thin and straggle out – but we could always hear the voice of Major Dodge. "Keep going lads. Only another mile. Keep going lads."

At Dalstein we managed to get a couple of hours sleep in some empty houses. We were awakened at dawn when our trucks arrived. Our next stop proved to be a village about ten kilometres away, which we were pleased to find was inhabited. Billets were not of the best but we were compensated by the fact that we were right next door to a real pub. All "D" Company had arrived so I think it can be recorded that during the course of the day, the proprietor did a remarkable amount of business.

Events that followed our withdrawal from Colmen were rather dull. I can vaguely remember travelling across France in an overloaded army truck after having spent a few days in a Maginot pillbox near Piblange. Motoring across France can be very pleasant but not in the way we did it. We would travel all night in a tiny truck crammed full of equipment with hardly enough room to sit, let alone sleep. Cramped and stiff, we would disembark at a new destination each day. Sometimes it would be a village. Sometimes a deserted chateau. More often than not though it would be in the woods where we would try to sleep tormented by mosquitoes. At night we would go on again until we got further from the front.

Then we began to travel by day. We passed the shell-holed

battlefields of Verdun and picturesque Vitry-le-François and still further west. This caused much speculation as to our ultimate destination for we were heading straight for Paris.[38] The German invasion of Holland and Belgium was now in progress and many of us believed we were going to Belgium to join the rest of the B.E.F.. We went round Paris in a huge semi-circle. All day we saw signposts – "Paris 30 kilometres" – but we never saw anything of the city. We turned north and west until, on May 29th, a fortnight after we had left the Maginot Line, we arrived at our destination, the small town of Foucarmont in the département of Seine Inférieure in Normandy.

Chapter 4: The Battle of Abbeville – and another withdrawal

INTRODUCTORY NOTE

Following the German invasion of France, the 1st Kensingtons, along with the whole of 51st Division, have been withdrawn from the Saar Front. They are now in Normandy, over 250 miles (400 kilometres) away from their previous location, on the opposite side of France. They have joined the largely French forces trying to halt – or at least disrupt – German progress towards the Channel coast. Germany's ultimate objective of course, is to take control of the entire coastline opposite southern England in preparation for the projected invasion of Britain. At this point in the fighting, Boulogne and Calais are already in German hands, having fallen on the 25th and 26th of May respectively. Although Ray does not mention this – indeed he may not even have known it – on its arrival in Normandy the 51st Division was placed under French command.

In this forthcoming chapter, Ray describes the Kensingtons' involvement in fighting around the town of Abbeville. As we have already seen, like the rest of his rank-and-file comrades, Ray is in no position to understand what is happening in the bigger picture. He simply gets on and does his job. The following – highly simplified – summary of events should help place his experiences in context.

The Battle of Abbeville

The town of Abbeville is situated on the River Somme, about 15 miles (24 kilometres) inland from the Channel coast. It had fallen to the Germans on May 20th. The Battle of Abbeville began on May 28th when Allied forces, attacking from the south, launched an attempt to force the Germans back to the north bank of the river. For a time, on the 29th and 30th of May, the Allies seemed to be gaining the upper hand. A second major attack by the Allies on June 4th was markedly less successful however. There were some minor local gains but these came at a cost, with over 500 casualties in the 51st Division. The following day the Germans counter-attacked and the Allies were forced backwards.

It gradually became clear to the Allies that the Battle of Abbeville was being lost. Over the next few days the French and British were pushed back, first to the River Bresle and then subsequently to the Béthune. For the British troops there then was no alternative but to make a run for the coast and the possibility of emergency evacuation back to the UK.

Ark Force and evacuation via Le Havre

The Commander of the 51st Division, General Victor Fortune, had recognised more or less from the time of the 51st's arrival in Normandy that the task of driving back the Germans might prove too much for the Allies. His view was shared by at least one of his junior officers, a young captain in the Camerons, who later observed that from the moment the 51st Division was ordered into position at Abbeville "...the stage was set for one of the greatest catastrophes in our military history".[39]

General Fortune's doubts about the viability of the Allies' position had led him to make contingency plans for a potential withdrawal to Le Havre, from where a large scale evacuation back to England might be possible. Le Havre had not yet fallen, although German forces were approaching the town rapidly. On June 9th, General Fortune split the 51st Division in two sections and ordered a force of over 4,000 men (perhaps around a fifth of the Division's strength) to move westwards and protect a route to Le Havre. The intention was to make it possible for the rest of the 51st and its French allies to make a fighting retreat towards Le Havre in due course. This detached force was known as Ark Force.

Among the units attached to Ark Force, were B and C Companies of the Kensingtons, plus the battalion's HQ Company. In a crucial decision from Ray Bailey's personal point of view, the remainder of the Kensingtons, around 300 men of A and D Companies (D Company being Ray's company), were left behind with the main body of the 51st Division.

In the event, Ark Force was not able to hold back the enemy for long enough to allow the rest of the Division to follow. The 7th Panzer Division moved rapidly from Rouen and on the afternoon of the 10th the road between the 51st Division and Le Havre was cut. The majority of Ark Force itself however, did make it to Le Havre and were among the 11,000 or so Allied troops successfully evacuated from there between the 10th and 13th of June. 421 members of the 1st Battalion Kensington Regiment made it home via this route.[40]

The retreat to St Valery

The fighting at Abbeville had been relentless and bloody. The week-long fighting withdrawal towards the coast by the Allies, chased every step of the way by superior German forces, continued in the same vein. Once the route to Le Havre had also been lost, there was only one option left for the remaining majority of the 51st Division. On June 10th an order was issued to make for the tiny fishing port of St Valery en Caux, fifty miles north of Le Havre and twenty miles south of Dieppe. Reaching St Valery would offer some hope of evacuation by the Royal Navy. If that were not possible however, every single man knew that it was at St Valery that the 51st must make its last stand.

Ray chooses not to describe the retreat in detail. It must have been a grim experience. The roads toward the coast were choked with military traffic and civilian refugees. German forces were never far behind and there were constant artillery and air attacks on the retreating columns of Allied soldiers. It is also widely documented that by this time significant numbers of French soldiers, believing that defeat was inevitable, had lost morale and discipline. Many were abandoning equipment and vehicles, and were looking for ways to avoid being trapped at the sea's edge. Some were even attempting to get away by travelling against the flow of traffic. In some places the narrow roads were jammed solid for long periods.

The result of all this was a mad, terrifying chaos in which even the more orderly British troops were unable to keep together. Cpt. Derek Lang of the Camerons for example, described losing the front half of his motorised convoy as they travelled towards St Valery in pitch darkness with no vehicle lights allowed. He set off on a motorbike to find them but failed to do so. He turned round to go back to the rear of the convoy and could not find that again either. For him, it was a "night of near despair".[41]

This vivid eye-witness account by Angus Campbell, formerly a private in the Seaforth Highlanders, gives just a sense of the experience:

> Who could describe in words, the horror of such a time? Your companions cut down alongside you; some blown to pieces, the wounded crying out in pain, trees torn out of the ground by the roots, the destructive power of the big guns, the terrifying explosions of the bombs – and yet the courage of soldiers clinging to hope in a desperate situation.[42]

Others described frequent strafing by German aircraft, not just of military columns but also of the straggling crowds of refugees. The objective of these latter attacks was perhaps intended simply to create physical obstacles on the roads.

Jim Charters, formerly of the Royal Northumberland Fusiliers[43] later described such an incident:

> Seeing refugees being machine-gunned and bombed was the worst moment of my whole war. The Germans did it to impede our retreat. It was a shock to see.

Charters also described the constant terror of attack and the all-consuming exhaustion as men struggled to keep going towards the coast:

> Mortars[44] and Stukas[45] were what we feared the most. The bombs had their sirens on and howled when they were

> coming down at us. But during the retreat I think we were in a stupor most of the time.

Ray lived through this mayhem, as did every other bone-tired British soldier, fearful – as each man must have been – of what the next day would bring. And yet, in this coming chapter, Ray mentions almost none of this. Even where he is directly involved in the action himself, he almost entirely avoids describing the distressing sights that he must have seen.

The Battle of Abbeville – and another withdrawal

Foucarmont was not a bad place. We had, as platoon billet, a barn arrangement next to a large house in a narrow street that ran up to the village square. It was clean and airy and evidently the property of a clog manufacturer. In the corner was a stack of wooden soles and along one side was a pile of small logs which I took to be raw material waiting to be carved. I mention it because I slept directly underneath it and even though it was stacked firmly against the wall, it wobbled and swayed when touched. Whenever I turned, I could imagine that one night the whole issue would collapse on top of me. I slept uneasily!

We hadn't been in Foucarmont twenty minutes when trouble arrived. It came in the form of the proprietor of the barn. I didn't know his name but we will call him "Dupont", as most Frenchmen in books seem to be called Dupont. Monsieur Dupont was furious. He came prancing into the billet and by the sound of him, cursing and swearing in the most fearful fashion. Fortunately no-one understood a word he was saying.

We sent for Murkin who could speak French. The two of them harangued each other for a full ten minutes but at last when Monsieur Dupont was compelled to pause for breath, Murkin was able to translate his troubles; some burly British soldier had walked across his back garden – there were big, hob-nailed foot-marks to prove it! He demanded that the man should be punished. He demanded he should see him punished. He demanded to see an officer!

"Better send for Ham," said someone.

In due course Platoon Commander, Second Lieutenant Hammond – "Ham" – arrived on the scene to find out the cause of the bother. No sooner did Monsieur Dupont catch sight of him than he opened up again with his pestiferous French.

"What did he say, Murkin?"

"Somebody has walked over his onion bed, sir…"

The Frenchman began again.

"…and he demands the man should be punished."

2nd Lieutenant Hammond enquired with resignation who had done this blackguardly act in time of war – and deep down in our hearts we realised the significance of this deed, especially now that the Boche had reached Amiens about a hundred kilometres away and were advancing like an express train. It was simply a horrid thing for a British soldier to do. Monsieur Dupont wanted the man punished. In the end 2nd Lieutenant Hammond had to promise that, as the culprit would not own up, all the British soldiers would be punished. It was an empty promise of course but it served to calm the situation.

The Germans were pressing heavily on the Somme. Amiens was bombed and bombed. Endless streams of refugees poured from Amiens into Foucarmont. They came by the thousand. They blocked the road with farm carts, motor cars, and bicycles. They came on foot. They pushed prams, pushchairs and wheelbarrows. Men and women, old and young. On they came, each and all clinging to a bundle of precious possessions. Westward, westward towards Neufchâtel.

It was hard to make them understand when we were on night patrol that they could not pass through the town while it was dark. Housed in barns and such-like they would be up at the most unearthly hours and ready to move off again. They would wring their hands and say they had to be away before it was light or they would be bombed again. But they had to stay put. They could not move before six o'clock. Regulations were regulations. The battalion did some good work though. Our transport was utilised to help the refugees on their way. Into the trucks they were crammed and whisked off to Neufchâtel. The main object was to clear the roads but the people were not ungrateful.

I was acting as section runner at one time and along with

Brewster, the other section runner, I was able to roam around a little more than the others. As a result, Brewster and I discovered a deserted Royal Army Service Corps dump. Whoever had occupied the place had left in a great hurry. Greatcoats and steel helmets hung in the proper places. Outside on a little bit of lawn was a round garden table with four chairs. It was all laid out and a meal had been finished. An after-dinner cup of tea had been in progress but for some unknown reason had been suddenly interrupted. A half-smoked cigarette lay by the side of each plate and an open packet lay on the table. They must have left in a tremendous hurry. We wondered why.

In one of the store sheds we saw a sight that nearly made our eyes pop out of our heads. Cigarettes! Thousands of them. And chocolate. Tons of it! We had been rather short of these commodities of late but we soon altered that by taking as much as we could carry back to the platoon. We filled our pockets to capacity and carried what we could in our arms.[46] I returned again later with a couple of chaps to make sure the platoon did not go short of cigarettes. That place must have been cursed though. We also had to leave in a hurry. The reason was that a battery of our own artillery was intent on destroying it before the Germans got there.

Around this time, Gus and I also succeeded in appropriating an excellent bottle of champagne – but to get it we had to overcome many obstacles. In the first place, the deed had to be done at dusk, which meant staying out after the seven o'clock curfew. It also entailed creeping past the anti-tank post, going through an empty house and over a number of fences to reach the cellar where it was hidden under an old boiler. Gus had been there previously with a few boys from his platoon. They had been disturbed and had had to make a quick getaway – that was how the champagne came to be under the boiler. A bottle of champagne was a bottle of champagne though. It was worth going after.

Our expedition was a success but on the way back we were intercepted by Platoon Sergeant Major Mullender who wanted to know what we were doing out after curfew. Of course, we could not tell him we had just bagged a bottle of champagne – that was plain looting. In any case, he would probably have drunk it himself. You can never tell with Sergeant Majors. We stammered some thin excuse and he told us to see him next morning…

It was June 3rd – our last night in Foucarmont – and had just gone seven o'clock. The mail had been issued. It was sometime since we had our last post and our letters had just caught up with us. I had a letter from home. Morris who slept next to me received a letter from his girlfriend. It had been posted some time ago. He read an extract to me:

"You boys in France must be enjoying yourselves," he read, "what with Gracie Fields and George Formby to entertain you at those concerts for troops, you must be having a marvellous time."

We did have a marvellous time. In fact it is marvellous that any of us were left alive to tell the story after what happened in the next few minutes.

All was calm and quiet when suddenly the bombers came. Junkers dive bombers. Down they came in a vertical dive, their engines screaming louder and louder. For a moment we did not realise what was happening, so sudden was their attack – until Sgt Pagan yelled, "Get down flat!"

Never was any command carried out with greater precision.

Then it happened, an ear-splitting explosion that shook the whole village. We crouched low, trying to press ourselves through the very floor. The first bomb was quickly followed by a second. Then another and another until the whole place heaved and rocked. Slates flew off the roof. The windows blew in. The door blew out and hung on one hinge. Even the floor seemed to tilt while huge cracks ran up the walls.

The screams of diving Stukas began to die away and I rose from my prone position to survey the room. The billet had not been hit and no-one was hurt – but looking round that little room with its forty-odd inhabitants I would have laughed had the situation not been serious. With their hands down and their behinds stuck up in the air my comrades looked so comical.

"Get down!" yelled Sgt Pagan, "they're coming back!"

They did.

Again the billet was rocked and shaken by heavy explosions. Through a patch of light where the door hung on its hinges I could see stones, lumps of masonry, wooden beams hurtling high into the air. Slates from roof-tops and glass from windows were flying in all directions. The noise was terrific. But even air raids can't last forever. This one was short but not very sweet.

When it was all over we put on our steel helmets and respirators, and were ordered outside. With the rest of the battalion in Foucarmont we were split into squads and went to work. Some to dig out civilians and others to fill in bomb craters on the roads. The whole town had had a bashing. There was hardly a house left intact anywhere. Three big craters were in a line up the narrow back street where our billet was. We could step out of the door into one of them. Our cookhouse next door had been bombed out. The cook was shell-shocked. We were lucky.

In the village square where our company transport park was, was a huge crater which would have held four army trucks without them appearing above ground level. The conical roof of the barber's shop at the corner had been blown off and set down intact in the opposite corner of the square. Foucarmont was in a mess. We hurried to fill up the craters in the more vital roads leading out of the town; we were going away. However, we did not pile into the trucks as was our usual procedure. As soon as we dug one out, off it went to some appointed rendezvous where the Stukas were not likely to find it again. When we had finished our task, very weary and fatigued, we trekked out of Foucarmont. Curling ourselves up under a blanket or groundsheet, we rested. During the night, German aeroplanes buzzed overhead and parachute flares floated around. We heeded them not. We were tired. Very tired. We slept.

The next morning came, we piled into our trucks and rode off to battle. Through Fallencourt we dashed. Past Blangy, around Huppy and up to the Somme. Our trucks came to a standstill under the protection of some overhanging trees. About a hundred yards away an artillery battery was laying down a barrage somewhere. It kicked up a devil of a noise. I thought it would split my eardrums. I stayed at the trucks while the gun teams went forward. Suddenly the artillery stopped. I wondered why. Then a squadron of German bombers wheeled across the sky. They twisted and turned, changed their formation and dived down on the unfortunate village of Huppy about half a mile behind. We could see them dive one at a time and drop their bombs. The bombs themselves we could distinctly see falling through the air and were followed by a number of loud detonations.

When they had competed their deadly work, the bombers turned and flew towards us. The last gun, which had just been unloaded from a truck, was hastily mounted in position for ack-ack [anti aircraft fire] but the planes flew away and did not bother to attack us.

We went into position that night in front of a wood near Huppy but that same night, having just dug ourselves in, we were ordered to withdraw. We went as far back as Biencourt near Martaineville. This time we did clash with the enemy but the Kensington guns gave a good account of themselves. Our positions were behind a line of Camerons. We gave them support by overhead fire when the Germans made a frontal attack from a large wood. Corporal Bartell insisted on firing the gun himself. He had just visited somebody's wine cellar and was slightly the worse for wear. He was in a very dashing mood so the boys willingly let him get down behind the gun; this prevented him from charging the enemy with fixed bayonet as he otherwise threatened to do.

The grey horde poured out of the wood and charged the Cameron line. Our guns opened up and a solitary field gun behind began laying shells along the edge of the wood – but the Germans were relentless and the Camerons were hopelessly outnumbered.

Nevertheless the Boche did not have it all his own way that day. Our machine gun fire had a telling effect on them for as soon as they ran into it, the grey line wavered. It turned and went back into the wood as fast as it had come out. Later that evening the Germans resumed their attack. Again we gave covering fire to the Camerons as the Germans came out. This certainly saved the Camerons from being massacred. I remember passing them later in the trucks. A Cameron major shouted as we went by, "Is that the Kensingtons? Thank God for your machine guns!" And he looked as though he meant every word he said.[47]

We withdrew through Blangy. We were heartened by the news that this retreat business was purely for strategic reasons and that two divisions of Canadians were moving up to relieve us. I thought if we kept going backwards at this rate, it would not be necessary for the Canadians actually to move up. Later we learned that these divisions were mythical and had been created only to keep our morale up. The streets of Blangy were crowded with soldiers – mostly French – marching away from the front. Civilians were loading up barrows and carts with furniture, blocking the roads in the town. Everywhere was a scene of chaos.

Once more we went cruising around France by night. A couple of foggy mornings made driving difficult but then we left for Dieppe.[48] God help Dieppe, I thought. The boys were not what they used to be. For one day, we took up position covering an aerodrome in case of German parachutists but the boys still showed signs of nervousness at the sound of diving aircraft. We were told not to be alarmed if we heard low-flying aircraft during the night as a squadron of Spitfires was due to arrive. It was another good attempt to keep up our morale but it fell short.

We did not like withdrawing day after day. To us it seemed to be without reason. They told us that it was a "strategic withdrawal to lengthen the lines of communication" and that we would not withdraw beyond a certain point. I don't know where this came from. Possibly it was yet another idea to keep our spirits up, I don't know.

We were the only division left in France. The one they forgot about. As my friend, Morris, the range-taker, said; we would probably retreat and retreat until we were cut off on that peninsular of France formed between Dieppe, Rouen and Le Havre. The result, he said, would be another Dunkirk. It was now a week after Dunkirk and the 51st Highland Division was still fighting a retreat. I agreed with him – although I still didn't realise how serious the situation was getting.

During the afternoon of the next day an unusual thing happened. An HQ Company truck came beating up the road about forty miles an hour. The driver – the sole occupant of the truck – pulled up abruptly causing the truck to skid about ten yards before it came to a standstill. He was very excited. "The tanks are coming!" he yelled. "HQ Company have gone.[49] You've got to get out of it! We're cut off!" Without further ado he turned his truck and tore back the way he had come.

Second Lieutenant Hammond was informed but as he said, he could not abandon his position without being told officially. In any case, he said, if the worst came to the worst we would ditch our machine guns and transport, and fight our way out like an infantry patrol. It was good tactics and had we done it there and then we would probably have won through. But fate stepped in. The cards were stacked heavily against us.

Word did come eventually through. We moved off silently at midnight. We were making for St Valery, a small sea-port further down the coast. They told us that from there we would get boats and evacuate. We were not sorry.

Chapter 5: The fall of St Valery

INTRODUCTORY NOTE

Arrival at St Valery

The great mass of the Allied forces arrived in St Valery throughout the morning of June 11th, beginning in the early hours. Estimates of numbers vary significantly but soon somewhere between 25,000 and almost 50,000 soldiers were packed into the small town.[50]

General Fortune established a defensive line around the entire perimeter of St Valery. Initially this line was a few miles outside the town. Later it withdrew to the outskirts. D Company of the Kensingtons (Ray's company) played its part in this defensive arrangement, providing machine gun cover for the infantry units deployed on the eastern side of the town. Kensingtons A Company was deployed on the western side.

The aim of the perimeter defences was to keep the Germans at bay long enough for an evacuation to take place. But in the town the situation was becoming increasingly desperate. There were intermittent dive-bombing raids by the Luftwaffe and regular shelling from German artillery situated in the countryside beyond the defended perimeter. Eventually in some places on the west side of the town German forces began to appear on the cliffs above the beach. Many of the buildings in St Valery were ablaze. Men were being killed and wounded all around. A proportion of French soldiers had lost discipline and openly given up preparing to fight the last stand. Some were even reported to be already trying to find their own way out of the town. For the British, ammunition was running out and food was in short supply. Many of the soldiers had not slept for days and were in a state of complete physical and mental exhaustion.

Making sense of events at St Valery

Events leading up to the final withdrawal to St Valery and events in the town itself were extremely complex and of course, developed in a fast-moving and unpredictable way. Inevitably perhaps, there is considerable inconsistency between the various published accounts of what happened over those last, terrible couple of days; this goes both for eye witness accounts and accounts by military historians. Different authors also offer differing analyses of why things unfolded in the particular way that they did. These chapter notes provide only the very briefest description of the sequence of events, the primary objective being to sketch out those aspects of St Valery that seem most relevant to the experience of a young private soldier like Ray Bailey who was caught up in the thick of things.

The experience of St Valery

To gain some sense of the visceral reality of St Valery, it is necessary to turn to accounts other than Ray's. As in Chapter 4, Ray again chooses for the most part not to describe the carnage and desperation through which every individual soldier had to fight to stay alive. For Ray and the many thousands of other men trapped in St Valery on those two early summer days in 1940, there was a glimpse of hell.

We cannot know why Ray sifted out the horror of these experiences and saved for his memoir only self-deprecation, wry humour and idiosyncratic detail. In taking this approach however, he offers us a highly individual view of events and in doing so, perhaps also gives us an insight into his personal means of survival. For the grim reality of what it was actually like at St Valery though, we have to go to other eye-witness accounts. These accounts make for sobering reading but unless we confront these descriptions we have no context for thinking about the absence of this kind of detail from Ray's own story or indeed, for trying to understand the relationship between Ray's experience at St Valery and the rest of his story.

As we have seen, the men of the 51st Division had been involved in a brutal running battle with the pursuing German forces some days.

As they were driven towards St Valery, the sense of madness and chaos must have increased exponentially. There was only one good road into St Valery and that was steep in places, narrow and twisting. Otherwise there were only back lanes and tracks. The good road was wedged tight with men and vehicles. Consequently just approaching the town and then trying to get down into it was a terrible ordeal for the desperate, exhausted men:

> All the main roads were simply choked with French troops on foot, and refugees, occasionally we passed piles of them dead at the roadside, having been machine-gunned from the air or just rolled aside by tanks. How we ever got out of that was a miracle.[51]

> ...the French transport appeared to be a heterogeneous collection from all their formations and was badly disorganised ... as a result the road was solid with vehicles from head to tail most of the night.[52]

> As we filed down from the hills above the town, we saw that it was ablaze. Great spurts of flame were visible ... and when we reached the outskirts we were confronted with streets jammed with every conceivable kind of vehicle. Men were rushing about in all directions so that the whole scene was hopeless chaos.[53]

By dawn on the morning of June 11th, the road into St Valery was no longer safe:

> As we were marching in threes along this narrow road, a machine gun opened up on us. We dived for cover in an orchard to our left but found it ringed with tanks .... Fifteen of us were captured shortly afterwards.[54]

Some men were trapped on the cliffs further down the coastline from the town itself:

> There was no way down the cliffs which were 300 feet high, and a sheer drop. Someone started making a rope of rifle-slings and I joined in. By the time we had made it, it was daylight, and the enemy was shelling from both sides. ...The first man to go met his death as the slings snapped, but it was either chance it or get caught so over I went. What a drop .... We were being machine-gunned and sniped all the time. What a lot of dead men on the beach – it was littered with them.[55]

Once in the town, the scenes that confronted the Allied soldiers were appalling. To make matters worse, during the early hours of the 11th, there was a heavy rainstorm:

> Every square foot was occupied by troops, some dead, some wounded, but most sound asleep in the torrential rain ... All the houses round the harbour were in flames ... Stretcher bearers were carrying bodies to the town square where a huge heap was steadily growing.[56]

> There were wounded everywhere and I could hear anguished cries from civilians inside their battered houses. At about four in the morning, I gave up and tried to find somewhere to sleep for the remaining hours before daylight. Eventually I found one of the few houses left standing. It was packed with bodies, whether dead or alive I did not care. Improbably a middle-aged lady appeared from somewhere and asked me if I would like her to dry my clothes. I was soaking wet but past caring. Within minutes I was fast asleep.[57]

> Thousands of drunken French soldiers were looting cafés, shops and houses, blazing away at anything with their rifles.[58]

We were in an open square. We could do nothing except take shelter. As they were bombing, these lovely coloured houses were being lifted up complete and collapsing to the ground in ruins. Then they started machine gunning us.[59]

It was the biggest cock up I've seen in my life. Blokes were getting killed everywhere.[60]

No salvation for the 51st Division

By the time the 51st Division and its French allies had arrived at St Valery, the outcome – surrender and capture of the entire division – was almost inevitable. The question of whether this catastrophe could have been avoided has long been a subject of controversy and debate. Understandably, a sense of bitterness lingered for decades, particularly in the Highlands and Islands of Scotland, where most of the British troops came from. The belief was that not enough was done to rescue the sons, husbands and fathers of those communities. Most would be lost to their families for five years. Some would never come home.

General Fortune had been in touch with British High Command over the days running up to June 11th, trying desperately to ensure that large numbers of rescue vessels would be offshore at St Valery when his men arrived. In the event, even though a large flotilla had set off from the south coast of England on June 9th almost no boats were available to the trapped soldiers.

The explanation is a complex one. It is not relevant to Ray's story to explore in detail the political and military decisions that proved so contentious – whole books have been devoted to these topics, so there is plenty of material available for anyone who wants to know more. It is however, helpful to know something of the reasons why such an enormous number of men were captured – not least because, in this chapter, Ray himself refers to the idea that the men of the 51st Division had been let down by the High Command. He says, "...we had not only been surrendered, we had been sold". The fact that Ray raises these questions, writing, as he was, so soon after the event, demonstrates that they have their origin in the immediacy of the captured men's experiences.

The first area of controversy is the very fact that the 51st Division ended up at St Valery at all, rather than at Le Havre, where their chances of evacuation would have been significantly better. It has been argued this happened at least partly as a consequence of the 51st being under French command – an arrangement that is believed to have caused delays to the Allied retreat. French commanders on the ground are said to have made poor tactical decisions and as we have seen, the morale of many of the the French troops seemed to be in a state of collapse. There was also a very practical reason why the retreat was slower than it might have been. The French army still relied relatively heavily on horse-drawn transport. French troops therefore moved at only about half the speed of the British army's motorised transport.

Without the various delays, it might have been possible for the 51st Division to get to Le Havre and – even if that had not been possible – it might have been that the British could have put further distance between themselves and the Germans and therefore had a better chance of evacuation from St Valery. It is also sometimes suggested that Churchill could have allowed the 51st Division to detach itself from the French command once the Battle of Abbeville had been lost but deliberately chose not to do so. This is said to be because of the long-term political benefit in showing solidarity with the French. It was also important to keep the French in the war for as long as possible. The longer the German army was tied up in France, the more time Britain had to prepare for a potential invasion attempt on home shores.

The men on the beaches however, felt more obvious and immediate grievances. Two questions come up time and again in eye-witness accounts – including in Ray's. Where were the ships that could have rescued them? And why did the RAF not appear over the horizon and help relieve the situation by attacking the German forces surrounding St Valery?

As far as the rescue by sea is concerned, the answer is not straightforward . A flotilla of 67 merchant ships and 140 smaller vessels, including warships,[61] had been put together by Admiral Sir William James, Commander-in-Chief, Portsmouth. As mentioned above, this flotilla set sail from the south coast of England on June 9th and by the following day on was anchored a few miles off the Normandy coast. Some boats from the flotilla approached the beach at St Valery on the evening of the 10th but found very few men there (Admiral James had no way of knowing precisely when the 51st Division and their French allies would arrive). The boats were able however to take away a small number of wounded men from the beach.

There is not complete agreement about what happened after that.[62] The following summary is primarily drawn from the account in Linklater (although it should be noted that his account is disputed to varying extents by some later commentators). Around midday on June 11th, some vessels from the flotilla assembled close inshore but were shelled by the German onshore artillery and bombed by the Luftwaffe. The group was forced back out to sea before any kind of rescue attempt could be made. By bad luck, a persistent fog fell over the sea in the late afternoon and the ships and boats of the flotilla lost sight of each other and of the coastline. Few of the flotilla vessels had radios and were therefore reliant on visual signalling. Consequently, the fog was enough to immobilise many of the vessels in the flotilla. One tug manged to get close to the shore just after midnight but the boats it landed were sunk by firing from the cliffs. Another small boat took around eighty men aboard just along the beach from St Valery but she was quickly sunk by shelling.[63] It was clear that the onshore strength of the German forces meant that it would be hopeless to make further attempts at evacuation.

There was, however, a little bit of good news. Some men (including some of those who had managed to descend safely from the cliffs) had been able to make it to the beach at Veules St Roses, a village about four miles along the shore east of St Valery. In the early hours of June 12th a small group of larger naval and merchant vessels plus a number of smaller boats came inshore there and were able to embark somewhere between 1,500 and 2,000 men before artillery and air attacks forced them to put back to sea. Shortly afterwards, Admiral James was able to report to the Admiralty that "every man found [at Veules St Roses] was taken off".[64,65] At the same time, he expressed his profound regret that only a very small number were saved from St Valery itself. Writing to a friend a few days later, he said this:

> I shall not easily forget that night. The last signals from the 51st Division were so tragic and bitter to read. "Situation critical", "When can we expect boats?", "Running short of ammunition", and I could do nothing.[66]

The matter of the non-appearance of the RAF has a simpler and more pragmatic explanation. On May 16th, Air Chief Marshall Hugh Dowding (Commander-in-Chief of Fighter Command), had written a restrained but emphatic letter to the Air Ministry outlining his belief that when the attack on Britain finally came, the RAF's strength would have been so depleted by its commitments in France that it would not be able to defend the homeland. He demanded the ministry set a minimum strength below which the RAF would not be allowed to fall, adding that:

> It should be made clear to the Allied Commanders on the Continent that not a single aeroplane from Fighter Command beyond the [newly agreed] limit will be sent across the Channel, no matter how desperate the situation might become.

Dowding concluded his letter with his famously stark warning that:

> If the Home Defence Force is drained away in desperate attempts to remedy the situation in France, defeat in France will involve the final, complete and irredeemable defeat of this country.

Churchill recognised that he had no alternative but to accept

Dowding's advice although he is thought to have done so only reluctantly.

At St Valery, on the night of 11th/12th June, General Fortune signalled Admiral James about his increasingly desperate situation, copying in the War Office and forcefully outlining the need for immediate evacuation. He added that "...air superiority is essential to neutralise shore batteries". But under the circumstances outlined above, air support was never going to materialise.

Surrender

The opening pages of the following chapter see the 51st Division forced to surrender. Ray is one of thousands caught up in this catastrophe. Like almost every other man present, he has no way of knowing the sequence of events that determines his becoming a prisoner-of-war – but to make sense of Ray's experiences, it is important to know how it happened.

At 8 o'clock on the morning of June 12th, in the face of vehement disapproval from General Fortune, General Ihler, Commander of the French forces at St Valery, surrendered to the Germans. In surrendering, General Ihler was accepting the inevitable. Apart from anything else and despite some brave exceptions, large numbers of his men had given up the fight many hours before their leaders and had been playing little part in the attempts to defend St Valery.

General Fortune himself had been desperately trying to formulate some kind of plan that would hold off the Germans for one more day. This would have given hope of a second evacuation attempt under cover of darkness on the night of the 12th. But the situation was hopeless, especially after the surrender of the French. In consultation with his senior officers, General Fortune, in the words of Eric Linklater opted for "the braver choice".[67] He made the decision to surrender at 10:30am.

In the confusion that followed, some small numbers of men were able to slip away to try their luck in making a run for it[68] but otherwise every single Allied soldier present in St Valery was forced to lay down his arms. As pointed out earlier, there is considerable variation in estimates of the total number of men present in the town but there is broad consensus about how many British soldiers were captured. Almost all authorities agree that the number was somewhere between 8,000 and 10,000. One among these thousands of course, was Ray Bailey.

There were tough, experienced, regular soldiers among the captured multitude but there were also large numbers of reservists and territorials. These latter men were generally older and many had wives and children. Only nine months before, they had been living steady, uneventful, family lives, most of them amid the beauty of the Scottish Highlands and Islands. They were men of the land and of the sea, and of the fresh air. The conscripts were more of a mixed bunch. They were of all social classes and came from all areas of the country. They had one thing in common with each other though. They were barely out of adolescence. Most of these lads, just a few months earlier, would have been living in their childhood homes with their mums and dads.

Whatever their background, whatever their age, whatever their rank, for these ten thousand, there was now only the bitter silence of the surrender and the slow-dawning unreality of captivity. In the words of one Kensington officer present, in these moments every soldier did the same. He simply "sank down on to the grass, wet, tired, miserable, dirty and hungry".[69] These thousands of men were in it together. But in those first moments, each was also a man alone.

Ray's personal experience, described in the coming chapter, demonstrates this sense of aloneness in a very literal way. At the beginning of the chapter, however, as he and his Kensington comrades begin to make their way down into St Valery, there is still a fragile sense of optimism about their chances of rescue...

The fall of St Valery

My training at Mill Hill had not included what to do in such an eventuality as the one we now faced. We were praying we would be evacuated once we got to St Valery but who could know what would happen? We might end up captured. The nearest approach had been a lecture at Ilminster on what to do if taken prisoner-of-war. I remembered having dodged that lecture in order to take Peggy somebody-or-other for a walk over Herne Hill.[70]

At first we were optimistic. We would be going home! Soon we would be in Blighty and it would be all over. That nightmare retreat would be little more than that – just a bad dream. Foolish ideas. But you could not blame us for that. The majority of us were young and inexperienced. Our training was not what it might have been. We knew our weapons – but good, valuable time that could have been spent on essential field-craft had been wasted blanco-ing up, polishing brasses and doing arms drill by numbers on the village square at Ilminster.

We moved off. The fighting trucks went first. They were needed. But the platoon did not go far – only into a little valley just outside St Valery itself. When I got there on the platoon commander's truck, our guns were already in action. The little port of St Valery, although out of sight from the position I was in, appeared to be undergoing continual bombardment. I cannot clearly remember everything that happened. It was one fierce whirl of action and excitement followed by despair. I can however remember every man-jack – combatant and non-combatant, truck driver and stretcher bearer – each grabbing a rifle and going up to shove back the Boche.[71] When darkness came, we were told to get back to our trucks, guns and everything. We were told finally that night, June 10th, that we would soon go down into St Valery and evacuate by boat.

There followed a period of waiting. I think waiting for something is the worst part of all. It is even worse than the "something" itself, no matter how bad that something might be. I remember sitting down with Gus and a few more and smoking Captain Salmon's cigarettes – keeping the lights low of course.

The French soldiers had been steadily trickling back from the line. They were a filthy, disgruntled lot. Unkempt and undisciplined, they threw away their arms and equipment. We told them what we thought of them, which wasn't much. To try and stop them though would have been like trying to stop the tide coming in. They went around grabbing what food they could find. We gave them some of ours, thinking they were hungry but next day we learned our mistake.

In the darkness I discussed the situation with Gus. Queer things went through my mind. I suggested we should scram because the future looked very black. We could make a run for it, south across France. We had our rifles and about a hundred and thirty rounds each in our bandoliers and pouches. So armed, we would be able to get food, transport, anything. We could deal with any Boche who tried to stop us. It was better, I felt, than waiting for evacuation that might never happen.[72] Also, the Germans having advanced so far west could not possibly have advanced very far south. I was all for it but Gus put me off, saying we had better wait and see what happened first. I wanted to be away there and then but I stayed with Gus. He was my pal. I hated thinking of the future. It seemed so uncertain. I noted the fact that even our officers, good as they were, seemed to have lost their polish.

At last the waiting was over. The following morning, June 11th, we were ordered to render our big guns useless and immobilise our trucks.[73] Sgt Jeacock saw to that. Led by Capt Salmon we tramped down to St Valery. When we got there the whole town was in flames. On several occasions we had to dash two or three at a time, down narrow streets where buildings were aflame both sides. Many lorries and cars were alight in the roadway, blazing furiously. As we ran, buildings were tumbling down. Showers of debris, chunks of burning wood, lumps of masonry and red-hot pieces of metal hurtled around as petrol tanks and ammunition dumps exploded. Covering our faces, we raced over the cobbled streets.

I remember reaching the harbour and standing at the end of a long queue – at least, there was a stretch of river or water of some kind on my left, which I took to be part of the harbour. I was told that the other end of the queue was actually going on the boats.[74] The main part of St Valery was now to our rear. Activity seemed to be dying down although Very lights[75] were being fired into the air by the dozen. The atmosphere was tense. Somewhere behind there was a deafening explosion that nearly shook us off our feet. A Service Corps bloke at my elbow said something about his petrol dump going up and then a strange quiet set in. That explosion rocked St Valery – and I think it heralded the end of the rearguard of the B.E.F.

The long dismal queue moved forward a few yards. It made me think of Dunkirk and all that had happened there.[76] I wondered how long we would have to wait before we got on those boats. In front was a gigantic column of tired men, waiting and hoping that they might be saved. And at the tail end of all this were a handful of Kensingtons.

The French soldiers seemed to have disappeared, yet everywhere, cluttering up the gutters were French packs, haversacks and carbines. We cursed them for this, throwing nasty reflections on their fighting qualities – but we might have saved our breath for it was us who were the fools. They knew more than we did.

The long black hours dragged by and gradually the streets of St Valery began to be littered with British equipment. Yet, although by now the British forces were as disorganised and in as great chaos as the French, not one British soldier threw away his rifle. Bren Guns could be had for the asking and ack-ack guns stood unattended. But every British soldier hung on to his rifle despite the fact that his chances of getting away were now impossibly slender.

The long, tired queue which had been moving only a few yards at a time now finally stopped. Men squatted down on the roadway and pavement, propping up their backs against anything that suggested ease. I don't know how long we waited there. It must have been hours. Then it started to rain. That steady drizzle that soaks you to the skin. We were all thoroughly down-hearted. I didn't know what to make of things. We took shelter from the rain under the trees in a terraced garden. Covering ourselves with ground sheets to keep out the big drops that dripped from the branches, we tried to make ourselves as comfortable as possible. But it was still uncomfortable.

I think I must have dozed off for I was awakened by someone calling for Kensingtons. We were then told that there would be no boats and it would not be possible for us to get away that night. It would be best if we went back to our trucks to get what sleep we could. It was still raining but the sky was turning grey and beginning to get lighter. I tramped back with Gus to where we had left the trucks. In the grey dawn St Valery was a scene of desolation. A scene of burnt out ruins, disabled Bren Carriers, and rows and rows of motor transport that had arrived more recently than we had.

So this was our "strategic withdrawal". The withdrawal they said would lengthen the Boche lines of communication. Strategic my eye! But we had withdrawn alright. The German Panzers had seen to that. We were cut off on all sides. The sea, which was to have been our line of retreat was now useless. No boats had turned up. Shoving off in small boats was out of the question anyway, since the Germans had taken the cliffs overlooking St Valery. From this strategic point they were able to sweep the entire beach with machine gun fire, making it impossible to evacuate by day. Tomorrow night, I thought, it may be too late.

But why hadn't the boats turned up as they should have done? That was the question we all asked. Later I read a newspaper account of what happened at St Valery. It was a glossily painted story and concluded with: "The boats at St Valery were unable to contact our forces because of the fog." There was no fog at St Valery. If there had been, we might have got away under cover of it.

Eventually we arrived back at our trucks. I found mine and

climbed inside. A couple of Jock infantry were already there and were snoring loudly but there was plenty of room. I rolled myself up in a blanket and followed their example. I must have slept very soundly for when I awoke, the sun was shining brilliantly. The two Jocks had gone and in their place were Morris and Feathers. Feathers was 2/Lt Hammond's batman. They both yawned, as I did. I fancied I heard a bugle call and just then a very noisy sergeant came running up the road. Through the back of the truck I could see him. He was carrying a small sack, into which he was thrusting a large tin of corned beef. He was shouting at the top of his voice, "Get all the grub you can! We are going to Germany!"

I watched him as he ran down the long line of trucks. I laughed. My two companions got out to see what was going on but I wriggled under my blankets and snuggled down. A few shots rang out among the trees and a chorus of voices yelled, "Stop that shooting you bloody fools! You'll make it all the worse!"

I was tired and still half asleep. I failed to comprehend what it was all about. I dozed but for some reason could not sleep. I could hear footsteps pacing up and down the road. Strange, but in my half-asleep state, I noticed the absence of the ring of heel and toe-plate on the hard road. Those footsteps had a different sound. They were Boche boots.

Something woke me. I sat up. Everything was quiet and still. Hastily I clambered out of the truck, grabbing my rifle. I looked around but there was not a soul in sight. A great deal of shouting was going on down the road, just around the bend. Slinging my rifle on my shoulder I sauntered off to investigate. I looked both sides of the road but I saw no-one. When I reached the bend, I stopped and stared. Behind the hedge was a tank. A grey tank with a big, black cross on its turret. One word flashed across my mind: "PANZER!"

Looking further down the road, I saw a German soldier. He was coming towards me, his rifle slung over his shoulder. He was shouting something. I strolled down the road to meet him. My hands were in my greatcoat pockets. My rifle was still over my shoulder. "Browning! Browning!", he shouted, pointing to his rifle and motioning me to throw mine away. I stood there regarding him. He pointed with his left hand. My eyes followed in that direction. There, in an open field, were rows and rows of British soldiers, unarmed. Someone recognised me.

"Get rid of your rifle Ray! Do as they tell you!"

Slowly it dawned on me that the whole position had been surrounded and every man-jack declared a prisoner of war. In which case, I reflected, I was also a prisoner of war and since I was still armed, the German who was telling me to throw away my "Browning" would be quite justified in shooting me.

I was completely stunned by this turn of events. Facing the German I felt like part of a Western film – ready to go for my gun the second my opponent made a false move. But he made no attempt to shoot me. His rifle remained slung over his shoulder the same as mine. With a "damn it all, what's the use" kind of attitude, I slung my rifle into a muddy ditch on one side of the road and my rifle bolt into the bushes on the other. Lee-Enfield no. G.1365 had come to an ignoble end – surrendered without firing a shot. It was with a feeling of great loathing and shame that I walked slowly over the field to join the ranks of prisoners.

I saw Gus and joined him but conversation was nil. Everybody seemed to be dazed. No-one was inclined to talk. The exception was a broad Scottish voice that that told the world what would happen to that fifth column bastard of a French General who had surrendered us if ever the Black Watch caught up with him. Gus spotted Captain Salmon and a few more of D Company. We went over to them. Then came an order that shook me to the very core.

"Get rid of your equipment! Dump your packs. You won't be needing them!"

This came from our own NCOs. Foolish lot of incompetent fools! Did they not know that the contents of those haversacks; that clean pair of socks, that warm cap, that comforter [scarf], that clean towel, that soap and that mess tin would have saved us from many hours and days of pain and privation?

I was disgusted with the whole show. I threw the contents of my pack in several different directions. "No knives," came the next order. I drew out my clasp knife and balanced it in my hand. It was one of those rare, extra-large models, and of Scottish origin. I had purchased it for ten francs from a Scottish fusilier at Rouen. With some regret, I dropped it in the wet grass.

The column of prisoners moved off out of the field. I noticed my rifle lying in the ditch, spattered with mud. I brought Gus's attention to it.

"That's my rifle," I said, rather brokenly.

"You mean that was your rifle," he replied.

Then someone in front turned round and said, "Cheer up Ray! You won't need that anymore. The war's over as far as you're concerned." I bit my lip at the thought. I wasn't so sure about that. We passed a couple of field guns drawn up on the side of the road, their breech blocks dismantled. We also passed a British general sitting on a milestone, His face was a picture of sullen defiance. "That's General Fortune," said somebody.[77]

"Do we salute?" asked a sarcastic voice.

A cat may look at a king. I looked at the General. He sat there, not caring a damn for the Boche. But the Boche in turn did not care a damn for him. I have often wondered how General Fortune must have felt. He was the commander of the most famous Division in the B.E.F., the "Fighting 51st". A division that had distinguished itself many times. To think that this was his inglorious end. I was in a tough spot myself – but he had my sympathy.

We marched on, passing a squad of French prisoners. They seemed to be taking things rather complacently. They were making a meal of what I recognised as Maconochie's. A solitary German sentry was standing over them as they sat on the grass. He was a typical Prussian, tall and hard-featured. He wore a steel helmet and a long greatcoat. He was the only German – other than officers – that I ever saw wearing a greatcoat. He stood there with his rifle at the secure, never moving or flinching. He looked hewn from a block of marble.

As we passed the French prisoners the boys gave vent to their feelings, telling the French, whose commander had let us down so badly, exactly what we thought of them. There was real barrack-room language flavoured with a few of the most choice swear-words in the Scottish vocabulary. But the French prisoners never even winced. They did not understand English – but I think they must have gathered that we did not like them.

Crossing a couple of open fields Gus and I were asked by a German if we would drive a captured Bren Carrier for him as he could not understand its workings. We looked into the cockpit, our eyes probing the mysteries of the Bren Carrier but shook our heads. We made it understood we did not know how to drive it, since we saw no chance of driving off with the vehicle.

There were a few stationary tanks dotted about here and there, with a handful of infantry. They were not large tanks by any means. They were painted dull grey with a large black cross and the insignia of a red devil on the turret. The uniform of the crews were of darker colour than usual and the piping round their epaulettes was different from the white piping of the infantry. Undoubtedly then, this was one of the notorious Panzer divisions I had heard so much about.[78]

When I saw these comparatively small forces to which we had been surrendered though, I became more and more convinced we had not only been surrendered, we had been sold. No doubt, if we had fought on, we would, after a time and owing to the poor strategic position of St Valery, been wiped out. The enemy would have brought up his heavier tanks and we had no tanks of our own left to counter such a weapon. But for all that, I do not think there was a single British soldier in that grim prison column who would not have fought on.

The June sunshine was what, under normal circumstances, I would have called "glorious". But to us, the hot sun was a torture. Our bodies sweated, our feet swelled and our throats became parched as we tramped over the narrow dusty roads of Normandy.

I saw Captain Salmon. He had fallen out by the side of the road in a state of exhaustion. We tried to help him but the German guards pushed us on. Our first instinct was to resist and to try and help our fallen officer but Capt Salmon insisted he would be alright and we had better go.

Hearing a plane overhead, I looked up and found to my surprise it was a British reconnaissance aircraft. It circled low over the prison column in a slow, leisurely manner. The Germans standing near their tanks opened up with their light machine guns but without any effect. On the other hand the presence of a British aircraft so low did not have the slightest effect on the Germans either. Those who were not guarding the column just stood where they were and looked up at it. Their faces were completely expressionless as the plane banked and turned before flying off towards the sea. It was the first RAF plane I had seen since we left Ilminster. It had arrived a little too late.[79]

My thirst was becoming unbearable as it was with everybody else. We tried getting water from a couple of German soldiers standing by the roadside. To my immense surprise they began to let us drink from their water bottles and I started to think these Germans were not such bad fellows after all. I had only succeeded in wetting my lips though, when the guards came up and interfered, causing the two soldiers to hastily withdraw.

Some of the men in the prison column discarded their respirators retaining only the haversack for the purposes of carrying such odds and ends as shaving kit (luckily I still had mine) or a bottle of water – that is, if they were lucky enough to find a bottle and some water to put in it. I followed their example and to make sure that no-one else would use the respirator, I tried to destroy it by jumping on it. Then I found out how strong a service respirator really is. 2/Lt Hammond saw me and in a sarcastic but good humoured voice said, "Surely Bailey, you're not throwing away your kit."

"No sir," I replied, "merely redistributing the load."

We followed what I thought was a very zig-zag course, mostly across fields and dusty by-roads until the column of prisoners came to a halt on a hill leading down to a small village. No sooner had the column stopped than we all sat down where we stood in the middle of the roadway to rest our tired feet.

The German sentries – who still paced tirelessly up and down the column – became a source of interest to us. We discussed their uniforms and equipment, comparing them with our own. We came to the conclusion that the German idea was much more sensible. Of course, we had to admit that their uniforms were rather the worse for wear and were darned in places, and the entrenching tools the infantry carried next to their bayonets were a little awkward ... but these trifles were overruled by the fact that the German soldier need never press his trousers and certainly never had to blanco up!

Ham made some witty remark about a hand grenade of the "potato masher" type, that one of the guards had stuck down the top of his jackboot and the conversation turned to the subject of hand grenades. It was so like Englishmen – discussing the advantages of various types of equipment – when they were bound for a Nazi prison camp.

The long column moved slowly forward again until we reached the village at the bottom of the hill. Here we were ushered into a large farmyard where we were allowed to rest while the officers were separated from the men. By this, we lost two good friends in the shape of 2/Lt Hammond, and Captain Salmon, whom the Germans had brought by truck since he had been incapable of walking the distance.

In the farmyard we threw ourselves down to rest, pulling off our boots and socks. We lay anywhere – some on the dirty ground, others on dung heaps. Gus and I chose an extra large dung heap on which to rest. Compared to our aching bodies, the tickling insects and the smell of the dung were only minor discomforts. I lay exhausted. A broody hen with a clutch of chicks began to investigate. One of her adventurous young perched itself on my head and started chirping in my ear. I had not the energy left to brush it off. We had lain there for about an hour when harsh German voices began to bawl, "Raus! Raus Engländer!"

I stirred myself. I pulled on my socks and boots. Hell! How those boots hurt me. My feet had swollen and felt as if a thousand red hot needles were piercing them. To put my weight on my feet was agony. Somehow I managed to stand up and – still in agony – hobble out of the farmyard. The column of prisoners was moving very slowly and I noticed that the guards were now considerably reinforced, not only by sentries on foot but by motorcycle combinations that patrolled up and down the length of the column. In the sidecars of the machines were mounted machine guns that covered us constantly as the motorcycles patrolled.

None of the prisoners could walk very fast and the Germans were getting impatient as we began to straggle out causing gaps to appear in the column. The guards and their NCOs were angry at our slow progress. They tried to make us double up [go faster]. By threats of force they succeeded to some extent. I saw one guard of the brutal type who had lost his temper completely. His face was red with rage. His harsh, guttural voice could be heard for some distance yelling.

"Raus! Raus!"

Seeing that the prisoners took little or no notice of his outbursts he reversed his rifle and clubbed them across the back, kicking them as they went down. We were made to double up like this on several occasions. In my anger, I hung back purposely but Gus pushed me on.

"Keep going Ray, they'll only make it worse!"

Not only did this exhaust what little energy we had but it was also degrading. Most Germans that we had seen so far carried cameras and some took photographs of us as we passed.

We marched many more miles. The day seemed endless. Several men dropped flat on their faces with sheer fatigue. I did not see them move again. It was hell. A truck passed us slowly. There were several men in the back that we recognised. Major Dodge was standing up, leaning on the tailboard. He was not wearing his own clothes. I later heard he had been in the sea a couple of times for already he had made an attempt at escape. Recognising us, he waved, telling us to keep our spirits up until the truck disappeared from view.[80,81]

By now, we were very hungry. I thanked heaven I still had a supply of the chocolate I had got from the deserted R.A.S.C. dump near Dieppe. I shared it with Gus. At last we reached our destination. This was a large orchard next to a farm. It had a large wall around it. As we went in, we were counted and searched for matches. These we were told we would have to surrender until the next morning when they would be returned. This was because we might start fires or signal to aircraft with them.

The column was split into three files and each one searched by a German private. The pile of matches began to grow bigger. Soon it was my turn. I had several boxes of matches and a considerable number of cigarettes. I knew there would soon be a shortage of these commodities and I had no wish to let the Germans have them if it could be helped.

My turn came. I handed the guard an old, half empty box, hoping that since I had voluntarily given up my matches, he would not bother to search me. But he was not satisfied. With the usual German thoroughness he began to search me anyway. My heart sank. It was then that fate intervened. At that critical moment, up came the German Feldwebel [sergeant]. It appeared the German soldier had done something wrong for the Feldwebel bawled and shouted at him in the manner of sergeant majors the world over, emitting a vocal venom that sounded like a string of blasphemous curses. The German soldier nearly jumped out of his skin. I felt glad I had never had that Feldwebel as my sergeant major.

While the guard was being reprimanded, I seized my opportunity and slipped past them into a batch of prisoners who had already been searched. Thus I saved my precious matches and cigarettes, which were of such quantity that I was able to keep the boys supplied for some time afterwards.

It was growing dusk. Sleep became a necessity. On this occasion and in the days that followed, the French prisoners who had joined the column were given preferential treatment. The majority had a barn to sleep in. Those that hadn't were given straw to lie on. We – the Engländers – had to sleep on the cold, hard ground, dressed as we were. Many of the infantry only had their battledress to keep them warm, having lost their greatcoats in action at St Valery.

I lay down near to Gus and tried to make the best of a bad job. Resting my head on my arm, I fell into a cramped, uneasy slumber. Thus ended my first day as a Nazi prisoner of war.

Part Three

CAPTIVITY

A PoW column is marched through northern France in 1940.

Chapter 6: "Gefangenenlager"

INTRODUCTORY NOTE

The PoW column

The battles fought in northern France during the spring of 1940 were the first major engagements of the Second World War. In addition to the 8,000 or so British captured at St Valery, many thousands had been captured on other battlefields or in the run up to the Dunkirk evacuation. There were also thousands of wounded men who found themselves left behind and reliant on the enemy for medical care. Most of these would eventually also become prisoners.

All told, it seems likely that around 40,000 British soldiers became captives of the German army in northern France during May and June of 1940[82] – and British prisoners were of course massively outnumbered by the French and French-colonial troops who had also been captured. The German military authorities had no detailed plans about how to deal with so many prisoners captured in such a short space of time nor was there any existing infrastructure to feed and shelter them, particularly in the immediate aftermath of their capture

The result was that these PoWs were formed up into huge columns, such as the one Ray found himself in, and marched off by their guards with no more detailed objective than that they should eventually be delivered to Germany or German-occupied Poland for long term incarceration. There are thought to have been hundreds of such columns of varying and shifting sizes on the roads of France during the summer of 1940, some containing hundreds, or even thousands, of prisoners. Almost without exception these men were exhausted, demoralised, starving and thirsty and many were sick. They were kept on their feet by abuse and beatings, with no choice but to drag themselves onwards step by agonising step, towards destinations that often even their captors did not know.

Gradually, the German military authorities established an ad hoc network of overnight stopping places for the PoW columns. These were typically in farm buildings, abandoned military facilities and sports stadia. In the worst cases though, they would be in open fields that had been commandeered for the purpose. Occasionally columns came together at these stopping places, merged for a while and then separated again. For the men involved, the experience must have been bewildering and relentlessly brutal.

The particular column that Ray was on seems at least initially to have contained several thousand men. It was estimated by eye-witnesses to have been between a mile and four miles long.[83] Accounts of the columns by other men who were on them, consistently confirm Ray's observation that the French prisoners were deliberately favoured over the British in terms of their treatment and material benefits. Conditions for the French were still poor but it does seem that they often received more and better food rations, were given greater access to shelter and were offered other minor comforts (such as straw to sleep on) that the British were denied. This was presumably a conscious policy choice by the German authorities, although it is not clear what the objective was (other than vindictiveness), since the men were already prisoners. The French were now out of the war of course – but singling out British PoWs for harsher treatment could not make it more likely that Britain would also eventually be beaten.

The distances covered by the column and the experience of being a PoW

Ray rarely indicates the passage of time. Towards the end of the coming chapter however, he reports that the news of the Armistice between France and Germany reached the column in Airaines. The Armistice was signed on June 22nd so, assuming Ray is remembering the location correctly, the march to that point had been going on probably for around ten days.

Ray also mentions in this chapter several places through which, or near which, the march passes. This makes it possible to track the route of the march on a map. It is interesting to note that the march does not proceed in even an approximation of a straight line. This is further evidence that at this early stage in the war, the arrangements for moving PoWs and the infrastructure for halting them overnight were nowhere near fully established. The places that Ray names and their approximate distance from St Valery are as follows: Yvetot (20 miles – 32 kilometres); Rouen (40mi – 64km), Buchy (45mi – 72km); Forges-les-Eaux (55mi – 88km); Gaillefontaine (58mi – 93km); Formerie (64mi – 103km); Abancourt (69mi – 111km); and Airaines (85mi – 140km).

It is not possible to work out how far the column travelled each day from these particular locations since not all of them are overnight stopping places – also, as we have seen, the column did not always take the shortest route from one place to another.

At the end of the chapter though, Ray specifically notes that that day's journey begins at Abancourt and ends at Airaines. That is a distance of around 16 miles. Ray also mentions that from Airaines, the march sets off the following day for Doullens. The distance from Airaines to Doullens is 25 miles (41 kilometres). It seems almost unbelievable that such large numbers of exhausted, malnourished men could cover theses kinds of distances in one day even under duress. That such long distances were covered however, is reiterated in Chapter 7, where Ray does give more detail about starting points and destinations.

Treatment of PoWs by their captors

As in the previous chapters, Ray's description is relatively benign by comparison with other eye-witness accounts. He concentrates on what might almost be called the "domestic detail" of life on the PoW column. He twice describes the march as "gruelling" but even that word is surely an understatement. With each day that passed, the march must have increasingly become an almost unbearable ordeal; an agonising test of each man's physical and psychological endurance.

Ray does not entirely shy away from the brutality of the experience however and this coming chapter gives a couple of examples of the casually vicious mistreatment that the marching prisoners experienced. For many of the other men who later wrote of their time on these columns though, it was this inhumanity – the starvation, the wilful refusal of water and the random acts of violence – that wholly dominated their recollections. It is widely reported for example that clubbing men with rifle butts to keep them in order was a regular occurrence. Slow walkers were also clubbed to "encourage" them to keep up (Ray describes this briefly too). Men who collapsed with exhaustion, many of whom were already injured, wounded or sick, were abandoned. Dead or alive, they would be gathered up by the trucks that followed on. Some were undoubtedly shot where they lay. Men who showed insubordination also risked summary execution. Attempted escapers could expect no mercy.

"Gefangenenlager"

In the morning Gus and I were able to arm ourselves with a supply of water by means of a couple of old bottles washed out and filled at the orchard pump. These we carried in our empty respirator haversacks , mine alongside my stock of cigarettes, chocolate and my shaving kit – the latter of which I had thrust into my greatcoat pocket at St Valery at the last minute.

I began to wonder when we would be fed, for the pangs of hunger were becoming acute. Gus noticed a number of Jocks clawing up a patch of garden with their fingers. We hurried over at once to see if we were missing anything and found they were digging up tiny potatoes. Some were eating them raw while others tried to roast them on fires made of straw and twigs. We joined the digging party for there were no signs of grub. Even raw potatoes were better than nothing. Clawing up the earth with our fingernails and little bits of wood, we were rewarded with sore tempers, broken fingernails and a dozen potatoes about the size of marbles. Although dispirited we were quite grateful.

Carrying off the fruits of our labours we returned to a group of our own regiment who were now lounging on the ground in the sunshine, which was already becoming warm. I ate a couple of the raw potatoes, chewing them very carefully but they tasted horrible. Being unused to such a diet, I gave up. Instead we filled out stomachs with water from the orchard pump. It gave us a feeling of fullness if nothing else. We then followed the example of the others and lay down under the trees to rest and wait.

As I lay, I looked around at my comrades. Most of them were completely worn out. Some were quiet and sullen, and regarded their captivity as a queer twist of fate. Others, like me, were angry and convinced they had been sold into slavery. There were some men – keen regular soldiers – who had put their heart and soul into their service. This was their ugly reward. I think these men must have been hardest hit of all. Among them was a warrant officer and as I watched him, I fancied I saw tears in his eyes. But there was no room for sentiment. We were all in the same boat even though that boat was a slave galley.

It must have been an hour later when we were ordered to "Raus!" and get on our feet ready to move off. Then, what I considered to be a very strange thing, happened. The Germans sorted us out according to our regiments. Then they lined us up ready to march off. I was surprised at the Germans knowing the names of our regiments but a still bigger surprise was to follow. The Kensingtons were first. We were to lead the prison column. So, with the Kensingtons leading, that gigantic prison column marched out of the camp.

As my boots crunched on the gritty road they reminded me of the previous day's gruelling march. I groaned at the thought, wondering how far we would have to go that day – but these thoughts were disturbed by the challenging voice of a German soldier. He was standing in the back of a stationary truck waving his arms and jumping about. I could not make out what he was saying at first but as we went by, his taunting voice shouted, "Ach, the Kensingtons! How many machine gunners left?"

He was answered with a timely raspberry and a hail of abuse. It amused me to think that a German should ask how many machine gunners my regiment had left, for even in England not many people had heard of the Kensingtons. However, we had put up a pretty good show in France so it is possible he knew the Kensingtons by personal experience rather than by regimental history.

Quite suddenly the column turned into a field where we were split into squads and herded into large diesel-engined trucks with railed sides that reminded me of cattle carriers. There was a great deal of speculation about what was going to happen next. One man said a German soldier had told him we were going to a camp near Rouen – this "going to Rouen" business was beginning to get monotonous.

It was destined to be a day of surprises. I was shocked when I found a civilian in the same truck as myself. He was a frightened little man who declared himself to be of Canadian origin. On his arm, looking strangely out of place, he wore the armband of the Imperial War Graves Commission. I asked him if he really was Canadian and how he came to be there but he motioned me not to talk so loud, in case the German sentry, sitting on a high seat on the back of the cab, might overhear. He did not want to advertise the fact that he was Canadian, saying the Germans did not like them. He seemed very nervous. I tried to assure him that Fritz, sitting up there with fixed bayonet and looking like a statue, was ignorant of all languages except his own but I failed to convince him. He firmly believed that we were being taken for a ride. For what other reason, he asked, would the Boche transport prisoners, except to line them up in front of a machine gun squad? I tried to calm him down by telling him that even the Germans couldn't do that sort of thing. Yet I knew they were just as likely to do that as anything else.[84]

The truck moved off, bumping and jogging across the field until it reached the road where it headed off towards its unknown destination. We sped across France, along roads littered with war equipment, wrecked field guns and dozens of dead, stinking mules. We passed another convoy even stranger than ours. It was composed of covered carts hauled entirely by horses. Someone started laughing and above the roar of the engine shouted a joke about the German army being mechanised. We all laughed but the German guard sat there as stiffly as ever.

We saw what once had been picturesque villages but were now nothing more than blackened ruins and heaps of rubble, still smoking from recent bombardment. I saw a signpost for Yvetot and wondered what Yvetot would be like under German rule. Perhaps they now occupied the same billets that we had. I could visualise them in HQ Company's chateau but I could not imagine them sleeping in our barn.

I saw signs that we were approaching a town. The roadside houses became more frequent and just ahead, over the brow of the hill, I could see a large column of smoke. When we reached the top a tall spire could be seen that I recognised as Rouen Cathedral.

The truck turned sharply off the main road and headed east through the countryside again. A large number of Messerschmitts flew overhead very low. Arriving at some crossroads we turned left, stopping at a farm. Here we were got out of the trucks and were hustled into another orchard.

A moan went up from the boys when they found it was already occupied by French prisoners. We thought we had got rid of them at the last camp. We cursed them again for already we could see that the "best places" were taken. Once more they had been given straw to sleep on by the Germans. For the British it was the hard ground. Even the trees in this orchard were small and stunted. They offered no protection whatever. The place was pretty crowded and it was only by good scouting on the part of Gus that we were able to find somewhere to lie down. This accomplished, we surveyed our new prison.

Some French prisoners were eating Maconochie's so I went over to see what could be had. I noticed that besides what they were already eating, they had their haversacks full of tinned food, such as corned beef and sardines. I pulled out about fifty cigarettes, knowing that there are few things a French soldier likes better than an English cigarette. I tried to do a little bartering with each one in turn but they laughed in my face. They told me that English cigarettes were good when times were good but now, when food was scarce, they were of little value. I pointed out that they had a good supply of English food, which really belonged to the British soldiers.

At that moment, a patrol of Jocks who were reconnoitring the camp in search of trouble, arrived on the scene. They saw me trying to barter with the Frenchmen and it aroused their suspicions, their appetites and their fighting instincts. When they spotted the British grub the Frenchmen had, they went off the deep end. They raved and roared at the Frenchmen, spitting out wicked Scotch curses that would have shocked the devil. They called them all the names under the sun, including robbers and fifth columnists. They called them ration stealers and accused them of looting our trucks at St Valery. But there comes a time when even a fifth columnist turns and this was one of them. Luckily there wasn't enough room for a fight but the Frenchmen rose to their feet in threatening attitudes.

Over on the edge of the orchard was the Feldwebel. He was red in the face from shouting. He did not like the idea of a rough-house in his prison camp. Some of the guards who stood near him shouted as well but none dared venture among the prisoners. At last the Feldwebel threw up his arms in despair and vanished from the scene.

I returned to Gus and had hardly sat down when crack! crack! crack! Bullets whistled overhead as a machine gun let loose a burst of fire. Nobody was hit. It was only a warning. But the Germans had not bothered to elevate the gun – or even sight it. They had just pressed the trigger. Had any tall man been standing up he would certainly have been shot through the head. The Jocks were in a slight hollow and at the first crack, threw themselves to the ground. The Feldwebel, standing by his machine gun, smiled with satisfaction.

Gus suggested we should replenish our supply of water in case we had to march again the next day. It was a wise move and off he went with both bottles while I stood guard over the two square yards of territory that was our sleeping space for the night. There was quite a crowd around the pump. Gus, who was by far the taller of the two of us, was more suited to elbowing his way through the crowd but when he returned he as looking very glum. The two bottles were still empty. I looked at him enquiringly but he was the first to speak

"No water in Nazi-land," he said. "All the water in London."

I eyed him rather queerly, thinking the strain had been too much for him. He explained himself.

"I couldn't get any water. I got to the pump but a Jerry came over and stopped me. He said, 'All the water is in London. This is Nazi-land!'"

I could not understand what manner of men these were – that

they would not allow their prisoners water to drink. Food I could understand. There was a scarcity of food. But water was plentiful. We smoked a last cigarette and lay down to sleep envying as we did so, the Frenchmen who had straw to sleep on and blankets to keep them warm. The night was cold and dark. Silent Scotsmen crept stealthily around the camp. French blankets were whisked away.

It started raining and I awoke in the night to find a young fox cub snuggled between Gus and me. I dragged it out and found it was wearing a collar. It was evidently a pet. Sleeping in a field is not nice under the most favourable conditions. On a wet night it is damned awful. But when foxes creep into your bed, I decided, things must be a little out of hand.

It rained until early morning. Men stood around in the grey dawn stamping their feet and swinging their arms to restore the circulation to their cold and cramped bodies. We were all very hungry and as soon as the sun came rose, we heard cries of "Grub up!" A good number of our troops who, by some miracle still possessed mess-tins, whipped them out and made their way to the entrance. Others, including Gus and me, hurriedly hunted about for old tins or anything that was capable of holding grub. Joining the end of an ever-growing queue, we reached the gate but discovered that we were the victims of a German ruse. There was no food and as the mess tins were held out, they were immediately seized and thrown on a heap. Precious metal. Aluminium for the Reich!

As we were marched out of camp, I noticed a pile of French helmets. More salvage. So on reaching the road I determined to get rid of my helmet at the first opportunity. I had no intention of helping the German war effort – not even in the way of scrap metal. Many others followed my example but first cut out the leather fittings to make a hat. I had no need to do this as I still had my side-hat folded in my respirator haversack (marvellous what you can get in a respirator haversack!).

The march that day was gruelling – as were the days that followed. We trudged along in the blazing June sunshine. When we were thirsty we would invade a water pump by the side of the road. By sheer weight of numbers we would succeed in temporarily quenching our thirst until driven off by the Germans, who fired shots in all directions. They were liable to flare up into a most towering rage and were masters in the art of shooting as close as possible without hitting anyone. It was prudent to move on.

I remember one guard on a bicycle who lost his temper completely. He raved and roared as he got off his machine, telling us to "Allez!" As he did so, he seized his bicycle and bounced it up and down on the road in sheer frenzy. Seeing that this had little effect, he whipped out his pistol and let shots fly all over the place. How he hit no-one was a mystery. But, as I said, in cases like this, it was wisest to move on – and keep moving.

The prison column reached the gutted town of Buchy, its ruins still smoking from the German bombs. It was midday and when we reached the centre of the town we were herded into cattle pens and allowed to rest. The rest was not a long one however and we were soon driven out again by harsh cries of "Raus! Raus!" As we passed out of Buchy our feet were more painful than ever through having rested. We passed a German soldier. He noticed our hobbling walk and took advantage of it.

"It's long way to Tipperary, ja?" he shouted.

A low murmur ran up and down the ranks of prisoners. Then with a stirring effect, a dozen cracked voices were raised,

"It's a long way to Tipperary,
It's a long way to go.
It's a long way to Tipperary
To the sweetest girl I know … Cor blimey!"

The effect on the Germans was amazing to see. The photographic-minded paused with their cameras in mid-air. The grinning young Nazis ceased to grin. The older Germans raised their eyebrows and stared. They had heard it before. The Engländer were singing their war song,

"Goodbye Piccadilly,

Farewell Leicester Square,
It's a long, long way to Tipperary,
But my heart's right there!"

It grew louder and louder until a thousand throats took up the song. Louder and louder still until the whole world seemed to stand in silence. In acknowledgement. It swept up and down that grim prison column as we marched on leaving the blackened walls of Buchy to echo and faintly re-echo the tune of "Tipperary".

We marched on past Forges-les-Eaux and Gaillefontaine. Footsore and hungry, we had been three days without food. Even our hardened Scottish comrades were feeling the strain. The Germans told us we would be put on a train the day after tomorrow and our marching would be over. But I soon learned that building up one's spirits and then breaking them down again is a favourite German method of undermining morale. I refused to believe them. It is as well I did for it was always "the day after tomorrow" and we never saw any trains.

Marching became a hell. Men dropped on their faces and lay still in the roadway. We could do nothing for them. The Germans did not even try, except to kick them and shout, "Raus! Raus!" Or else, let a pistol off next to their ears to see if they really were unconscious. Many who had previously served in the East lay white-faced and stricken with an attack of fever brought on by these barbarous conditions but they did not receive any medical aid.[85] They were left lying where they were until an open lorry came along and they were thrown in and carted off like so many sacks of sand.

Besides our usual guard of German infantry, there were a number of despatch riders who patrolled up and down giving instructions to the guards. I remember one stopping just after we had left Formerie. He was asking directions of someone and I heard him say "Gefangenenlager". I learned from German-speaking prisoners that this meant "prison camp". Passing the village of Blargies, we saw signs marked, "GEFANGENENLAGER". They appeared at every road junction until we reached the next camp at Abancourt. Every night after that we would look for that grim but welcome sign. It may have meant "prison camp" – but to us it also meant a rest.

When we reached Abancourt, the column came to a halt as the leading prisoners filed into the camp. I could see about half a dozen field kitchens near the entrance. This was to be our first meal. But I did not look forward to it in the least. I had forgotten what it was like to eat.

While we squatted on the road awaiting our turn to be fed, a German came up in a car and endeavoured to take a ciné film. I say "endeavoured" for his efforts did not meet with much success. He tried to film my little group as we sat on the road but as soon as he set up his apparatus, having no desire to become film stars, we rose in a body and turned the other way. He tried to coax us but gave it up. The next time I saw him he had his camera perched in the top of a tree and was taking a view of the camp.

A few of the boys tried getting into conversation with a German soldier who stood by. They asked him how the war was going – his version of it. He replied telling them that all twelve divisions were advancing on Paris where there had been a change of government and a minor revolution was in progress.[86] Someone in the queue then recollected the French having said that if the Germans ever reached Paris, they would give up the war. This was gloomy news indeed.

The queue moved forward and I was issued with my ration in a rusty tin I had picked up that morning. The meal consisted of a ladleful of bean soup – which became a dirty brown coloured bean soup. It was not nice to look at but it was not too bad to taste.

There were no incidents that night except the Germans let fly their usual burst of machine gun fire as a signal for us to settle down for the night. The next day we marched to Airaines where we had to sleep in a boggy field. It had a horrible persistent smell as if some dead bodies had been buried too near the surface. A stream flowed through the camp so we were able to wash and shave. It was here that I met Humphries, my pal of Mill Hill days. He borrowed my razor and looked as though he needed it.

At Airaines – as was usual – the French prisoners were given straw to sleep on. They also had sheets of corrugated iron that they rigged up to shelter themselves from the rain. But here, I think the Germans had ideas of keeping the peace for they put the French in a separate field. We had another ladle of bean soup as at Abancourt. This time, by skilful manoeuvring I was able to get a second helping.

We got news of the French Armistice.[87] The Froggies heard about it first and gave a loud cheer. They honestly thought they would be released and allowed to go home. They laughed at us but they were fools, for they were not released – neither then nor for a very long time after.[88]

The next morning we set out for Doullens and picked up turnips from the roadside that had probably fallen from a farm cart. I tried eating them but they were long past their prime and only suitable for pig food. Gus selected one of the best and declared he would boil it at the next camp. Under ordinary circumstances I would have laughed but my stomach reminded me it was no joke.

The prison column crossed the River Somme and had not gone far when I heard a rifle shot. I had heard no shots for several hours and, as everything had been quiet, I decided to see what was going on. A Jock was dashing across a field. The shot was probably a warning or a miss. In any case, the Jock kept on running. The sentry guarding my section of the column, raised his rifle, took aim and pressed the trigger. I saw the Jock fall. He pitched headlong on the ground and lay still. The guard slung his rifle and walked slowly over to him. He shoved the Jock with his boot but the Jock did not move. The guard turned and walked away, leaving on the ground the broken form of the brave, dead Scotsman. I did not mourn him. He did not need it. He had accomplished his object. He was free.

Chapter 7: "La Citadelle"

INTRODUCTORY NOTE

The Citadel at Doullens

The PoW column is marching towards Doullens. Doullens is approximately 110 miles (180 kilometres) from St Valery en Caux where the prisoners were captured and around 75 miles (120 kilometres) from the Belgian border.

Doullens, a small town in a largely rural area, is the site of a massive, sprawling fortification, *La Citadelle de Doullens*. The citadel (which is still standing) was begun in the 16th century as part of the defences along what was then France's northern border with the Spanish Netherlands. Over the centuries the site had had a number of uses including, during the First World War, as a Canadian military hospital. After the fall of France, the site had been commandeered by the German army and quickly brought into use as a temporary PoW camp. Its size and location made it a place where columns sometimes came together before being marched onwards, as seems to be the case in this chapter. In 1941, after the mass movement of prisoners captured during the Battle of France had subsided, La Citadelle became a permanent internment camp for French prisoners.

Daily distances marched by the PoW column

In this chapter Ray specifies the locations of the three camps between which the PoWs are marched (i.e. rather than just naming places through which they pass en route). This gives us a little more insight into the distances that prisoners were forced to march each day and confirms that the 25 miles implied in Chapter 6 was indeed correct. From Doullens, the prisoners are marched to Saint-Pol-sur-Ternoise, where they sleep on the racecourse. From St Pol, they are marched to Béthune and from there to Lille. The first of those journeys is about 17 miles (28 kilometres). The second is around 20 miles (33 kilometres) and the third is over 24 miles (38 kilometres). It is interesting to note also that the PoW column arrangements are sufficiently loose that Ray and Gus are able to gain an extra day's rest at Béthune by simply swapping to another column. Presumably when more than one column was present at a particular location the guards would have had no real hope of keeping the same prisoners in the same columns.

“La Citadelle”

We arrived at Doullens that evening. I remember going down the slope that led into the town, passing on our left what had once been a group of British army Nissen huts. A few were still standing but none was intact. A stick of bombs had been laid across them, wrecking the whole area.

Up the hill from the town came a couple of trucks laden with bread. It was indeed a rare sight. Some of the boys who were nearest tried to grab a loaf as the trucks went by but a German pistol intervened and put an end to any ambition they might have had in that direction. Turning sharply left we went up a rough drive, passing under an archway in a high stone wall. On the wall, in the now familiar script, was the sign, “GEFANGENENLAGER”.

Having passed through the archway, we were separated from the French prisoners. They filed off to the left while we turned right and were sent down a steep incline into a deep hollow. This had evidently once been the moat of the old castle or fort whose walls rose steeply in our right. This was *La Citadelle*, The Citadel.

An old marquee stood in the centre of the hollow. By the time we got there though, it was already full of men who had booked themselves a place to sleep for the night. I had to sleep out in the open again but that night the weather was fine. I sat down and watched the rest of the prisoners as they came trickling in. The Feldwebel was there again and as I watched, a rather amusing incident took place. That blustering German was not satisfied at the speed the prisoners were going into his camp. Once more he shouted and raved until he was red in the face. Then he began pushing them down the steep slope in an effort to make them go faster. The first two he pushed violently so that they slipped and rolled to the bottom. At that, the Jocks got their backs up and the fun started. The Feldwebel tried to push a third man but as he did so, someone tripped up the fat German and he went rolling down to the bottom himself. He landed on his backside – a picture of outraged dignity. He sat in a cloud of dust bellowing at the hundreds of squaddies who stood around laughing at him.

I found Gus again and we decided to boil the turnips we had found but first we needed a tin and some water. I got the water in our bottles while Gus hunted round for a tin. I toured our small but over-populated camp and found a queue of about two hundred men waiting to have their water bottle filled from a single tap that just dripped and dribbled. I waited patiently, noticing that a good many of our soldiers now had French water bottles. They had not been wasting their time.

I returned to where I had left Gus and found he had managed to get a tin of a sort. It was an empty five gallon petrol tin that had been cut in half. Of course, he explained, it still smelled a little of petrol. But it was all he could find so we rinsed it out. The turnips we peeled with a blunt, rusty penknife that I had found in a house in Martainville and had forgotten I had. I had picked it up because it had a corkscrew attachment. There would be no use for a corkscrew here!

We sliced up the turnips and discovered to our disgust that the insides were rotten but we made the best of it by cutting away the bad portions and using what was left. Gus stoked up a little fire, threw a few nettle leaves in the pot for flavour, and put it on to boil. The smoke didn't help it any – but it kept away the mosquitoes. Neither of us had any idea how long it took to boil turnips so we followed the simple method of testing it every few minutes to see how it was getting on. At last it was ready. We drained off the water and Gus tasted it. He said it seemed alright. I tasted it and complained about it not having any salt.

Thus we conjured up a buckshee meal under the shadow of the swastika. Unfortunately, it, had the delicate flavour of petrol. After a few mouthfuls, I gave up. My stomach was turning upside down. Gus felt the same way. A little bloke shuffled up to us where we sat. "Got any of that to spare, chum?" he asked. I handed him the whole potful. I wasn't being big-hearted. I just couldn't stomach my own stew.

I was rather disappointed by our failure as cooks. I lay back, crestfallen. Gus suggested I should have my feet dressed. I had forgotten about them. They were covered with blisters and in a bad way. There was a French first-aid post in a yard just beyond the bank the Feldwebel had been pushed down. It was not a very clean yard. In the corner stood a row of stagnant latrines which smelled as though they had not been cleaned out for years. Some filthy French soldiers still using them did not help matters. This was our first-aid post.

I took my place among the queue of sick men. Both French and British were waiting to receive attention. The first-aid I received was simple but nonetheless effective. It consisted of a piece of lint and a bandage. The French officer in charge examined the men's feet and chalked on the uniform of some, a white cross if he considered them too bad to walk. This was their passport to a truck the next day. It gave some men ideas and they began looking round for bits of chalk but he warned them that if there were more than the proper number of crosses tomorrow, they would all have to walk.

I thought I had seen that French officer before. I studied him as he went from man to man and I heard someone ask him if he knew where we were going.

"To Poland," he answered. Then he turned so everyone could hear. "To Poland," he repeated. "All British prisoners of war go to Poland!"

He then started to tell us the war news. According to him, London had been bombed – in fact, wiped out. I felt sorry for Gus when I told him what the French officer had said. Gus's family lived in London – in Kensington. He was worried as to what might have happened to them.

After a little careful thought, I decided not to believe the French officer. Only a little while previously I had seen him hobnobbing with some German officers, so it was not surprising that I regarded him with suspicion. It was his job to tell us these things to undermine our morale. He was a fifth columnist[89] and even though France had fallen, he was still very active.

Returning to the camp, I found most of the platoon had gathered together and were singing popular songs, such as *Roll Out the Barrel, Somewhere in France* and *We'll Hang Out the Washing on the Siegfried Line.* Strange to say "Siegfried Line" was still a favourite – and no Germans interfered.[90]

Soon, the singing died down and I noticed a couple of German soldiers leaning over a railing on a parapet. One of them was throwing scraps of bread to the prisoners below. His companion took photographs of them as, with wild eyes, they fought and clawed for these scraps from the Nazi table. It was a revolting sight.[91]

When they had finished their photography, the French officer appeared and told the rest of the camp what he had already told us. He moderated his "War News" a little and it was as well he did. He was booed and howled down by the prisoners, who shouted for food. Unable to make himself heard, the officer held up his arms as a gesture for quiet. After a talk with a German officer, he announced that there would be food that night and that next morning, we would be allowed to buy food from the townspeople. We were cheered by this news and the various sergeant majors present organised their food queues, for that was the only way of preventing a riot.

The food arrived. It was bean soup again and very dark in colour – but being hungry, we enjoyed it. After our meal we lay back, still hungry, and had a quiet smoke. I discussed the question of escape with Gus. At first he was not too keen but after we had discussed the matter thoroughly, he agreed it would be an idea if the opportunity presented itself. As we talked, many of the boys and some of our NCOs heard our conversation and vehemently condemned it. One even went as far as to say we would get a dozen bullets in our back before we even got ten yards.

I pointed out that it would be better to die by a bullet while trying to get somewhere, than sit around doing nothing and die of starvation. Someone spoke up and said conditions would be better once we got to a proper prison camp. But by that time, I said, if conditions were not better, we would all be too weak to attempt an escape. This failed to convince them. They all murmured disapproval at our plans.

Gus asked what would happen in the event of us being separated during an attempt to escape. He suggested a rendezvous where we could meet and discuss old times and eat tremendous meals. The problem of a meeting place cropped up for we realised that neither of us might have the same address after the war. I suggested Eros at eight o'clock on the first Saturday of any month. He agreed. Our imagination ran riot. We planned the most gluttonous meals – breakfast, dinner, tea and supper all rolled into one. He talked about lovely roast lamb but I said I wanted roast pork with sage and onions and heaps of roast potatoes. For tea, a plate of big strawberries with lashings of cream … and so it went on until a voice yelled, "Hey, can't you two stop yapping about grub? You'll send us all mad!" We both laughed and turned over to sleep.

That morning rather earlier than usual, we were marched out of the camp. As we passed through the gates, we were given a chunk of bread and a quantity of something they called coffee. We were highly delighted about our rations being increased to two meals a day. It was the first time we had had bread – and anything other than water to wash it down with. I was very pleased until I tasted this so-called coffee, then my estimation of German army cooking went down considerably. I took one taste and spat it out. It was undrinkable.[92]

Outside the Citadel on the other side of the road we were paraded on the green and made to sit down. Remembering what the French officer had said about allowing us to buy food from the townspeople, I wrangled my way to the front of the column. I had ideas about getting served before they sold out but I was disappointed for nothing happened. I think it was too early for anyone to be about. We must have waited there for about an hour. Most of the time was spent listening to a couple of Frenchmen who argued monotonously about a bicycle bell. Then we moved off and in the cobbled streets of Doullens I saw my first Nazi Stormtrooper.[93]

The long column of prisoners left Doullens and the daily trek began again. By now we had ceased to bother about where our next stop would be. All we worried about was when we would get there so we could ease our aching feet. Passing through a small town, which I think was Frevent, between Doullens and St Pol, I witnessed a rather pathetic scene. We were proceeding very slowly along a cobbled street when a woman with two children left the kerb and came running towards the column of prisoners. With tears running down her cheeks, she clasped her arms round a French prisoner and began kissing him. The children danced around clapping their hands. It was a touching scene. As I watched an older man came over and handed the French soldier a bag of food – bread, sausages and red wine. I felt sorry for them. Being a prisoner is bad enough. To march through your home town as an enemy prisoner and to meet your own wife and children and know that you will not see them again for a very long time, if ever. Surely this is a worse torture than the devil himself could devise.

The prison column stopped at St Pol. I knew it was St Pol by the numerous signposts we had passed. Here we were herded on to the racecourse and parked for the night. We were fed and watered again with the familiar bean soup. This took more time than usual as there was only one queue. While we were waiting I heard a German who claimed to have been to school in England, say that we were going to Poland. "But first", he added, "you will march through the streets of Berlin!" They seemed very definite about this Poland business …

Gus and I had just settled down for the night – heads to the wind to keep out the draught – when there was a sudden cacophony of aircraft engines and three Spitfires raced over the treetops. It was an unexpected sight for us – and must have been even more unexpected for the German with the machine gun, perched high on the tower near the grandstand. Although he swivelled his gun round quickly, the Spitfires were gone before he could take aim.

Next morning, we left St Pol Racecourse and took the long straight road to Béthune. We passed many people working in the fields. They waved to us as we went past. Because of our physical condition, progress was very slow. About halfway to Béthune we stopped and were put into a field, where we rested. From the villages around came people with sandwiches, bread, cubes of sugar and little twists of tobacco screwed up in pieces of newspaper. They came up to this field full of prisoners and threw their gifts over the hedge. Quite naturally there was a scramble and shots were fired. Our benefactors were driven off and order restored.

We remained in the field for an hour before moving off again. News of our coming must have travelled fast for, from then on until we reached Béthune, the road was lined with people whose only ambition in life it seemed was to give us food. We felt we had never eaten so much in all our lives. But suddenly I heard a woman scream and I looked in that direction.

A Jock had run right out of the column and was being given food by a knot of women on the opposite side of the road. I can understand the Jock being desperately hungry but after the last few kilometres of plenty, I thought he was going a little too far. A German sentry intervened. He yelled and shouted at the Jock who took no notice but went on eating. Then he fixed his bayonet and the women screamed again.

The Jock continued wolfing food and scrabbling around in the women's baskets for more. More Germans arrived and made a fierce rush at the women with fixed bayonets. They fled, screaming as they disappeared down a side-street.[94] The Jock who had been the cause of the trouble ran back across the road and re-joined the prison column and I lost sight of him.

I realised how wonderful were these people of Pas-de-Calais who had gone to immense trouble and taken such grave risks to help us. I remember passing through a village where, for some reason or other, the prison column had slowed down. We were on the pavement and progress was zero when I saw an open window. I looked in and shouted for bread. To my surprise, a voice answered in English and said it was alright to ask for bread but my French pronunciation was terrible. A woman and a young girl came to the window. They explained that they were a Scottish family but had been living there for some years. The woman said she regretted that it was not baking day until tomorrow but said she had a loaf her daughter had baked that was so heavy no-one would eat it.

Gus eagerly grasped the loaf as it was handed through the window – "tomorrow's rations," I thought – but I noted the look of surprise on Gus's face when he felt it. The column moved forward again and casually, he handed the loaf to me. I held it in one hand and almost dropped it. It must have been the heaviest loaf ever made!

The prison column marched into Béthune that evening. Somehow Béthune was different from the other towns we had passed through. People lined the streets as we went by. We felt as though a thousand eyes were watching us. It was not nice. It made me feel uncomfortable. As we went along a chap in front of me – a little more cheerful than the rest – spotted a coal miner with a bicycle. Looking at the miner's black face he asked, "What are you up to chum?"

He never expected an answer but he got one. "Same as you chum," came the quiet but definitely English reply. I blinked my eyes and trudged on, wondering who the miner was. Anything could happen now.[95]

We turned into a back street which led to a sports ground. This was to be our camp for the night. It was a fairly large place, oval in shape, with high walls, reminding me of an arena. On one side was a large pavilion and a grandstand. Encircling the arena was what once had been a racetrack. No-one was allowed on this. It formed a kind of no-man's land between the prisoners and the outer walls.

There was no issue of food that night but thanks to the kind people of Pas-de-Calais we were far from hungry and still had a little food to spare. I thought they were very brave people. Silently I thanked them again.

Sitting on the ground I saw a fellow prisoner wearing a trilby hat.

I approached him about it, thinking it might be useful sometime in the future but unfortunately it was not for sale.

Collecting civilian clothes in a prison camp is a very useful hobby. One that I can recommend.

My failure as a fashion buyer was soon forgotten by an unusual announcement from the loudspeaker on top of the grandstand. Up to the present it had been monotonously gurgling in French but now it was different. Like Radio Bremen, it had an announcement to make in English.

It began by stating that a British soldier had made a most vulgar gesture while passing through the streets of Béthune – and the German officer at whom it was intended, was furious. The next man caught doing it would be severely punished. I glanced at Gus. It tickled us so much we nearly split our sides with laughter. Late in the evening we were all settling down to make the best of sleeping on the hard ground when the loudspeaker made another announcement in English, "Anyone who wants a good bed for the night," it said, "should make their way over to the gate on the right."

We did so. Leaving the arena we went through the gate and down a short drive guarded by German sentries. We reached a collection of huts. On our left was a stretch of grassy land about a hundred yards wide with, on the far side, an ordinary fence and an ordinary gate. Behind the fence was a crowd of French girls, who waved and shouted to the prisoners. Beyond that gate, I thought, lay a covered retreat and safety. But between me and the gate was a good hundred yards of open ground. I remembered the Jock who had been shot before he got thirty yards. Not yet, I thought.

On reaching the huts, we turned right into a long concrete building that I decided was a rifle range. Into this we filed to sleep. The floor was covered quite generously with straw so that, even though it was rather dark in there, we made ourselves quite comfortable.

A good deal of bartering started when we got inside. Perhaps a chap with a bit more bread than he needed would swap with another who had an egg to spare and so on. It was because of this bartering business that the French and British became friendly for the first time since that disgraceful show at St Valery. I think by now the French realised the Germans had no intention of setting them free even though their country had capitulated. The British, on the other hand, had nothing to lose – and a lot to gain – by being friendly with the French. The French are good allies and awkward enemies, even in a prison camp.

A quartet on the other side of the billet struck up a chorus and the rest joined in. A Tommy who didn't care for red wine he had been given, gave it to a Frenchman and he joined in the singing. After the hell march from St Valery, it was a great sight to see the British and the French friendly again. We all sang and sang. We sang ourselves to sleep that night.

Next morning we paraded for our morning meal. It was bean soup again but we had some bread with it and a little more than we had at Doullens. Half a round loaf of bread was given to every three men and they were left to share it out themselves. It fell to Gus, me and a Frenchman. Between the three of us, only the Frenchman had a knife so it was his lot to cut it into three equal parts. I look back with some amusement on how we held on to that Frenchman in the crowd in case he absconded with the bread.

A great number of the prisoners went on again that morning including most of the Kensingtons. Gus and I hung back among the French to gain a day's respite. We were getting too near the Belgian frontier for my liking. I pointed out to Gus that if we did not make a break before we reached Belgium, we would have an additional frontier to cross on our way back. The day passed without any undue excitement. One thing that interested me was how the prisoners communicated with the people outside by giving them a few francs wrapped in paper to buy them cigarettes. To do this, they had to run across the race-track to reach the outer walls. For some reason, this race-track, which formed a kind of no-man's land was not so well guarded on the second day. At the bottom of the wall next to a bush was a hole just big enough for a packet of cigarettes to be pushed through. I watched one chap run across several times, crouching low behind the bush waiting for his pals to signal to him it was safe to return.

Again we slept in the rifle range. We left Béthune the next morning. By now, I had formed a detailed plan of action. I decided to make a dash the very first time the guards showed any signs of relaxing. I still had my money and a small compass that I had hidden in my battle dress on the first day. I intended to make my way to Spain, that being the only neutral country on the way home. I believed at that time that all of France had fallen and was in German hands. I had never heard of unoccupied France. I imagined getting civilian clothes from the first clothes line, marching hundreds of miles across country avoiding towns and villages, and living on what food I could get from isolated farms. How very different it was to turn out.

Béthune was soon left far behind as we tramped further across conquered France towards Lille, which was to be the next stop. Our guards, I noticed, had not decreased in number. There were still the usual infantry guards who marched by the side of the prison column and when not on duty, rode behind on bicycles. At the head of the column was a lorry with a Bren Gun on the back. This lorry was used to set the pace. Up and down the length of the column toured a motorcycle combination with its machine gun ready for action. I felt a little disheartened when I weighed up the odds. The Germans, with their traditional efficiency showed no signs of relaxing their vigilance.

We had not received any food from French civilians since our arrival at Béthune. But quite unexpectedly, out of a roadside cottage came a woman carrying a big pot. It was stew. Thick delicious stew. Disregarding the Germans, she dumped it by the roadside and turning, ran for her life. The result can be well imagined. No-one had smelled stew like that since leaving civvy street. There was one mad rush but the Germans didn't mind that sort of thing happening every once in a while, so long as the prisoners kept to the middle of the road and didn't take too long. Not that they could stop them anyway, except by shooting them all stone dead and they would never do that with British prisoners. They might need hostages to dictate the peace terms.

Being a little chap, I couldn't get anywhere near the stew pot, so I weighed up my surroundings instead. But the Boche were eagle-eyed. There was no escape here – and my biggest disappointment was just about to come. I had lost my pal Gus. Though I searched up and down the column, I could not find him. That was the last I ever saw of him.

About noon the Germans turned us into a field to rest. I glanced ahead down the road as I went in. I knew that the time for action was getting near. When we left that field, I thought, if I could get anywhere near the head of the column my chances of escape would be greatly increased because the bulk of the German guards would be busy getting the tired prisoners to their feet and driving them out. I noted all that I saw in that glance down the road. There was a railway bridge a hundred yards ahead and beyond that a field of tall green corn. Good. Further still was a small, dense-looking wood. My pulse was beating quicker. It wouldn't be long now.

I looked around the field for Gus but again failed to find him, so I sat down to think. I smoked innumerable cigarettes. It was like waiting for what in the last war they called "going over the top". The minutes dragged by. Then, at last, we began to move again. I took good care to get in the front of the column – but not so near the front as to be in view of the truck with the Bren Gun. The column tramped off down the road. My companions now were mostly French with a sprinkling of Jocks.

Now we were passing the cornfield. Five yards inside that corn, I decided, a man would be invisible. Five seconds, I calculated, to get there and be still. Five seconds to freedom if, for such an infinitesimal time, those German sentries looked the other way… if.

I wrangled my way to the inside file of the column next to the cornfield but a German sentry marched just opposite. The precious cornfield was slipping slowly by. Then Providence intervened. There was some confusion to the rear. I looked and saw a disturbance among the prisoners. Above their voices, I heard the angry German yells of "Raus! Raus!" This was nothing uncommon. Perhaps someone had gone down and his pals had refused to leave him lying there. Or perhaps the Jocks had deliberately "tied a knot" in the column for they knew the Germans didn't like us being on these narrow roads because it held up their transport convoys.

I watched my sentry. I saw him turn. He looked back, seeming anxious. Then he took a couple of paces in the direction of the disturbance.

It was now or never.

I turned back quickly but we had passed the cornfield and in front of me was a hedge. A low ragged hedge. I doubled into a crouch. Suddenly I felt myself going forward. I jumped. I sailed through the air. I was over. I grazed my knuckles on the bark of a tree. A few more steps and I dropped face downwards among the bramble bushes, hardly daring to move. From the road came the noise of the prison column. But there were no shots. I had not been seen.[96]

How long I lay there I don't know. The prison column moved slowly by. I was stiff and cramped but I did not dare move until the hubbub died away in the distance. Then, cautiously, I ventured to lift my head and look through the bushes. I could see a couple of German soldiers on bicycles talking to some French girls. They were two of the guards who were not on duty and were riding behind the column.

I sank back again, cursing my luck. Either of them might easily spot me where I lay. I hoped the feminine charms of the French girls held their attention until they had to go. A few minutes later – it seemed like hours to me – I heard them mount their bicycles and ride off. When the tinkling of bicycle bells had died away, I rose from my hiding place and crept silently into the woods.

I was free.

Part Four

ESCAPE THROUGH FRANCE

The demarcation line between Occupied France and the Zone Libre near the village of Cormery, south of Tours. It is impossible to know for sure but examination of wartime maps of the area suggests this as the most likely crossing point for Ray.

Chapter 8: Madame Benoit

INTRODUCTORY NOTE

Escaped British prisoners-of-war in France

As we have already seen, in the weeks leading up to the fall of France, around half a million largely British soldiers were evacuated (almost 350,000 from Dunkirk and a further 160,000 or so from various French ports further to the south and west). 40,000 others were much less fortunate and were taken prisoner by the German army. For these men, the only way to avoid five long, terrible years in captivity was to escape. Some, like Ray, reasoned that it was best to act at the earliest possible opportunity.

Before considering those men who escaped from the forced marches, however, it is important to note that there were far more British "evaders" than British escapers at large in north-western France and western Belgium during the summer and autumn of 1940. Evaders are those combatants who have never been captured in the first place. There are several ways in which individual soldiers or groups of soldiers become evaders: they may have got lost or become separated from their units during the fighting; they may have been part of a outlying group that failed to receive a signal to lay down their arms; they may have been wounded and unable to keep up with the retreat; or they may have slipped away during the latter stages of fighting when defeat had become inevitable and the order given "every man for himself". Fairly obviously, they may also have been deserters.

There is no count – or even a particularly reliable estimate – of how many British soldiers were in hiding near the Franco-Belgian border during the summer and autumn of 1940 but it is broadly accepted that the number was comfortably into four figures.[97] During June, the evaders were subsequently joined by a sprinkling of men who had had the same thought as Ray – that there would never be a better chance to get away than here in France, out in the open, with potential hiding places all around, the minimum of occupied territory to travel across – and a sporting chance of help and support from a sympathetic local population.

Evaders and escapers were significantly more likely to be captured (or recaptured) than to make it back to Britain. Some, as was the case for the Scottish infantryman whose attempted escape was witnessed by Ray, would enjoy no more than a few seconds of freedom before they met with sudden, brutal death. Of the 170,000 British PoWs taken in Europe during almost six years of the Second World War, fewer than 1200 escaped and made it home.[98] Nerves of steel, a resilient nature and a hell of a lot of good luck were required.

Ray strikes very lucky, very quickly. He will have his scares, and his share of misery and pain. It is a long and hazardous road back to Bedfordshire. But if he owes his successful escape to anything, he owes it to what happens in the first 24 hours...

Madame Benoit

I had not gone far into the wood when I heard the cracking of a twig underfoot from the direction of the cornfield. I stood perfectly still, camouflaged by my uniform. Someone else was in the wood and I did not dare take an unnecessary risk. For a full five minutes I stood completely motionless, then I heard the noise again. This time it was nearer. Then nearer still. It reminded me of the Germans in the Bouzonville Forest. Surely though, this could be no conquering German creeping furtively through a little French wood. The only way to find out was to do a little stalking of my own.

I got down on my stomach and wriggled round to the rear of where I had heard the last noises. It took me some time but I was quite successful for I knew he was now in front of me. I rose from the ground. I saw him – at least I thought I did for the bushes were moving as if someone was pushing through them. I went forward quietly and it did not take me long to catch up with him. Suddenly he turned round and I have never seen an expression of greater surprise on any man's face than I did on his.

I was equally surprised. He was a French soldier – young – about my own age I imagined. Walking over to him I began talking but he shook his head vacantly. He did not understand English. I ignored this language difficulty for I needed a friend – and in this fellow escapee, I saw a very useful friend. He could speak the vitally necessary French and I couldn't.

I decided to pave the way to his heart with a cigarette and by signs we got on splendidly. I discovered his name was André Legrande. I watched him cast off his tunic revealing an orange pullover. Out of his haversack he took a couple of white shirts which I recognised as having been issued by the Red Cross at Béthune. I hadn't tried to get one myself as the shirts of some men were in ribbons.

André handed one of the shirts to me, so I began disrobing. Off came my greatcoat and battledress tunic. I was about to dispose of my army pullover but he stopped me by making signs that it would be cold at night so I should roll it up and carry it under my arm.

While André was making his change I scouted around the vicinity. What I needed was a pair of trousers and I found a pair – of a kind! I dug them out of a rubbish tip. They were very well worn and they were crawling with cockroaches but a good shaking got rid of most of those. I pulled them over my battledress trousers and tried to look like a civilian.

I reckoned I might pass at a distance except for my respirator haversack. I decided to get rid of it. It meant carrying my shaving kit wrapped up in a rag of towel, and stuffing what cigarettes and tobacco I had left into my pockets. André was ready when I rejoined him and he led us to the other side of the wood. I looked back at the spot we had just left, with its heaps of khaki. It looked like a quartermaster's store. Perhaps some villager would come along and find a thick army greatcoat that would keep his bed warm at night – or take it home to show his wife and together they would wonder what happened to the poor Tommy who owned it.

No sooner did we reach a clearing on the other side of the wood than I remembered that I had left my money and compass stitched into my battledress. They were too valuable to leave behind for, with André's French and my money we could buy what food we wanted for some time. Making signs for André to remain I made my way back. I still moved very cautiously for although I could neither see or hear any Germans I knew that in more ways than one, I was not yet out of the woods.

When I returned, I found to my surprise that André was talking to a civilian. He looked friendly so I joined them but could not make head nor tail of their conversation. André was doing most of the talking and by the way he gestured, I could see he was discussing the question of clothes. This was confirmed when André indicated me and the civilian stepped back, measuring me with his eyes. He indicated some bushes and motioned for us to hide – then off he went. It was here I really got down to brass tacks with André. Hidden under the bushes we tried to form a plan of campaign. I tried to ask him in French where he lived but failed miserably at first. Then, by drawing a map of France on a scrap of paper and marking most of the prominent towns, I was able to ask him where he was going. He indicated Cherbourg and told me his home was there. By various methods and a little practice we soon improved our sign language so that we could converse. I learned his age was nineteen and he had also been captured at St Valery.

So far I had asked all the questions but André's turn came. He wanted to know my name. I told him and he tried to imitate but somehow he could not get his tongue around it. He then asked me where I was going. I thought hard but I did not know what to say. I didn't like the idea of telling him I was on my way to Spain – about 800 miles away – because it sounded so ridiculous. I pondered for a while but I could see he was still waiting for an answer. Not being able to think of one, I shrugged my shoulders. He looked rather disappointed.

Presently the civilian returned carrying under his arm a bundle of clothes. Seeing him approach, we came out of hiding. He had a blue serge suite for André. It fitted him perfectly. He had a jacket and a pair of trousers for me. I was delighted with them despite the fact that they were several sizes too big – they were clean, which was much more important. Once more we changed our clothes and thanking the civilian, we made our way from the wood up a narrow cart-track. Here André stopped two small boys on bicycles. A conversation followed during which the two boys seemed very interested in my head. Suddenly they dashed off on their bicycles and we sat down on the grassy bank to wait.

The two boys returned bringing with them a shopping bag. The first thing they had brought was a beret for me. This explained why they had been so interested in my head. I put it on. Now I looked like a Frenchman! After the beret followed a stream of sandwiches, bread and butter, a litre bottle full of coffee and a few eggs. The two boys gasped with wonder at our appetites. I don't think they had ever seen anyone eat like that before. The eggs were raw but that did not matter. Eating raw eggs was a habit I had already become accustomed to.

We finished our little picnic and managed to save a couple of sandwiches for later. Then we exchanged addresses with the two boys. They wanted my address especially. André had told them I was "un soldat Anglais" and although it was only two hours since I had escaped, I was expecting terrible hardships but I was already amazed at the number of people who wanted to help me. I was sorry for the things I had thought of the French at St Valery.

Leaving the two boys, we went on our way, taking a westerly direction. I decided to accompany André probably as far as Rouen, where I would have to cut off if I wanted to reach Spain. We followed cart-tracks and by-roads until dusk fell, when we slept in a haystack. All during that day since leaving the wood we had not seen a single German.

We had quite a comfortable sleep in the haystack. The next morning we finished off our sandwiches and resumed our trek. This time André walked about a hundred yards ahead of me, stopping at every corner and signalling if the coast was clear. He realised as well as I did that my ill-fitting clothes would arouse suspicion – especially since a column of prisoners had passed that way.

Once I watched him stop a couple of cyclists – a man and a woman on a tandem. In less than no time he was examining their map. About dinner time, I watched him go into a rather lonely house by the roadside. I judged he was after food for he seemed not the type to go hungry for long if he could help it. I walked slowly towards the house expecting André to come out any minute. But no André appeared.

I walked past the house but there was no sign of André anywhere. I was beginning to get alarmed. I walked on up the road. He had been in the house far too long. Finally, I sat down on the grass verge, screened by a bush. I could see the house but no-one in the house could see me. I thought something must have happened to André but then suddenly the door opened and two women appeared.

Very strange, I thought.

Then I saw André. He dashed out and I stood up so he could see me, wondering all the time what was going to happen next. When he saw me he stopped running and began waving his arms. He was very excited.

He shouted to me, "Madame speak English! Madame speak English!"

The women were waving too, so I decided to investigate.

No sooner did I reach them than I was ushered through the yard and into the house.

The gate was locked behind me. Very unusual.

I was given a chair at one end of a table and André sat down at the other. A conversation ensued between André and Madame. The other woman was obviously her daughter. Madame asked me a few things in broken English, including whether I was hungry. Quite naturally I answered "yes" – and a meal was prepared.

Madame Benoit (as she was called) went on to tell me that when that part of France had been occupied by the British, several officers had been billeted there. Judging by the amount of British army food she had in stock, she must have had several Quartermaster Sergeants as well!

Madame Benoit did not speak good English, mind you – but it was understandable. While we talked, I noticed that her three sons aged about eleven, fourteen and fifteen looked on with interest. From the youngest, the boys were Clément, Jean and René. Jean looked at me and Madame in turn, puckering his brow now and then. I learned later that he was the budding linguist of the family.

André and I had dinner in the garden with the boys. Madame said it was safer that way in case any inquisitive Germans came to the house and found too many plates on the table. I guessed that was why the back gate had been locked behind me so quickly. It was an extra precaution. An outer defence so to speak.

The dinner itself I can say was the best I had tasted for a long time and was followed by a liberal quantity of red wine.

After dinner René brought a pack of cards from the house and André and I simply had to accept the invitation to play. The garden was rather secluded so there was no fear of intrusion.

Of course, we did not play for money, which was lucky for me. Boy, oh boy, could those kids cheat! They had also learned something from those officers – or quartermaster sergeants, or whatever they had billeted upon them – for now and again they would, quite innocently from their point of view, come out with English words that could definitely be labelled "Aldershot".[99]

After our card game we talked (or tried to talk) and smoked until tea-time arrived. All three of the boys smoked – and at such a rate that the garden resembled a saloon bar. The tea was as good as the dinner. It included jam. I remember Madame saying, "All Tommies like Tickler's jam".[100]

After tea, it wasn't quite so warm so we all went back into the house. It was then that I realised I wasn't making much headway on my way to Rouen, Cherbourg, Spain – or wherever I was going.

Madame's husband had returned home though, so I forgot all about Spain for the rest of the evening. I found M. Benoit a very interesting person. He could speak German fluently which was a valuable asset in occupied territory. He was much older than Madame and had been in the last war. He always said – in common with most Frenchmen – *La Guerre Quatorze* was a good war but *la guerre contre Hitler* was no good.

Whenever he said that he always shook his head. Before long I realised the whole family believed that one day the British would return to drive back the Boche. The Benoits, not having seen the fiasco at St Valery, had more faith than I had at the time.

When darkness fell, I began to think in terms of haystacks but Madame said we must stay there for the night. She gave us a large bedroom and the bed was a real one – not a haystack or a folded camouflage net – but a real cosy bed. The window faced north. I pushed it open and looked out.

Down in the valley I could see the village of Acheville with its mines and slag heaps, reminding me of the north country.* As I looked I heard faintly the noise of a bugle – a German bugle. It was lights out.

The following morning I had a pleasant surprise. I was awakened by young Clément bringing me a cup of coffee. Clément was a cheery little chap and as my stay lengthened, which it did, we became quite attached to each other. Regularly every morning he would be there with this cup of coffee. I regarded this as an extravagant luxury. Never before had I ever indulged in coffee in bed. After ten days or so of privation with the Germans, this was yet another something to be thankful for – another little debt I must certainly pay back to these kind people who had befriended me in time of need. These foreigners – no, we were not foreigners really, neither me to them nor them to me – who had taken me in and fed me. Me, an escaped prisoner of war, when my very presence if discovered would mean a firing party for all concerned. This struck me very keenly for in my opinion, even under peace conditions, to take a hungry stranger under your roof, to feed him, to give him a bed for the night and trust him without question is undoubtedly the grandest deed a human being can possibly perform. I had much to be thankful for.

Yet more was to come. During the morning Madame took me into the room adjoining the living room. Without offering any explanation or expecting any thanks she raised the lid of a big old-fashioned chest. Out of it she brought a grey suit. It fitted me

---

* The Pas-de-Calais region of France was at this time, an important coal-mining area. Acheville, near which the Benoit family lived, was a tiny pit village of only 295 inhabitants (French Census, 1936). Acheville is about four miles (6.5 kilometres) south-east of the city of Lens and about eleven miles (18 kilometres) south of Wingles where Ray had made his escape. Ray's father had been a miner in Chester-le-Street, County Durham and Ray had been born in that town, so – depending how old he was when his family moved to the south of England – it is probable that Ray was familiar with scenery of the kind around Acheville.

perfectly and was a big improvement on the clothes I had been wearing.

André and I stayed there the next night and the next until a whole week had passed. But André was impatient to go home. The Benoit family wanted me to stay longer – for the duration of the war if necessary! Not having any definite plans – that is to say, not any sensible plans – I accepted their offer.

One morning André left on foot for his home. Before he went, he gave me his address, a farm in the hills behind Cherbourg. Clément and Jean escorted him as far as Acheville, a couple of kilometres away. When they got back, they had quite a tale to tell. Very excitedly and with Madame Benoit acting as interpreter, they told me how André had got off the mark. It appeared that on reaching the village André had decided Cherbourg was much too far away to walk so he had stolen a bicycle. Jean described how he had stolen it from outside an estaminet and how, as André rode off, the half drunk owner went staggering up the road trying to chase him.

During my stay with the Benoit family, I was very well looked after. I was not allowed to get bored, they saw to that. One day when Madame Benoit returned from the village she brought me quite an assortment of English books to read. She explained she had got them from an English lady and gentleman who lived there. I don't know how they managed to live there under German rule but I didn't ask embarrassing questions. I just took it for granted that in Acheville there lived an English lady and gentleman. Who they were or what they did was none of my business.

The three boys also kept me pretty busy. Like all children they had crazes from time to time. First it was wooden pistols. These had to be carved with a knife and they insisted on having two each. The next craze was catapults to shoot sparrows. Then came kites. Each one wanted a kite of his own. No sooner would I finish René's kite than Clément would discover his kite was not quite so good and he would want a better one. And so it went on, each boy wanting a better kite than the other until the kite business got out of hand and

I prayed that the wind would drop.

I was reading in a secluded corner of the garden one day when the three boys crept up and started to use their catapults to good effect, causing me to make a hasty withdrawal. I guessed what they wanted was a little fun so my retaliation would be welcomed. Without further ado, I constructed a catapult and a pitched battle was fought in the garden. Now I was in an unfortunate position. Not wishing to hurt anybody, I had to aim as near as possible without hitting them. But when the boys aimed they aimed to hit. I soon found myself on the retreat with my back to the little wooden gate when Madame suddenly appeared. She was accompanied by a strange young woman who split her sides with laughter at our catapult duel.

Madame called to me, saying the young lady wished to see me. I thought it very unusual. I called a truce with the boys and went over. This was "Jacqueline". I shook hands with her, told her I was pleased to meet her etc. but no sooner had I done so than I realised she had not come to see me in that sense. She merely wanted to look at me. Instead of talking to me, she talked about me with Madame. Evidently there was something about me that called for a great deal of conversation – so much so, in fact, that they completely forgot about my presence and began strolling back to the house still talking about me. It was not a breach of etiquette. They were simply too interested in something. I sensed a conspiracy in the air.

I was sitting in the house that evening when Madame asked me to stand against the wall while she measured my height. She then wrote down my description on a piece of paper; fair hair, brown eyes and so on. I decided it was time to get to the bottom of this mystery so I asked her what it was all about. In reply, she went over to a drawer and took out her identity card. She handed it to me saying that I must also have one, as they were very necessary and this was the reason for Jacqueline's visit.

I opened her identity card and examined it. It was the first time I had ever seen one. On the top left hand corner was her photograph.

Opposite was a small square for a thumb-print. The card contained her full description, her signature and the signature of the Prefect of Police. I asked what on earth Jacqueline could have to do with it. She explained that Jacqueline worked at a German office, *Acheville Kommandantur*, the local centre of Nazi government. She would not tell me much more than that but it was quite sufficient. I saw daylight.

The following afternoon, Madame took my photograph in the garden but I never heard anything of the identity card for a while – until one day, she gave it to me. I opened it and found it was similar to Madame's except that it stated I was *muet* – or dumb. This was arranged because I spoke no French. It was deficient of one thing however. The signature of the Prefect of Police. But this was soon made good, for the next day there arrived at the house a man – a strange man, who spoke few words. He scribbled a signature and, looking at my age, a serial number at the top. I don't know who the strange man was. Maybe he actually was the Prefect of Police himself . At the first opportunity I compared his signature with that on Madame's card and strange to say, they were both the same. I examined it but I could see no flaws. Not that I expected to find any. It was not a counterfeit really. It had been issued from the Germans' own office.

Strange things were going on in Pas-de-Calais, I thought. The Germans had occupied it for only a few weeks, yet already forces were working against them. Agents in the German office itself. Strange men who signed signatures. Germans – friendly Germans who visited the house and to whom Monsieur Benoit talked in their own language. Rifles and ammunition were buried in the garden. I knew. I had helped to clean them on several occasions. Yes, already forces were at work against the Germans and the encouraging thing was that they were organised. All Pas-de-Calais believed – indeed knew – that one day the British would come back.

Once or twice, I heard the air-raid siren in the village. The boys regarded it as an excuse to get excited and keep a lookout for Bristol

Blenheim bombers. But no British bombers ever appeared, except one lone plane which flew low over the house, rocking from side to side, in a rainstorm.

Time passed very quickly and before I realised it, I had been with the Benoit family for six weeks. I had been looked after very well and was quite fit. I began to grow restless. Madame usually told me of rumours or news that she had heard in the village. One item of interest she told me was that in the village estaminet, a German officer had said the population of Pas-de-Calais would soon have to be evacuated as it would become a forbidden military area. One day, he had prophesied, the British would invade – and in the Pas-de-Calais, there would be a great battle.[101]

This I regarded as just interesting. But rumours of a real British attack turned my thoughts towards Calais. For three days I had heard the monotonous roll of gunfire and it was rumoured throughout the district that the British were attacking Calais. It might be a good thing, I thought, to try and get to Calais. In a modern war, it is not impossible to cross through the lines from one side to the other. I had seen refugees do it – and I could look like a refugee.

The idea of the British attacking Calais at that time may sound ridiculous now but to me, with no news except rumours, it was different. Besides, I could hear the guns. For three solid days, a continual bombardment. I talked to Madame about it. She was quite enthusiastic about helping me but emphasised that if I failed, I could always come back again.

I had nothing to lose, so next day I made preparations for my journey to Calais…

Chapter 9: The Road to Calais (and back)

The most important thing of all that I received from the Benoit family was a bicycle. It was an old bicycle and a ladies bicycle but it served me very well. They had several bicycles but they were all ladies bicycles so it was a case of Hobson's choice. The day before I left, Monsieur Benoit made the bicycle ready for the road while I spent my time studying the map of Pas-de-Calais they had given me. It was a small map about the size of a pocket handkerchief but it had all the by-roads and small villages in detail and it served my purpose – until it got me into trouble near Calais.

I was up early next morning anxious to be away before the world awoke. I remember eating quite a large breakfast while I watched Madame packing still more food into a bag which she tied up on my bicycle carrier. Before I left she also gave me an overcoat to keep out the cold at night and a few German pfennig notes to create a "pro-German" atmosphere if I was ever searched. At last I was ready for the big adventure. Monsieur Benoit was to accompany me as far as Béthune. After that, I would have to rely on my little map and my own good luck. I said goodbye to the rest of the Benoit family. This was quite an ordeal as it entailed kissing them all on both cheeks.

During the journey to Béthune I rode close behind Monsieur; there was hardly room to do otherwise. We avoided the village of Acheville for there were prying eyes and prattling tongues and Monsieur Benoit was well known. We got through Lens safely and stopped at an estaminet for a breather. Before Monsieur Benoit went in he warned me that whatever happened I must never speak and must live up to my role as a dumb youth. Luckily however, the place was empty so after a glass of vin rouge and a smoke we pushed on.

I was still riding behind him when we went through Béthune. We were just passing a German barracks when I felt my bicycle chain snap. I was annoyed but also afraid at the same time. There were

Germans everywhere. Worse still, Monsieur Benoit was still riding on straight ahead! I was opposite the German sentry at the barracks gate and I could not shout to attract my friend's attention for I was supposed to be dumb. I began pushing my bicycle – anything to get away from those barracks. So once more I tramped over the cobbled streets of Béthune. After I had gone a couple of hundred yards I saw Monsieur coming back. He had missed me.

I showed him what had happened and when we left the busier part of the town behind he borrowed a hammer from a house and we tried to knock the links together but failed miserably. This held up my progress. It was as if bad luck was to dog my journey to Calais from the very beginning. Instead of getting nearer I could see Calais getting further away. Monsieur Benoit suggested looking for a cycle shop.

We walked up the road together, my friend asking where the nearest cycle shop was. It was then that I had quite a shock for as we pushed our bicycles, I saw on the other side of the road a German military building with a large swastika flag hanging from the upper window. There was nothing unusual in that. They were everywhere. But beneath the flag stood a sentry. There was nothing unusual in that either but as I drew abreast of him, I recognised him as one of the guards from the Béthune prison camp. I could not mistake that hard sunburned face. Fortunately he did not recognise me.

At last we found a cycle shop, right on the edge of town. It was crammed full of spare parts; mudguards, wheels, handlebars and the like. The proprietor came out, took the chain that had caused all the trouble, measured it, then disappeared inside behind the heaps of paraphernalia. Monsieur followed him to supervise the job, leaving me behind outside.

I realised I was in a delicate situation. I could not go into the shop for there were children in there who might innocently give me away. Children always ask questions and I could not pretend to them that I was dumb for they might easily think I was playing a game. Outside it was dangerous. All I could do was loiter while German soldiers strutted up and down the pavement. I felt the cold, clammy hand of fear. Then I remembered I still had a part to play; the part of a dumb Frenchman. A sort of half-wit. A simpleton. I sat down in an undignified position on the step holding my head in my hands, looking through my fingers at the jackboots that pounded by.

At last my bicycle was ready. Monsieur and the proprietor came out of the shop. He had evidently learned all about me for he looked upon my dumbness with pity. Monsieur offered him a couple of francs in payment but refusing them, the proprietor gave them to me.

We left Béthune and Monsieur Benoit showed me the road to Calais. But before we parted company he insisted on drinking a toast to good luck. We stopped at an estaminet and went in. I chose a vin rouge although I hated the stuff. Monsieur Benoit wanted to pay for it in German money but the lady behind the counter was rather sceptical about receiving the currency of the Reich. We both drank and after much cheek kissing I managed to say "goodbye" once we got outside. I cycled off giving a last wave of farewell. Then I turned towards Calais.

I followed my map through Lillers, Norrent and Saint-Omer. Saint-Omer, I found, was a garrison for Stormtroopers. They marched round the streets in their brown shirts and swastikas, singing songs. The main road was thick with German transport; heavy lorries, staff cars and infantry carriers. I rested for a while at Les Attaques then pushed on again. Approaching Calais I was rather puzzled for everywhere was quiet and peaceful. Houses began to appear with more regularity. Finally there were the cobbled streets and tram-lines of Calais itself. But of war, there was not a sign.

Alert and very wary, I rode further into the town until I reached some crossroads; one to Boulogne and one to Dunkirk. A German staff car came round the bend. Two officers sat in the back laughing and joking. Calais was perfectly normal. There was no British attack or invasion anywhere near Calais.

I was disappointed, amazed and puzzled all at the same time.

It was getting dark by now, so I decided to retreat and retire for the night. I found a little barn just off a cart-track near Les Attaques. It contained a farm cart and some clean straw. I made myself quite comfortable but it was some time before I fell asleep. I was worried and in a bit of a dilemma. I had come to Calais expecting to find a war and to run into a British advance but had found nothing. Something had gone wrong somewhere. Maybe the Germans had started the "British are attacking" rumours themselves. I did not like the idea of going back to the Benoit family at Acheville despite their invitation for me to stay with them for the rest of the war. They were very kind and generous but it would be unfair for me to thrust myself upon them. If they were ever discovered hiding a British soldier they would be punished. Under these circumstances I could not bring myself to go back. On the other hand I did not know where to go. I had reached a dead end.

I took my map and studied it intently in the fading light. I came to the conclusion that the only way to cross the Channel was under my own steam. I decided next morning to make my way to the coast where I might be able to find a small boat or even knock a raft together. Having a plan of campaign for the morrow I felt much easier and soon fell into a sound sleep.

I awoke next morning. It was a glorious morning. Some German cavalry cantered past the barn where I lay. I watched them from behind the cart which conveniently blocked the doorway. One soldier rose in his stirrup and look keenly in my direction. His eyes seemed to pierce the blackness of the little barn making me feel rather uneasy. The cavalry were followed by a light tank which kicked up a loud noise and a terrible stink.

Having made sure that they were out of sight I got ready for my journey to the coast north of Calais. I cycled back through the village of Les Attaques taking the first road on the right heading towards Dunkirk. As I approached Marck on the Calais to Dunkirk road, I was stopped by a German officer in a car going in the opposite direction. He hailed me and I pulled up, got off my bicycle and walked back to see what he wanted. He wanted the road to Ardres, a town I had passed the day before. He spoke in French but by now I could understand simple questions in that language. I pointed straight ahead and he drove off. I watched him until he disappeared and I smiled; I knew that if he failed to turn right at the first fork he might never get there.

Reaching the village of Marck I crossed the main road and went straight on towards the sea. The road became narrower and the houses each side became clustered. I passed a German soldier standing by the side of the road with a rifle and fixed bayonet. Coastal defence, I thought. He shouted something as I went by but I did not understand him so I just bluffed by nodding my head and cycled on. It was a pretty desperate bluff but it worked. I had learned already that half the battle was to keep moving. To pause is to invite trouble. While moving the chances of being caught are tremendously reduced.

I think I must have been riding in a daze after that for when I looked up the houses had disappeared and I was in the middle of a large, flat field. I stopped and got off my bicycle. I looked around. On my left was an endless stretch of green. On my right was a line of Messerschmitts with their engines ticking over, ready to take off! I immediately realised I was in a jam. I was on a German aerodrome and hardly knew how I'd got there. Looking back the way I'd come I saw the German sentry was still watching me. I was at a loss for what to do next. Fortunately I saw some civilian workmen digging a trench and laying pipes. I saw at once what had happened. This sentry had thought I was one of them and had let me pass thinking I was a plumber's apprentice or something.

Not wanting to attract attention by standing about, I walked over to the workmen and as I did so I had an idea. I decided to pretend I was a workman. I had to get off that aerodrome somehow. When I reached the men, who were laying metal pipes and too busy to notice me, I took the bag from the back my bicycle and began fumbling about inside. Now, a plumber's mate, no matter what his nationality, is always supposed to forget his tools. This gave me an idea. There was no reason why I shouldn't have forgotten something – and of course, have to go back for it.

Besides tins of sausages and sardines, I had in my bag a tin opener, an assortment of spanners and a couple of tyre lifters. I turned them over and over inside the bag to create the desired sound effects that might issue from a plumber's kit. By my actions, I made it plain that I could not find when I was looking for. I made a few well-feigned gestures of annoyance; I stamped my foot, bounced my bicycle on the ground, mounted it and rode off. The sentry was still watching me. I cycled brazenly out into the street. He just stared at me. I think if he had been anything other than a German, he would have seen the funny side. I could hardly help laughing at the utter daftness of the whole show myself.

Going back to Marck I took the Dunkirk road once more, trying to find the road to the sea – but I failed again. The roads I tried either led to farms or petered out before they went anywhere. I began to feel very depressed. The result of one failure after another was beginning to have an effect. I cycled inland towards Les Attaques. By the side of the road I found an overturned van. I went behind it and sat down, for here I was screened from the road and could sit in quiet and think. I stayed there for some time just thinking. I did not know where to go, what to do or how to do it. My mind was in greater agony than the worst headache.

I pored over my little map in vain. I even knelt and prayed that I might find the right road. But the road I was eventually fated to find was far beyond anything I could have then imagined. It was to be a long and adventurous road. Not that I would have minded that for it was the road home. It was the road to "Tipperary" as that German called it. That jeering German who stood on the back of the truck yelling "'It's a long way to Tipperary', ja?"

The very recollection of that incident made me angry. My anger roused me from my lethargy. I rose, stretched myself and rode off to find the road to the sea on the other side of Calais. I made my way to Guines, passing sentries who guarded canal bridges but they never stopped me. On and on I went but still I could not find the sea. In the end I got tired of it. I turned my wheels towards Ardres and the road to Acheville.

I slept that night right in the middle of a cornfield where no farm labourer was likely to stumble across me in the early hours. Next morning I was away through Saint-Omer with its Stormtroopers and on past Norrent. I took to the back streets when passing through Lillers and found myself near the railway station. What I saw brought back memories, for there was a line of cattle trucks on the same siding where I had waited so wearily while going to Metz with the reinforcements. Everything seemed to be in the same place; the cattle trucks, the heaps of scrap iron, the bales of straw. It was as though time had been pushed back to when I first arrived in France.

I left the place behind and there were no more incidents until I reached the other side of Béthune. In Béthune itself I had no trouble. I did not meet the German who had been my prison guard nor did my chain snap – but once outside the town the fun started again.

I was going downhill near Nœux-les-Mines when I became involved in an unusual accident. By now my bicycle had no brakes. It had had only one to start with but now that one was worn out and ineffective.

Being in a devil-may-care mood, I let the old bike rip down the hill. Coming up the hill in the opposite direction was a heavy German convoy of big diesel trucks. I thought nothing of them until behind me, travelling even faster than I was, came a French civilian lorry. I tried to slow down and pull over but before I could complete any such manoeuvre, the lorry was already squeezing between me and the German convoy. It carried sacks of coal which protruded over the sides and as he swung by, one of them caught me on the shoulder knocking me flying off my bicycle.

With my clothes all torn up and my arms badly scraped I sat up, dazed, in the middle of the road, amid the tangled wreckage of my bicycle. Badly shaken, I looked up the hill at the disappearing German convoy and saw to my horror, fast bearing down on me was a German staff car. I tried to move but couldn't. I could only stare at the oncoming car like a hypnotised rabbit. Then suddenly there was a screech of brakes and the car rocked drunkenly and pulled up. Its bumpers were only a few inches from my head!

I tried to sort myself from the tangled wreckage of my bicycle for in the back of the car I could see two German officers. They were very Prussian-like with their hard-features, their monocles and their Nazi swastikas on their arms. Together they leant forward, then rose and stepped out of the car. They came round to the front and looked down at me, regarding me as just something that blocked the road. But then to my intense surprise, still very dignified, they stooped down, picked me up and carried me to the side of the road.

They looked me up and down, examining me, displaying such interest as they might over a horse which have had a fall and satisfying themselves that I was in one piece. Then, without saying a single word, they turned, climbed stiffly back into the car and were driven off. I watched them until they disappeared, still unable to make them out. Their actions had shaken me much more than the accident.

When I had recovered from this, I straightened myself out and examined my bicycle. It was in a sorry state. The front wheel was buckled and the pedal cranks were bent. From then on it was a long walk back to Acheville, pushing my bicycle as I went. I remember surveying the Benoit house from a distance, hating myself because I was a failure and hating to go back because of the possible consequences and trouble my presence might bring upon them.

I was received much better than I expected. Madame Benoit seemed glad to see me back, saying once more that I could stay there for the duration. But even this assurance and the attention of the whole family could not sweeten the bitterness of failure.

My sleep that night was troubled. I would dream of the jeering German on the back of the truck. He would leer, thrusting his face into mine and yelling, "'It's a long way to Tipperary', ja?" To me it was the darkest hour.

But I need not have worried. Next morning Monsieur Benoit brought good news. Overnight, RAF planes had dropped leaflets over the Lille and Béthune area. I did not pay much attention to the leaflets at first as they were in French but as I glanced through them I noticed one of them showed a map of France. This interested me very much for although it was a very rough map – being of a scale so small it ceased to be a scale at all – it showed France divided in two. One half was white; the other was shaded black. I asked Madame about it and was very surprised by her reply.

She explained that one half of France was not occupied by Germany for, after the fall of Paris, what was left of France had signed an armistice with Hitler. So southern France was at peace and not occupied by the enemy. I could hardly believe it. I had been under the impression that all of France was now German. That was what they told us in the prison camp. This was great news. Already I could see a way of escape – and already I was making plans.

Later in the day I ventured to approach Madame again on the same subject and I learned the useful points to remember. First, if I reached the *Zone Libre*, as they now called the southern half of France, even if I got no further, I would be safer, as there were no Germans to dodge. Secondly, at Marseilles in the extreme south, I would probably be able to contact a British Consul who would no doubt be able to put me on a boat. With these beliefs in mind, I began to plan my journey. Little did I know that both beliefs were so very misleading.

By supper time I had completed my plans for a journey to Marseilles. There was nothing very startling in them, except that I must cross the demarcation line near Tours. This was Madame Benoit's idea. She had it on good authority that this was the easiest place to cross from occupied to unoccupied territory. I took her word for it. She knew more than I did. I mentioned that I did not know Tours except that it was somewhere south of Le Mans. She advised me to go first to see André at Cherbourg where I could rest and he would help me to find my way to Tours.

My bicycle was duly repaired – and I think it was on the third day after my return from Calais – that I set off on the long trek to Marseilles. This time I knew there was no turning back.

It was Blighty or bust!

Chapter 10: Adolf Hitler Bridge

INTRODUCTORY NOTE

Air-dropped leaflets

Air-dropped leaflets like the one picked up by M. Benoit in the last chapter were widely used by both sides in the Second World War. A single aircraft could distribute hundreds of thousands of leaflets over a very wide area in a short space of time. Leaflets dropped on military installations and battlefields were invariably propaganda, intended to demoralise or strike fear into those who read them. British air-dropped leaflets aimed at the French civilian population however, were generally intended to offer encouragement, boost morale and deliver important information that local people could not obtain elsewhere (for example because more familiar means of mass communication such as newspapers and wireless broadcasts might be under the control of the German authorities).

"Vichy France"

It is not clear what was the main content of the leaflet brought home by M. Benoit at the end of the previous chapter. Its value for Ray though, was that it happened to include a small sketch showing the division of France that had been agreed between Adolf Hitler and the surrendering French Government some weeks previously. The terms of the Armistice ceded northern France (including Paris) and the whole of the Channel / Atlantic coast to German control. The remainder of France (the *Zone Libre* or "Free Zone") was to remain in French hands.

In theory, the Zone Libre was an independent territory under the control of an independent French government. In practice, it functioned effectively as a client state of Germany, subject to an authoritarian form of rule, led by those senior French politicians who had opted to go along with this aspect of the German-dominated armistice. The seat of the new government was at the small spa town of Vichy about 250 miles (400 kilometres) south of Paris and 290 miles (470 kilometres) north of Marseilles. The regime in the Zone Libre was officially known as *l'État Français* (French State) or more commonly, "Vichy France".

It is surprising that Ray was not already aware of the division of France into occupied and "free" territories but clearly he was not. Once he had the idea straight in his mind however, he concluded, naturally enough, that in order to reach safety and a possible passage home to England, he need not make it all the way to Spain. He had only to reach the border between Occupied France and the Zone Libre, and find a way to cross it. Assuming he could do that, he believed he would be free to travel wherever he wished in Vichy France and, of course, that he would be safe from the threat of recapture.

Adolf Hitler Bridge

I left Acheville and made towards Arras, joining the main road on the other side of Vimy. From here I could see the Vimy War Memorial – or what was left of it – along the now wooded Vimy Ridge. Nearby I saw a little road running off to the right with a signpost in English stating that it led to the trenches used by the Canadians in the last war. The road was littered with German signs; military signs, evidently for the benefit of transport drivers, stating that a whole list of things were *Verboten!*

I cycled through Arras without mishap. German transport was almost everywhere. Every warehouse had been turned into a garage. Work seemed to be going on all over, yet no-one questioned me. I saw mechanics under trucks and tinkering with tanks but I rode through the town unmolested. Once outside Arras I left the main road which runs by Bapaume and Albert and took a secondary road to Puisieux and Contay, thinking that on this road I would meet the least Germans but they were as busy as anywhere, mostly Luftwaffe personnel dashing here and there on lorries.

I saw bombed Amiens where French prisoners were working down by the river. I calculated the distance I had travelled by means of signposts and I think I did well over 100 kilometres that first day. This brought me as far as Abancourt where I spent the night behind a hedge in a field. This particular field was next to one with a lot of barbed wire around. I remembered having spent an unpleasant night there in German hands. But now the cage was empty. In fact the whole village was almost deserted.

I was up early next morning retracing the steps of the prison column to Rouen but I did not get far before I had my first setback. It happened at Forges-les-Eaux. I had a good look at the town as I rode through. It had been bombed pretty badly. Of the main streets only one narrow thoroughfare was left intact. It contained the only shops left in the town and was a very busy little street. Crowds of people were shopping and I was tempted to stop – for there is something very peaceful about people shopping – but there were German soldiers about and, wishing to avoid detection, I pushed on. The lowest German private seemed to exercise a certain amount of authority over the civilian population. This, combined with a natural bullying tendency, made them men to be avoided.

I was to see much more of Forges-les-Eaux, for no sooner did I reach the other side of town than I had a puncture. I felt glad it had not happened in the street but I was sorry it had happened at all. I pushed my bicycle down a narrow side road and stood it upside down to find out the extent of the damage. To my horror I discovered the tube was split right round where it joined the valve. It was impossible to repair.

My first thoughts were despairing but remembering my trip to Calais, I hastily banished them. At the same time I did not like the idea of marching halfway across Europe. In any case, that was impossible in the canvas slippers I was wearing; on the rough roads, it was like walking in bare feet. I recalled having seen that many of the people shopping in the town had bicycles. Pushing my now useless machine, I walked back to see what could be done. Reaching the busy, narrow thoroughfare I parked my bicycle by the kerb and strolled up and down. There were not many German soldiers about now – not that it would have mattered, for now I had much bigger things at stake. To be recaptured was one thing; I might escape again. But to walk to Marseilles was something I wasn't keen on trying. Thus it was that I descended to the depths of crime. I decided to steal a bicycle.

In that little street I had dozens of machines to choose from. Almost everybody seemed to do their shopping on a bicycle – a fact about which I felt very pleased. But as I studied the situation I saw a flaw. I noticed that the time between the owners going into the shops and their coming out again was hardly long enough for me to make a getaway. I would have to transfer my overcoat and bag of food from one machine to the other so, in the crowded street, a really quick getaway would be almost impossible.

As I stood on the pavement I would watch someone come along on a bicycle and I would rehearse the crime in my imagination. The result made me feel nervous. In my mind, I was caught every time. Finally I was in such a state that when I discovered an estaminet surrounded by a riot of machines I was afraid to take one for fear the owner came out at the crucial moment.

Just then, down the street came a man on a bicycle. I eyed his machine, for now I scrutinised all bicycles. He stopped at the estaminet, stood his bicycle against the wall and went inside. I decided that this was to be the bicycle. It was a ladies model and Frenchmen are averse to riding ladies bicycles. I decided therefore, that the type of Frenchman who would ride a ladies bicycle would be the type of man who, once he went into an estaminet, would not come out again for some time. I was not far wrong.

I walked past the estaminet a couple of times, making a visual examination of the machine each time. I noted the tyres had a good tread and were not liable to puncture. I had a good look at the brake-blocks, remembering that little incident I had with the German officers near Béthune. I could only see the front blocks but they seemed quite new. Exchange is no robbery. I fetched my own machine, transferred my kit and rode off as fast as the crowded street would allow. Once clear of the town, I went hell for leather without a pause until I had passed at least two forks in the road which I calculated would put any pursuit off the scent.

I slowed down to examine my prize, then for the first time I noticed my front wheel was going "bumpety-bump, bumpety-bump" along the tarmacadam. I became alarmed, thinking it was another puncture, so I hastily dismounted to make an examination. Instead of a puncture, I discovered the tyre was split and to prevent further damage had been bound to the rim with string and wire. It was still serviceable but I cursed loud and long, for I had thought I had a good bicycle. A German dashed past in a truck so I cursed him as well. He drove a British Bedford and had my thoughts been powerful enough, that German will still be driving his swastika-painted Bedford through the flames of hell.[102]

I halted a few kilometres from Rouen for something to eat, taking advantage of the stop to strip the owner's name and licence disc from my bicycle. I found Rouen a very different place from when I was stationed there. The bridges were all destroyed and the once popular cafés on the riverfront were gutted. A couple of ships lay on their sides in the river. This brought my attention to two pontoon bridges flung across the river. I had been wondering how I would get to the other side.

On the first bridge I found myself pushing against a thick stream of pedestrians. I had gone some distance when I came up against a Frenchwoman who seemed very concerned about my progress. She told me to go back and cross by the other bridge before the Boche got me. It was only then I realised I was trying to cross a one-way bridge. I hastily withdrew and tried the other pontoon. This time I met no resistance. I was swept forward by the crowd.

Once over the bridge, I mounted my bicycle and made hard going over the rough cobbles. I passed the old lady who sold newspapers. She still sat at the corner shouting, "Paris Soir! Paris Soir!" The only difference was that this time I didn't stop to buy one… I wasn't supposed to be able to read.

I soon found the road to Caen. I remembered it forked off the road that led to the camp. On the way I had made notes of all the boulangeries that I passed, for I was running short of bread, however I did not stop until I found one on the outskirts of the town. I wasn't too keen on going into the shop at first and I thought of waiting until the shop was devoid of customers but if I had I would have probably waited all night. The old lady behind the counter was doing quite a lot of business.

At last I ventured to go in. There were there were about four women in the shop. They did not haggle over their purchases but each one in turn had a long, monotonous conversation with the old lady. I watched them carefully, trying to make myself as inconspicuous as possible, fearing they might try to involve me in the conversation. It was only by skilful manoeuvring on my part that they didn't.

They would walk all over the shop, which was fairly large, feeling loaves here and there to see if they were fresh. When it was my turn I imitated them, then placed my loaf on the scales as they had done. I didn't care whether it had been baked last night or last week. The older the better; it would last longer. I gave the old lady the money and turned to go but she began talking to me. I shook my head vigorously pretending I was dumb and as a kind of support act, I showed my identity card, pointing to where it said *muet*. Just then, two German soldiers opened the door. As they walked in I walked out. I breathed more freely when I got on my bicycle. I had only just got out in time.

Two kilometres further on I came upon a village. I had had my second puncture by then but I just kept riding on. I had no misgivings. The old tyre had done its work well – much better than I had ever expected – but I felt it getting lower and lower, bumping harder and harder on the cobblestones. Then I saw, standing by the kerb, another bicycle. I had no qualms about stealing it – I may as well be hung for a sheep as a lamb. I cycled up to the bicycle, grabbed my kit, jumped on it and rode off. It was all done smoothly in a matter of seconds. I had become an expert.

I slept that night in a wood on the hills overlooking the River Seine. I chose the location because it was nearer some forks in the road; one road south to Le Mans and Tours, and one left to Caen and Cherbourg.[103] I was at cross purposes with myself. I wondered, since I had found this road, if it would be better for me to try to reach Tours on my own. It might save me a long journey to Cherbourg to try and find André. The next morning I decided to risk it and go south to Tours.

In the first village I passed a few German soldiers having an early parade but the rest of the day was uneventful. There were many hills and I made little progress. The following day I decided to check my bearings on my pocket compass and discovered to my amazement I was no longer going due south but south-east. I began to get anxious, for the road did not show any promise of turning south again. A few more miles and I re-checked my compass – but I was still travelling in the same direction. Realising that I was on the wrong road and had probably been on it for some time, I took the first right hand turn and cycled on hoping that I would find the correct Le Mans road.

I was in for a surprise, for the road led right through a German flying field. There were about forty Messerschmitts pegged down by the side of the road.[104] Except for a single mechanic who was tinkering with an engine, there was not a soul in sight. No guard. Nobody. At the bottom of a hill I found the village of Beaumont. I made a note of the name. I thought it would be useful to know one day that two kilometres east of Beaumont was a German fighter field; perhaps the RAF could visit it? But I had made one mistake. I was lost. I did not know where Beaumont was!

There was a notable absence of German soldiers in this area and turning south-west from Beaumont, I passed some beautiful forest scenery. I lost count of the days – although I remember eating my last sausage sandwich as I sat by the roadside, thinking how lucky I had been to get this far without any breakdowns. But I counted my chickens too soon for no sooner did I ride off than I discovered I had a flat tyre. I actually tried to repair it this time but failed miserably. That meant a walk to the nearest town. I saw a big sign as I entered: "Évreux".*

Évreux proved to be quite a busy town. Finding a shopping centre, I decided to repeat my bicycle-exchanging performance. I even found what I wanted, a large shop which sold gowns. Being situated on a corner, it was where everyone parked their bicycles, for there was too much traffic on the main streets. By now of course, I realised the folly of just taking any old machine. I was determined to

---

* Évreux is about 180 miles (almost 300 kilometres) from Acheville and a similar distance from Ray's present destination of Tours.

get a good bicycle this time. The newer the better.

Examining them carefully I found the bicycles were all in more or less the same condition, with the exception of one, which stood out above all the others. Unfortunately, this was also a ladies machine – but since I had been riding only ladies models so far and since I wouldn't have to pay for it, I saw no reason for grumbling.

I was attracted to it by the fact that it had a three speed gear, which would save me a great deal of work on the hills. Also, it was so new that it looked like an exhibition model in a dealer's window. Altogether it was a magnificent machine. It was painted maroon and had large red tyres, mudguards and chromium-plated wheels. But it was someone else's. That night some mademoiselle must have broken her heart, for I was soon winging my way towards the hills behind Évreux.

I had an annoying problem to deal with before that day was over. I discovered the road I had taken was of the circular type and found myself heading back to Évreux. I tried hard to find the road going south but without success. I made a detailed reconnaissance over the whole area but gained no satisfaction. At last when I camped down for the night in a thick wood, I decided to go back north to Rouen and then to Cherbourg – where I should have gone in the first place.*

Settling down I made myself as comfortable as circumstances would allow but found great difficulty in hiding my machine, for although the sun was low it was still shining bright and reflecting on the chromium parts of the bicycle. It shone like a mirror. Being afraid it might attract attention, I covered it with grass and branches but despite these precautions it still shone with such brilliance that I felt decidedly uncomfortable. However these difficulties were compensated by the discovery of a receipt in the tool case. I hadn't realised the machine was as new as all that. But later that receipt came in useful.

---

* Given his recent frustrations, it is easy to understand why a visit to André and his family now appeals to Ray. The journey to Cherbourg however, necessitates a detour of well over 200 miles (320 kilometres).

Next morning I went north until I reached the River Seine near Elbeuf. This was further up the river than Rouen but I was unable to cross the river for all the bridges had been blown up. I reckoned it was essential I should cross the river because from the other side I would be able to find Rouen more easily. I did find one bridge – but it was not the kind of bridge I expected to find there or anywhere else. It was unique among bridges. It was a long wooden structure on many pylons, built across the river where it was widest but most shallow. It was accessible by a rough, narrow road which led steeply down from a village. Approaching the bridge, I saw it was guarded by a German sentry. Behind him I could see a large board on which I could read in the distance, in German and in French, the following words, *Verboten!* and *Interdite!* [Prohibited!] but above all this, stood the legend ADOLF HITLER BRÜCKE.

This was the only bridge across the Seine. I wanted to cross it but it was *Verboten!* For some time I stood regarding the sign, and not knowing what to do. Finally, a black car went past. I had a good view of the occupants. They were civilians. The car stopped by the sentry for a few minutes before proceeding across the bridge. I watched it until I reached the other side and decided to have a try myself. I cycled up and was past the sentry almost before he realised – but I didn't get far. A loud yell made me turn around. I stopped. The German had unslung his rifle so I reckoned it would be safer to go back. He questioned in French, "Avez vous les papiers?"

I pulled out my identity card. "Nein! Nein!" he barked. "Les papiers …" He pointed up the hill, "le Commandant …" He showed me a square piece of white paper; written permission from the local *Kommandantur* to cross the bridge. I took this is my cue to withdraw. On my way back up the hill I looked back at the bridge but it was no place for me. It was Adolf Hitler's bridge.

Chapter 11: Vichy France via Cherbourg

Eventually I found my way back to Rouen where, after purchasing more bread, I took the road to Caen. I spent the night right in the middle of a large cornfield where I was least likely to be disturbed. It was about the only cornfield that had not so far been reaped. When I awoke the next morning I found the whole place littered with RAF leaflets telling the French people (more or less) that General de Gaulle[105] had signed a pact with Churchill, forming a Free French Force. It gave details of the pact, a letter from de Gaulle to Churchill, and Churchill's answer. At the end, it called for volunteers for the Free French Forces, stating terms of service and so on. It ended with: *Vive la France! Vive L'Angleterre!*

Arriving at Caen, I found signs pointing to the centre of the town and, although I tried to avoid these, I still found myself right in the middle which was hardly what I wanted. I came upon a large square where four or five roads converged and from an island in the centre, a gendarme controlled the traffic by waving a little baton. Taking no notice of him and ignoring the island roundabout on which he stood, I rode straight across the square to where I saw the sign for Cherbourg. I had almost reached it when I heard him shouting at the top of his voice.

At first I did not realise he was shouting at me and even when I did I took no notice whatsoever. I tried to hurry away from the scene but that gendarme believed in getting his man. Then he pulled out his whistle and began blowing it frantically. I looked around and saw that he was waving his baton wildly in the air. He was very excited and angry. Dismounting, I went back to find out what was annoying him. I felt anything might happen if he didn't stop blowing that whistle.

I reached the island on foot. He was not a big man but from where he stood, he looked down on me. During my stay with the

Benoit family, I had begun to learn a little French but I could not understand the half of what he said. He spoke much too quickly for he was mad with rage and red in the face. I expected him to have a fit at any moment. He spluttered and fumed, all because I had not cycled around his roundabout. I fiddled with my beret and just gaped at him. Seeing that I said nothing, he calmed down and began to fire questions at me. "Don't you understand?" he bawled.

I continued to gape and look foolish.

"What is your nationality?"

I still said nothing but just stared at him vacantly, tapping my mouth with my clenched fist. Instantly the gendarme's expression changed.

"Muet?"

I nodded my head vigorously.

"Have you your identity card?"

Again I nodded, taking my card from my pocket to show him but to my surprise he waved me to be off, looking almost ashamed of himself for having been so angry with a dumb man.

Outside Caen, I took the right fork and had a hard, uphill ride against the wind. Down in the valley I could see an aerodrome full of German bombers. At Bayeux I tried to buy bread but unfortunately it was a Sunday and when I went into the shop, the woman asked "Avez vous le ticket?" Of course, I had no tickets or coupons so I left. But it worried me for a while because I thought rationing must have come into force. However, it was not so. I discovered later that one only needed a ticket on a Sunday.

Later in the day I approached Cherbourg and was a little worried for I could find no sign of André's village which was supposed to be in this approximate locality. Fearing I had missed the road, which I knew could not be far away, I stopped for a breather – conveniently next to an orchard – and standing my bicycle against the wall in a spot where the most branches overhung, I systematically devoured every apple I could reach.

It was by sheer chance, when I remounted, that I discovered the road I was looking for. I happened to glance at the farm buildings as I rode off and there I saw a tiny sign pointing to the village, only a few yards from the spot where I had been unceremoniously stealing apples. The road was a ten-foot gravel track with loose stones that made riding awkward – and sometimes dangerous – as it sloped steeply downhill. I was compensated however by the beautiful scenery. I have always admired pleasant scenery and this was among the prettiest I had ever seen.

The road became rougher. It ran uphill and downhill around farmyards and through farmyards until, at length, I wondered if I was on the right road after all. I practised the little French I had learned then, quite openly, I spoke to some farm workers who I thought I could trust, and asked my way. At last I reached the village but no one had heard of André's farm, nor had they heard of André. Thinking they did not understand me, I wrote his name and address on a piece of paper but still I had no success.

It was getting quite dark, so I made a reconnaissance of the whole area and found to my utter dismay that it was like looking for a needle in a haystack. The whole district was covered, not by dozens but hundreds of tiny farms and all of them were linked by picturesque little paths. I scoured a good many of these paths then, growing hungry again, I made a meal of the abundance of large blackberries which grew on the banks and the stone walls bordering the way. My bed at night was of dry leaves under a thick, overgrown hedgerow. Hiding my bicycle, I found myself a small hollow between two bushes. Pulling the bushes back into place behind me hid me from view.

Despite my precautions I was not allowed to sleep that night. The Nazis did not bother me nor did the French police. This time it was the RAF! They started knocking the hell out of Cherbourg and made an awful din in the process. That's what I dislike about our air force – they won't let escaped prisoners-of-war sleep at night.

Poor Cherbourg! I could not see the bombing but the night was lit up and the sky was a mass of fireworks. I was glad when it was all over and the last bomber flew away. It passed directly overhead. Instantly a nearby anti aircraft gun went into action. I could plainly see the shells exploding but when it stopped I could still hear the drone of the bomber as it flew back home.

When the sun came up I was able to find a stream and have a good wash. It was about the first I had been able to get since I set off so I made the most of it. Having plenty of time I washed my feet and socks and the canvas slippers I wore. When I had done this, I once more tried to find André's farm. Among the people I had passed was a padre. I felt safe asking him. Following the directions he indicated I came to a crossroads. Here I decided to wait until someone else came along. Presently a boy came by. I spoke to him but gained no information. He spoke with a very pronounced accent that was surprisingly different from the accent of Pas-de-Calais. Gaining nothing I tried all four of the roads but it was the same story. André's farm was nowhere to be found. In the end I still didn't find it but I knew it must be there. It was impossible to believe that no one knew where it was especially as the padre had been able to point the way.

By now I felt very hungry, which reminded me that I was going somewhere and must not delay. Riding like this from one end of France to the other I felt like a bumble bee imprisoned in a glass jar, flying from one side to the other knocking its head against the sides in an effort to escape. But escape I must. After another meal of blackberries – which would have to last me until I reached the first convenient boulangerie – I gave up my quest to find André's farm and set off south once more.

The next stage of my journey was uneventful and was merely a repetition of what had now become my daily routine – strange as my routine was. At night I would choose my resting place with great caution and often describe a complete circle around a selected spot, approaching it from all angles to see if it would be safe to lie there. Sometimes I would sleep in a hedgerow, sometimes in a cavity clawed in the bottom of a haystack or, when I was denied the luxury of a haystack, cover myself with sheaves of corn or just lie down on the damp grass.

During the day I would ride and ride, stopping only to buy bread, again with the same caution, or to have a snack or a few puffs of my pipe but that was rare because I had few matches. Matches were scarce.

At Caen, I saw again the gendarme waving his baton at the traffic. This time I cycled right round his little island. He looked as cocky and impertinent as ever. Finding a signpost to Alençon and Le Mans, I followed it. Without a hitch, I reached Le Mans. Once more I was surprised by the strange absence of German troops south of the Seine. They were there of course but in very small numbers.

I was coasting leisurely down the gentle slope that leads into Le Mans when from a garden gate, I heard a woman shout. I took no notice of her at first until I heard her shout the words "Allemands" and "Velo". I put the words together – "Germans" and "bike" and remembered how Madame Benoit used to talk of the Germans requisitioning bicycles for their infantry. The woman was evidently trying to warn me. I stopped and hastily dismounted for I ran a great risk if I entered the town. Not only might I lose my bicycle but also my freedom. Even if the German authorities took only my bicycle without suspecting me, I would not find it very easy to get another bike in such a place – and if the gendarmes caught me, I would be charged with stealing the bike and lose my freedom in any case. It did not take me long to come to the conclusion that the Nazi city of Le Mans was not a very healthy place to cycle through.

It seemed the best thing to do was to detour around Le Mans. But that was where the sticking point arose for this would mean an extra ten miles or so – and I was not likely to find the right road where it emerged on the other side of the town. I turned around and went back. I had a plan in mind. I must make a reconnaissance of Le Mans on foot to ascertain my chances of running the gauntlet.

About three kilometres away I stuck my machine behind a hedge and walked into town. I saw nothing unusual although I noted the absence of bicycles. Reaching the river, I turned back again. A platoon of German soldiers overtook me. They sang lustily as they passed. I marvelled at their deep bass voices. It was then that I saw a man on a bicycle. I watched him and no sooner did he reach the corner than a gendarme stepped out and waved him to stop. They talked for some minutes, the gendarme taking down particulars. Presently they both walked off. Curious, I followed them two or three hundred yards down the street where they went into a police station.

After five minutes the man came out – minus his bicycle. I wondered what would have happened if I had been in his shoes. But I didn't dare dwell on the subject. I had seen enough. It was the long way round for me. But somewhere south of Le Mans I got lost. I can't tell you where I went. I don't know. I just kept going south by my compass. I was also on a bread and water diet – my tinned food had run out somewhere near Elbeuf. I could always get bread but for many reasons, other forms of food I could not. It was a poor diet for such a rigorous journey. The nights were cold and my stomach often empty.

I continued going south until I thought I was level with Tours then I turned my wheels south-east for I had no intention of cycling until I found myself going down that narrow neck of occupied territory on the west coast.[106] Instead, I turned south-east in an effort to find the demarcation line. I expected to find it somewhere near Tours, so the day I saw a signpost that said "Tours 27 kilometres" I felt very relieved indeed*.

I passed a line of fortified German positions which seemed to stretch away into the west as far as I could see. Going down the hill to the city I also saw some camouflaged German artillery. Their muzzles were pointing over Tours – towards Vichy France, I guessed. Owing to Madame Benoit's none too good English, I had come to believe that Tours itself was in Vichy hands so, after passing these

---

* Bearing in mind his lengthy detours, by the time he has reached this point Ray must have cycled well in excess of 600 miles since he left Acheville.

German guns I expected any second to come across a frontier post. Because of this, I proceeded with great caution but even when I reached the bridge on the other side of the city, I still found no signs of a frontier.

Reaching the edge of town I passed a gendarme at a fork in the road. It didn't matter now which road I took for I was bound to hit unoccupied territory sooner or later. I chose the left fork which followed the river, chiefly because to take the other meant going uphill. I rode very slowly exercising great caution, especially at corners, in case I might run into a frontier barrier. I had no intention of going through one. It would be much simpler to creep across in the dark. This would mean leaving my bicycle behind but I would not need it so much on the other side.

About five kilometres further on, I reached a small town – but still no sign of the frontier. I stopped by the kerb and looked at the things around me. A couple of German army trucks went by. They turned left. They were quickly followed by some private cars carrying mattresses on their roofs. These were refugees. So was I. I followed them. They turned right.

The road went uphill and I soon lost sight of them but I kept going in that direction. Reaching the top, I saw a field full of vines. Large bunches of grapes hung from their branches. Here was a luxury, I thought! The feast of a lifetime. I forgot the war and could think of nothing but grapes. Lovely, luscious grapes! I stopped and, making sure there was no one about, I slipped over the fence. I grabbed two of the biggest bunches I could see and nipped back again, my mouth watering in anticipation. I put a grape into my mouth but that was as far as it got. They were the most horrible vile-tasting grapes I had ever tasted. Sour. With disgust and disappointment I threw them in the ditch.[107]

I rode a little further and began wondering where on earth the frontier had got to. Then I became careless – and came upon it sooner than I expected.

The "frontier" comprised two German soldiers standing by the side of the road. I came across them quite unexpectedly. I rounded a bend in the road and suddenly I saw them in front of me. And they saw me. It was too late to turn back. Remembering my earlier success at bluffing it out (the more brazen the better), I rode straight up to them. As I approached, the taller of the two waved his hand in the downward motion. He wanted me to stop. This was it!

"Demandez papiers!", he rasped when I stopped.

I took out my identification card and handed it to him, hoping for the best. He was the first person really to examine it – a frontier guard, of all people. A big frontier guard. If it passed him, I was OK.

I waited and waited. I looked ahead down the road. It was too much of a strain on my neck to look up at him. He looked from one side of the card to the other. I remembered that the ink was a slightly different colour on one side. I wondered if he had rumbled it but he didn't. My friends at Acheville had done their work well.

He looked at the photograph then at me. Without saying a word he returned the card and waved me to go. I did not need the second telling. I had had my foot on a raised pedal for the past five minutes. I was off! I had outwitted the *Reichswehr*![108]

Two hundred yards or so further round the bend, I arrived at the Vichy side of the demarcation line. Being slightly more advanced than the Germans, the French had gone to the trouble of erecting a small hut and throwing a barrier across the road. A solitary French soldier was on duty. Seeing me approach, he opened the barrier and smiled, like a shepherd letting another of the flock into the fold. I stopped and voluntarily took out my identity card then almost fell off my bicycle, for he just laughed. He didn't want to see it!

Loches was the first town I came to in Vichy France. It was very quiet although occupied by French cavalry. I still had some tobacco left when I reached Loches but no matches. I had not had any for some time so, seeing a likely shop, I decided to buy some and sort of celebrate by having a smoke. An older man came to the counter. I asked for two boxes. I risked speaking, for now the nearest German was twenty five kilometres away. The old man had matches alright but was horrified when asked for two boxes. He said I could only have one. They were rationed. I was satisfied with that but I also realised that, as soon as I opened my mouth, by not knowing about rationing, I had branded myself a stranger.

Outside Loches, I found a quiet spot by a hayfield where I lay down in the sun to read and have a peaceful smoke. I had a pleasant feeling of contentment. I did not know that further south there were hundreds of big, sneaky gendarmes just waiting to pounce on little fellows like me. Just then I knew nothing. I puffed happily at my pipe. For the second time since I left Béthune prison camp, I thought I was free!

Chapter 12: The "British" Consul

I passed Châteauroux before nightfall and the next morning I decided to keep going south-east. I had an idea that on this course I would sooner or later reach the river Rhône, which I knew flowed into the Mediterranean near Marseilles. Here I hoped to see the British Consul or even get a boat.*

South of Châteauroux I lost my way completely and followed tiny roads and cart-tracks for several days. I passed through some wild but very beautiful country until I came to a pleasant valley. It was really a very pretty place where a slender stone bridge traversed a deep, rocky gorge. At the bottom of the gorge flowed the river, sparkling brilliantly in the sunshine, so that the very rocks themselves seemed to take on different colours. Further downstream I could see men wading in the river, fishing. As the day was hot I was tempted to go down and have a bathe but I decided to push on. I did not know exactly where I was during those few days but I remember passing a town somewhere that was full of picturesque chateaux.

Passing over an arched bridge spanning a broad river, I decided it was time for a wash and shave. However on going down to the riverbank I found it difficult to reach the water, so I had a wash in a nearby ornamental pool. I think it belonged to a girls' school or something similar, for I could hear them inside the building. I think

---

* From Loches, the pretty little town just inside the Zone Libre where Ray begins this next stage of his journey, it is 500 miles (around 800 kilometres) to his intended destination, Marseilles. Much of the terrain between Loches and Marseilles is mountainous with the roads consistently climbing above 1500 feet (around 450 metres) and occasionally much higher. It is probably late August to mid-September by this time. Daytime temperatures in the mountains of southern France are similar to those at lower levels (in the mid-twenties Celsius) but it is a good deal chillier at night. The cycling and the sleeping out therefore must have made for some very tough conditions, especially for someone who had limited access to food. You wouldn't know this from Ray's account though.

they would have been very surprised had they looked out of the window and seen a very dirty, bedraggled, little tramp, shaving in their fish-pond.

I finally found myself at Aubusson and was more or less able to ascertain my position, for there I found signposts pointing to Clermont-Ferrand and Saint-Étienne. I was overjoyed at this but I am afraid my joy didn't last long for I ran into a series of mountain ranges. No sooner did I ever get to the top of one of them than in the distance I would see another range ready for the next day. Tortuous roads wound steeply uphill, too steep to ride up – and when I reached the top I would find them too steep to ride down the other side.

The nights were bitter cold and I usually slept among the thick heather or bushes, soaked by the thick damp mist. One afternoon when I must have been cycling rather high up I found myself riding through a cloud. But at last, I found myself arriving at Clermont-Ferrand. I first saw it from high up in the mountains. It was spread out far below in the hot sunshine, making indeed a very beautiful picture. I had never heard of Clermont-Ferrand before and I did not know it was the home town of the traitor, Laval.[109] But then, at the time, I had never heard of Laval either.

Descending the steep winding road, I entered the town, stopping only to glance at places of interest. I had already found the road to Saint-Étienne and judging by the signposts, the next towns I would have to pass through were Ambert and Montbrisson.

Cycling through a small village on the outskirts of town I passed a couple of gendarmes who stood talking outside the local lockup. This was a formidable looking affair with massive iron bars across the windows and being built of rough grey stone, it looked cold and wicked. I should hate to be in there, I thought. A casual glance at the two gendarmes caused me to think how lucky I had been so far to avoid capture – but I cast away those ill-boding thoughts. Cycling along in the sunshine on France's central plateau, why, I might have paid good money to do that in peace-time. Behind me, I heard the swish of bicycle wheels. Automatically I put more weight on my pedals, for I couldn't stand anyone overtaking me. Then I heard a shout. "Arrêtez!" ["Stop!"]

I looked back. It was a gendarme! He rode alongside me and said something. I just grinned – so he said it again. Smelling trouble, I decided to stop. It was his turn to grin now. He was evidently tickled by some huge joke but personally I couldn't see it. He wanted to know where I was going. "Ou allez vous?"

I waved my hand down the road in a rather vague manner but said nothing. He then asked me where I came from but I remained silent, tapping the thumb of my clenched fist against my open mouth. It certainly shook him but he was determined not to be outdone. He pointed to my shining bicycle and then to scruffy me. He wanted details of ownership! I explained as best I could by signs, that it belonged to a woman. This made him grin more than ever. I pretended it was my sister's bicycle by making a "ssss" noise, which in my imagination was the nearest a dumb man could get to the French word for sister. I then made signs, placing one hand so-high from the road then placing it a little lower, then a little lower, making out that she was one of the family. He seemed quite satisfied with that but next came the inevitable question which always arises when apprehended by the French police. "Avez vous les papiers? Carte d'identité?"

Taking out my identity card, I handed it to him while he produced a thick notebook and copied down every detail of information it gave. Looking at my front bracket he also took my bicycle number, so it was obvious – although he could prove nothing – that he was still suspicious and wanted to know why my bicycle wasn't taxed. I pointed out though, that it was not really my bicycle and he let me go.

I hit up a good pace until I was well past Ambert and this part of my journey was uneventful. Reaching the top of a high range where there was the sign stating it was the highest point in the whole chain, I found a beret lying by the side of the road.[110] It was an improvement to my wardrobe so I made good use of it. I found Saint-Étienne just as I expected to find it – a busy, grimy, industrial town full of iron and steel-works. Steering my way between trams and taxis, I reached the other side of town. Here I felt much easier in my mind but as I left behind the last few houses, I was again apprehended by the police.

A gendarme seemed to appear from nowhere. He also wanted to know why my bicycle had not been taxed. The French police must have been having a purge on bicycle-tax dodgers that week. He was a nasty-tempered individual and it looked as if I was in for a rough time but the situation was saved by the appearance of another gendarme who was an older and kindlier man. He wore a different uniform and must have been the superior of the two for he took charge immediately. When I showed him the word "muet" on my identity card he became very sympathetic and explained to me by signs, that I simply must get my bicycle taxed. Tapping the front bracket where that tax plate usually is, he showed me 25 francs and pointed back to the town, saying, "Bientôt!" ["Soon!"]

The two gendarmes left me and I climbed the steep, winding road which led over the last range of mountains before I reached the river Rhône. Here I noticed a series of automobile signs belonging to the Touring Club de France, stating that this road was the Paris to Côte d'Azur route. Somewhere on the Côte d'Azur was Marseilles. I decided my luck was in.

Passing through Bourg-Argental and Annonay, I reached the river Rhône at Andance. I knew that from now on, as far as the direction was concerned, my journey would be easy. All I had to do was follow the Rhône until I found Marseilles. And following the course of the river, I would have no steep hills to climb. It was somewhere in this locality that I found a small vineyard. The grapes were not yet all ripe but by practice, I was soon able to sort the sweet from the sour. I was busy in this process, sitting down with my back against a tree, when from across the fields came an old man with four children. Not wishing to start a conversation, I did not look up at him as he passed but he wished me a good day so I answered him. That started it. He said something I did not understand. "Je ne comprends pas", I replied. He became curious.

"Pas parler Français?" [You don't speak French?].

"Non"

"Quelle nationalité?"

"Belge" [Belgian], I replied, trying to give an excuse for not being able to speak French while not disclosing my real nationality. In saying that though, I made the biggest mistake of all.

"Sprechen Sie Deutsch?"

I shook my head for I could see that he could.

"Vlaams?" [Flemish?]

"Non."

He started laughing and said since I spoke neither French, German nor Flemish, I could not possibly be a Belgian! At this, the children also started laughing and between them they enjoyed a huge joke at my expense but I didn't mind for they were a happy, inoffensive lot. The old man then told me he was a Belgian himself. I felt such a fool but I was able to enjoy the joke as well. Presently the laughter died down and he asked me if I was Italian or Spanish, insisting that I was Italian but ashamed to admit it. I was very sunburned at the time but although I guessed the old man could not speak Italian, I hated the idea of pretending to be from that country.[111]

At that, he and the children began a kind of guessing competition as to my nationality. They asked me if I was Russian so, seeing this conversation wasn't getting anywhere, I confessed I was English. The old man raised his eyebrows and shook his head. I had told him the truth but he didn't believe me! He said a few simple phrases in English that he had probably learned from the soldiers in Belgium and I answered him in English – but he still did not believe me. After the old man and his children had gone, I realised how I had got through France so easily – because I did not look the least little bit like an Englishman – at least not the continental idea of an Englishman.

I went by way of Tournon-sur-Rhône and Bagnols-sur-Cèze until I reached Avignon. There were many beautiful scenes on the river just north of Avignon but I had little time to admire them. For me it was on and on. Marseilles or bust!

One morning south of Avignon, I found a signpost "Marseilles – 85 kilometres". It was like nectar to a man dying of thirst. I rode like the devil all day in an effort to get there by nightfall. And I did it! From the hills behind Marseilles I could see a ship coming into port. I wondered if it was British. It did not take me long to find the centre of the city and once there I cycled around looking for the British Consulate. After about an hour's fruitless search, the enthusiasm wore off and I absentmindedly turned down a one way street against the traffic. I did not get very far before I was stopped by a gendarme. He sent me back. Taking advantage of the situation, I asked him anyway, "Où est le Consul Brittanique?"

Strange to say, he replied with a smile.

"Une, Rue de Arcole."

He pointed in the direction of the street. Following his instructions, I found it without undue difficulty. It was not an imposing building but it had double oak doors, above which was the royal coat of arms. It was the doors that held my attention. In the centre of each was posted a notice, one in French and one in English. They stated that owing to the collapse of France, the British Consul had evacuated and that British affairs and the consulate itself were in the hands of the American Consulate.

It looked a sad state of affairs. I had come a long way to find this. For the few minutes I stood staring at the notice, I thought I had come a long way for nothing. The brass plate by the side of the door gave the Consul's office hours. I saw I was a couple of hours late. Next morning I would return to see if there were any signs of activity. If not, I would go to the American Consulate and see what could be done there.

I went out of the town that night and slept in an old quarry. Next morning about nine o'clock I was back at 1, Rue de Arcole.

This time I did not take my bicycle. Instead I parked it against the sandbags of an air-raid shelter down behind the Vieux Port [Old Port] and proceeded to the Consulate on foot. If there was anything doing, I did not want to be encumbered by a stolen bicycle. The Consul might not like it.

I felt very much out of place walking through town. So ragged and grimy was I, that I was almost ashamed of my own reflection in the big plate glass windows of the shops. Arriving at the Consulate, I found to my utter dismay the doors were still shut. Everything was just the same as I had seen the night before. It was perfectly true then, I thought – the British Consul had evacuated. Not having much else to do, I read the notice again. After running my eyes over it several times I turned to go but then I heard a voice behind me.

"Are you English?"

I turned round quickly, very surprised. In front of me was an old lady. "How the devil does she know I'm English?" I thought. Then I remembered – how careless of me – I had been reading the English notice, not the French.

"Are you English?" she asked again.

"Yes," I replied.

"Do you want to see the Consul?"

This was very helpful I thought. I said "yes" again.

She half turned. "Then come along with me," she said. She spoke excellent English. "I'll show you where to find him."

I went. And so it was that a kind old lady saved the day. I told her who I was and where I come from but she showed no sign of surprise. It was I who was surprised, when she said, "Well, I'll take you to the Consul and then you can state your case to him. But don't take his manners to heart as he is a very abrupt and impetuous young man!"

"Oh!" was all I could say.

"But he'll be able to fix you up. We've had quite a few soldiers like you here. They stay at the Fort where at least they have a bed and food, and are allowed into the town for a few hours each evening."

"Um," I said, rather mystified.

"They are interned, of course – but they are allowed out certain times and they get 100 francs every month from the Consul."

Every month! Those last two words jarred my train of thought. I had no wish to get interned or to stay in any one place for months. I had come too far for that.* I would rather have stayed at Acheville. I turned to give a hot reply. But she was a dear old lady and so I decided to see the Consul first. Instead of taking me through the oak doors, she led me round the back, under an arch and up some steps to a waiting room. On the door of the waiting room, was a notice stating that only British subjects were allowed in. The room was pretty full and inside I was accosted by a bald-headed man whose job it seemed, was continually to dash about here and there.

"Are you English?"

He spoke rather haughtily, rather as though he didn't really think I was.

"Yeah!" I answered. I was getting all worked up by now.

He blinked behind his spectacles and asked me to take a seat. The Consul would see me soon. A few minutes elapsed while the bald man attended to two young women. All three talked rather loudly.

"Here are your visas", I heard the bald man say. "You will go via Perpignan to Barcelona."

"Oh, Perpignan!", exclaimed one of the girls, "and to think, we've just come that way from Carcassonne."

"Well, I'm sorry", replied the bald man – but it's the only way out. I believe there's a boat at Barcelona for such people as you. It leaves on Wednesday I think."

That little bit of information gave me an idea. It was Friday and surely I could make Barcelona in five or six days on a bicycle like mine. If there was one boat at Barcelona, then there was bound to be another sometime anyway. But there was the Spanish frontier to

---

* Ray had indeed come a long way. Including the various lengthy detours, his journey from Acheville in northern France to Marseilles must have been at least 1,200 miles (2,000 kilometres).

cross. I didn't like the idea of that.

Soon it was my turn to see the Consul. I found him exactly as the old lady described. If he was an American he certainly didn't talk like one. Seated behind a desk he asked me to sit down and to explain my difficulty. He listened very intently at first but when I explained I had crossed the demarcation line by means of a forged identity card, he sat back in his chair as though he had seen a ghost. He was horrified!

"Get rid of it! Get rid of it!" he said. "I don't know anything about it! You'll get five years if the French police catch you with it."

I was amazed. A stickler for international law, was that Yank. That is, if he was a Yank, which I doubted. When I nodded and half-agreed to do this, he came out with the cruellest stroke I had ever heard. "Well," he said, "you'll have to intern yourself."[112]

Despite what I had heard from the old lady, I was startled. He must have noticed, for he went on, "Of course, understand you will not be a prisoner. You will be allowed out at certain times and have certain privileges."

I opened my mouth to protest. But he continued.

"You won't have to beg or scrounge for your food and you'll have plenty of company. There are some other soldiers interned – so you won't be lonely. You might even find someone of your own regiment. In addition, you will get 100 francs, through the Consulate. It's a sort of pocket money."

I stood up.

"But I've come a long way and I'm determined to get back to England. Home!"

He waved aside my protest.

"My dear fellow. You don't seem to realise the conditions that exist here. No ships leave here except for Italy and North Africa. The only way you could get to England is by going through Spain and Portugal and you are liable to be detained in either of those two countries.[113] It would be much better for you if you interned yourself here, in a more friendly country.

"Of course, I can't compel you, you know. But I strongly advise you to.

"Now, I'll tell you what to do. Here is the address of the Sailors' Club. It is run by Padre Caskie. He's a very nice man. I think you'll like him. His place is a sort of centre where civilians who can't leave the country stay. No Englishman of military age is allowed to leave France. That is one of the terms of the Armistice. Padre Caskie will be able to give you a good meal and put you up for the night. Then, in the morning," he paused here and I imagined somebody being shot at dawn, "...an Inspector Gallibourne of the Marseilles Police will call."

He paused again, tapping the end of his pencil on the desk.

"He visits the club every morning and he will 'arrest' you."

He said the word "arrest" as though it didn't mean anything whatsoever and was merely part of a routine.

"Of course, having arrested you, he will take you to the *Sûreté*[114] for a routine interrogation. Then he will take you to the Fort."

I didn't like that word either. In fact I didn't like the whole idea at all. It sounded too much like surrender. Heaven knows I had had enough of that already.

"Now, at the fort – Fort Saint-Jean – you will find more soldiers like yourself.[115] A number were left behind during the evacuation from Dunkirk. Some escaped and others got lost. I think you will be alright at the Fort."

I nodded but not in approval. Inwardly I was still thinking of that boat from Barcelona. The Consul gave me a slip of paper.

"Here is the address of Padre Caskie. Go there now."

He told me how to get there and the interview came to a close. I left.[116]

My mind was in a whirl as I walked back to the Vieux Port. I thought I had overcome the worst difficulties – but now I realised the worst was yet to come. That German was certainly right when he said it's a long way to Tipperary. I returned to where I had left my bicycle and did a little maintenance on it, such as pumping up the tyres and adjusting the brakes. I was preparing for a long journey.

It was just then that I noticed three men sitting in the back of a motor launch. They eyed me rather peculiarly and when I went to wheel the bicycle away, they started shouting and kicked up a devil of a noise. They thought I was stealing the bike! Ye gods! What a situation to be in! I could not understand a word they were saying but their meaning was obvious. I yelled back, telling them exactly what I thought of them in ripe army vocabulary. But this brought a gendarme to the scene. This complicated matters, for now I could not pretend I was dumb.

First, the gendarme listened to the three Frenchmen. Then he asked me about my bicycle. Fortunately Marseilles gendarmes seemed to be of the rare, tolerant, type. I started babbling in broken French, using more actions than words. I think this is the secret of putting over something in a foreign language you don't understand. Finally I brought out the bicycle's bill of sale that I had found in the tool case shortly after I had stolen it at Évreux.

The gendarme asked me my nationality.

"Belge. Réfugié," I bluffed, remembering the last time I had tried that one.

This time it worked. He looked at the receipt and nodded. Turning to the three men in the motor launch, he shrugged his shoulders and walked away.

I cycled out of the city. I had five or six days to reach Barcelona. My plans were made.

On reaching the outskirts of the city, I halted. I read the slip of paper the Consul had given me. It read:

Padre Caskie
The Sailors' Club
36 Rue de Forbin (off Place de Jolie)
Marseilles

I thrust it into my pocket and turned my bicycle wheels west – towards Spain!

Chapter 13: Detective Inspector Gallibourne

I had a reasonable idea how to reach Spain before leaving Marseilles. I had taken a good look at a map in a shop window and my memory of it gave me a rough idea of the route. To the west of Marseilles is a large lake, *la Étang de Berre*, which is separated from the sea by a narrow isthmus and connected to the sea by a canal. This lake had to be passed to reach Montpellier, Béziers and Perpignan. I memorised their names and approximate positions on the map, then set off, trusting to luck. Little did I know, that luck does not last forever – and that the sands of physical effort were rapidly running out.

At Martigues, the first village, I decided to buy a pair of shoes. For some time I stood looking in the shop window weighing the situation in my mind before I finally decided. I did not know how to say "shoes" in French and would therefore brand myself as a foreigner. But I trusted they would not turn a cash customer over to the police and so I simply walked in and asked in English for a pair of shoes. I knew well the saleswoman would not understand a word I said but I had to say something to start off with, if only to convey the fact that I could not speak French. Luckily however, she was an intelligent woman and soon I got what I wanted.

Passing Istres, I reached the main road to Arles. By now I was feeling signs of weakness. For some time I had been living on a bread and water diet – and sleeping outside in all weathers had not done my health any good. On top of this I had a stroke of bad luck. I ran into a terrific wind, against which I could not cycle. It was impossible for me to make any progress. I tried to make some headway, hoping to reach more hilly country where I would be sheltered from the wind. But this part of France was a flat plain with nothing on it whatsoever to break the rush of wind. Try as I may, I could not ride more than a few yards without having to dismount. Walking was just as bad. In the heavier gusts it was all I could do to hang on to my bicycle and keep my balance.

The whole plain was covered with locust-like creatures, huge grasshoppers about 3 inches long. They swarmed over the dry grass and across the road, which was spattered thickly with their bodies, crushed by the occasional cars that passed that way. They would leap into the air in swarms and come sailing down in the wind at express speed, hitting me in the face and head. At that speed, creatures of that size could hurt.[117]

The great wind showed no signs of abating. It raged and tore across the flat plain. On the first day I felt myself growing weaker and weaker until night fell, when I slept under some scraggy bushes on some rough scrubland. At the end of the second day I decided to give up. It was useless to persist. I was too weak. I would to return to Marseilles to find Padre Caskie and to get myself interned. I would stay long enough to regain my strength. Maybe too I would find a friend before I hit the trail again. I was feeling very lonely.

The wind dropped as I lay resting on the second night but in its place came a worse evil – mosquitoes that tortured me throughout the night. By morning my face was a mass of bumps and blood. It was hell in its worst form. That morning though, since the wind had died down, I decided to continue towards Spain. Finding a small stream, I washed my socks but lost my only piece of soap in the process. It was going to be a dirty journey I thought.

Beyond Arles I got within a few kilometres of Montpellier. But the going was too hard now. It was like the last effort of a dying man. I did not have the strength to go further. After another night of hell with mosquitoes, I started my return journey to Marseilles. To have gone on would have meant driving myself to a state of collapse. I began the pitiful journey back. It was failure. I hated every inch of it.[118]

Pedalling very slowly in order to conserve what energy I had, I suddenly became aware that I was on the wrong road. But I didn't worry. Up to now I had done quite well, finding my way across a strange foreign country. I just kept going. I was bound to get somewhere. That somewhere proved to be Nîmes, miles north of my proper route.[119] In Nîmes, I had quite a shock. Walking down a street were two German soldiers. They caused me to worry that the rest of France had been occupied! I later learned the German soldiers would have belonged to the German Armistice Commission, whose job it was to see that the terms of the armistice were carried out.[120]

I found my way back to Marseilles and on the hills behind the city, I decided to hide my bicycle. I had a good reason for doing this for otherwise, on being interned, I might lose it and I would need it for future operations. If I was condemned to travel across Europe as a tramp I might as well be a mechanised one. It took me some time to haul it up the steep, bushy hillside to a suitable spot where no one was likely to stumble across it. I stuck it between the rocks and covered it with foliage until it was impossible to detect. It was a job well done, even though it cost me two hours.

A five mile march brought me once more to the centre of Marseilles. My feet were feeling very tender by the time I got there and I was glad when I found the Rue de Forbin and was standing at the door of the Sailors' Club.[121] A woman, the caretaker, who was obviously French, opened the door.

"Could I see Padre Caskie?" I asked.

She looked at me for a full minute, "Are you English?"

That infernal question again!

"Come in," she said and led me to Padre Caskie.

Padre Caskie was a benevolent-looking man, short in stature and with grey curly hair. He was a padre of the Church of Scotland.[122] He led me into a large room, where a number of men, young and middle-aged, were reading or playing billiards. Padre Caskie introduced me to some of them. Saying something about a cup of tea, he left me talking to Humphries – Frank, I think his name was.

While Padre Caskie was seeing about the cup of tea (and something to eat, for he was horrified at me living on bread and water for such a long time), I learned from Humphries that he was an Englishman but had lived in America for some years. He had been on his way over to England from the States to do his bit when the cattle boat on which he was working his passage was torpedoed. Landing on the French coast, he had made his way to Marseilles but that was as far as he had got. I did not attach much importance to this – but I soon found Marseilles was as far as most Englishmen got.[123]

Actually Humphries's story was very interesting. I think the padre must have asked him to keep me entertained for he went on to tell me all about America. He asked me if I had been there. I said "no" but that I had relatives in Springfield, Illinois. He told me all about the place, saying he used to go there every Fall to some kind of fete they used to have. I then had a kind of private tea in the kitchen with Humphries and Padre Caskie. Padre Caskie wanted to know all my late history.

And so the day passed. Padre Caskie told me, just as the Consul had, all about Inspector Gallibourne and what would happen when he visited the club. I gathered from Humphries that others before me had been through the same routine. I also learned that Gallibourne was only half-French, his mother being English. He could speak English perfectly.

Dinner was not until six o'clock. Padre Caskie arranged the timing like this so the boys from the fort could come up afterwards and have anything that was left over. I met a few of the boys from the fort that evening but it was soon "lights out" for although Padre Caskie was a kind and generous man he ran the place with great discipline.

Next morning Humphries suggested I should dodge the Inspector and stay at the club for another day – but our little plan did not work. When I least expected it, I felt someone tap me gently on the shoulder.

"Would you like to come along with me?"

Turning round, I found a short, plump man with a reddish face.

"I'm Inspector Gallibourne."

He sounded as if he was apologising for the fact. I think they should have called him "Mother Gallibourne" as he was so awfully fussy.

"Now, don't be afraid," he said before I could say a word. "You're not under arrest. I'm only going to take you to the station as a matter of routine. Just a formality, you know. Then I'll take you to the Fort where you'll meet the boys."[124]

I was amazed at his command of English and noticed he said "station", not "Sûreté", and that he said it as casually as any London copper might have said it. Probably, that was why he had that kind of job.

I went with him. Padre Caskie said I could leave my bag there and collect it later. This I did. There wasn't anything of value in it, except a tin opener, a bicycle pump and a German water bottle. Perhaps one day they would come in useful...

As I walked through the streets with the Inspector, he would continually say, "You are not under arrest. If you were you would be walking in front of me, not behind me." Entering the Sûreté, which was a large building just behind the cathedral, he led me up a flight of steps to a waiting room. Here he produced a couple of forms, which he proceeded to fill in by asking me questions. He wanted my name, rank and number. He wanted to know where I had escaped from the Germans and what route I had taken to Marseilles. He also wanted to know how I had got to Marseilles and where I had crossed the demarcation line.

I told him I had had a bicycle given to me and that had brought me almost to Marseilles but that it had crocked and I had dumped it, making the rest of the journey on foot. This story conveniently accounted for the absence of the bicycle. But the Inspector had his doubts about this bicycle. He said it didn't matter if I had stolen it from the Germans. It was one less for them and one more for us – but he would rather I had stolen a motor car or a tank. Or maybe three or four bicycles. I smiled to myself. Perhaps one day Inspector Gallibourne will read this and he will realise how near he was to the truth.

He asked me my age and I told him I was 21 but he looked at me slyly.

"You know," he said, "not long ago a chap came here saying he was eighteen."

I listened intently wondering what was coming next.

"Obviously, he was a soldier but he was trying to get past by saying he was under military age. I didn't believe him so I locked him up for the night and in the morning when the bristles were beginning to show on his chin, he told me the truth."

I agreed with the Inspector's policy. British soldiers should not tell lies to the French police.

"But you look young," he said. "Now, if you had told me you were eighteen, I would have believed you."

My thoughts immediately flashed to my identity card, which said I was eighteen. I found Inspector Gallibourne to be an amazing conversationalist, who could easily win one's confidence. You had to be continually on your guard. He proceeded to tell me all about himself. He said his job was to round up any British soldiers who came that way and see that they were interned. He was personally responsible for them. He had to go to the office of the German Armistice Commission in La Canebière[125] every so often and report the number of British soldiers interned at Fort Saint-Jean and whether any had escaped.

"Escaped?" I asked. He was now talking my language in more ways than one. "Then what?"

"They tell me to go and find them. But when I see them, I never recognise them."

I expressed disbelief at this, so he went on to prove it. He told me of two men from the Fort, Hills and Caldecott. One night they stole a boat, a luxury motor launch, and loaded it with stolen petrol until they had enough for a very long journey. Unfortunately for them, they set sail in very stormy weather and were blown ashore further up the coast. They were lucky enough to escape injury and reached dry land. The motor boat however had her bottom torn out when she hit the beach. It was a very expensive motor boat and a warrant was issued for their arrest.

A few days later, they were arrested at the Sailors' Club to be interned again, in the usual way. They did not even bother to give false names. Gallibourne said he told them he had a warrant for their arrest. But he did not serve it. Then he purposely forgot about the matter – and as far as anyone else was concerned, he had not recognised them. Later, I met Hills and Caldecott. They told me that Inspector Gallibourne's version was perfectly true.

Gallibourne finished filling in the forms, making me sign them both with my thumb-print next to my signature. He took both forms away and then came back. There followed a period of waiting, which he did not explain. While we waited, he took me to the window and showed me where the Italians had dropped their bombs.[126] He pointed to where one had killed thirty gendarmes. I sympathised with him although, except for a few shrapnel holes in the walls of the cathedral and the Sûreté, I could see no damage whatever. He seemed very distressed over the Italian bombing so I looked sorry – but at the same time, I felt like telling him he should have seen Neufchâtel after the Stukas had finished with it.

Inspector Gallibourne was wanted by somebody, so he handed me over to a Detective Sergeant who took me to Fort Saint-Jean. It was a formidable looking place on the seafront next to the docks. Of sandy colour, it had a drawbridge, high walls and battlements. From the south-west corner rose a tall, mosque-like tower, making the whole place look like a scene from "Beau Geste".[127]

Crossing the drawbridge, we went up several flights of stone steps – for it was a rambling place – until we reached the highest level of the Fort. This was the *dépôt* of the Foreign Légion.[128] It was a flat, irregularly shaped area with a couple of barrack blocks. It was halved in the centre by a high wall, painted ochre. In the middle of the wall was the statue of some Légionnaire and the regimental motto.[129] Painted on the wall were these words:

LA LÉGION ÉTRANGÈRE

"The Foreign Legion!" I thought. "I'm certainly getting around."

In the wall, to the left of the statue, was a little arched gate, guarded by a sentry. The Sergeant took me through this gate to a small office situated in one of the barrack blocks. Here, he handed me over to a Foreign Legion corporal, who merely wrote my name on a piece of paper and then showed me into a room next door. It was as much as to say, "This is where you live."

I hardly knew what to make of this internment business. I was about to regard it as a huge joke until I saw the room. It was a large, airy place with a narrow shelf running round all four walls. It was completely devoid of furniture. The beds consisted of blankets laid on the floor – the bare concrete floor.

There were only about three chaps in the room at the time. I walked over to one who sat reading, "Hullo", I said, not knowing what else to say under these strange circumstances.

"Hullo," he replied, glancing up. "Just got in?"

"Yes. What's it like here?"

"Not bad. You'll get used to it – but don't put your bed too near the wall, especially at night."

"Why not?"

"Bugs," he said quietly and went on reading.

Chapter 14:
Life at Fort Saint-Jean

INTRODUCTORY NOTE

In order to place Ray's experiences in Marseilles in their context, it is helpful first to know something about the city itself during this period, and second to understand the circumstances of the "voluntary" internment that Ray has had no alternative but to accept. It is also important to know something about a man whose name first appeared in Ray's story two chapters ago, the Reverend Donald Caskie.

Marseilles in 1940

Marseilles in 1940 was a place of hope and despair; of intrigue, adventure and violence. The city had long been an intercontinental crossroads and a home to communities of many nationalities. During the Second World War it was even more a melting pot. Countless people from scores of nations crowded the city looking for a route away from France. Displaced people had travelled from every corner of Europe to get there, including, of course, many Jewish refugees seeking to escape the Holocaust. There were also foreign residents of France trying to return to their homelands and young men of all nations – including from France itself – hoping to find a passage to Britain where they could join the free forces fighting against the Nazis. All this was in addition to the merchant seamen whose ships were in port and the shady figures of the city's ever-present criminal underworld. There were also some numbers of German soldiers in the city. Their presence occasionally met with a violent response from organised groups of local people.

Fort Saint-Jean

After his "voluntary" arrest, Ray was taken to Fort Saint-Jean. Fort Saint-Jean was (and still is) a monumental fortification situated on the Marseilles harbourside, at the entrance to the Vieux Port.[130] It had formed a crucial part of the city's seaward defences since the 17th century.

In 1940, in an ad hoc response to the trickle of escaped British soldiers who had begun to turn up in Marseilles, a small internment camp had been established in one of the buildings enclosed within the fort. Already there, under the supervision of the French Foreign Legion (Fort Saint-Jean housed a Legion barracks), were around thirty other escaped British PoWs who had been drawn to Marseilles for much the same reasons as Ray. As a large city, with a thriving port and a British Consulate, it seemed – in theory at least – a promising place for finding a passage home.

The little band of escaped British soldiers at Fort Saint-Jean was but a tiny fraction of the chaotic mix that made up Marseilles' population at that time. They were however, as determined to get away from the city as anyone else. Because they had been documented by the authorities and their movements were monitored, the situation of the British soldiers was more challenging than that facing civilians who were also trying to find an onward passage. On the other hand there were no armed guards, no barbed wire perimeter and there were no searchlights sweeping the surrounding area – those imprisoned in Poland and Germany later in the war would face far greater hazards if they risked an escape. The men in Fort St-Jean knew they had already done the most difficult bit – getting out of occupied France. They just had to work out the next move. As Ray says in this coming chapter "...escape was virtually the sole topic of conversation at Fort Saint-Jean".

Rev. Donald Caskie and the "Sailors' Club"

Escape was probably also the main topic of conversation at what Ray calls the "Sailors' Club", the seamen's hostel at which he spends his first night back in Marseilles following his failed attempt to cycle to Spain. The hostel, more properly known by its official name as the British and American Seamen's Mission, was where many of the interned British servicemen spent their evenings, when they were allowed to leave Fort Saint-Jean and move freely around the city.

As we saw in the previous chapter, on his arrival at the Seamen's Mission, ragged, exhausted, malnourished and dispirited, Ray had been welcomed and cared for by the man in charge, the Rev. Donald Caskie. Rev. Caskie (1902 – 1983) had formerly been the minister of the Scottish Kirk in Paris. Forced to leave for his own safety when German forces occupied Paris in June 1940, he had eventually made his way to Marseilles, where he had been offered the Seamen's Mission as a building from which he could offer practical and pastoral support to British citizens who had drifted to the city.

Rev. Caskie was destined gradually to become a hugely important figure in managing the onward journeys of escaped PoWs and stranded airmen who had found their way to Marseilles. Working at enormous personal risk, eventually in conjunction with British Military Intelligence operative and escape specialist, "Lieutenant-Commander Patrick O'Leary RN" (the alias of the Belgian army officer, Albert-Marie Edmond Guérisse), Rev. Caskie is believed to have helped facilitate around 500 escapes from southern France via Spain before his expulsion from Marseilles by a Vichy Military Tribunal in 1941.[131]

At the time of Ray's internment however – probably late August or early September 1940, only a short while after Rev. Caskie's own arrival in Marseilles – this escape infrastructure did not yet exist. Rev. Caskie seems to have played no role in the various escape attempts from Fort Saint-Jean described by Ray in this chapter, apart from providing the tacit support of making the Seamen's Mission a place where all the internees were welcome, and where they could speak freely and openly.

Life at Fort Saint-Jean

When I went outside, I found most of the boys on the battlements next to the tower. They were standing up, staring intently out to sea and shouting. Suddenly, they all gave a cheer and began waving. I was curious, so I joined them. For some time, in their excitement, they did not notice me. Then I discovered they were watching a ship sail out of harbour. I could distinguish the name of the ship, *Sidi-Bel-Abbès*.[132]

"He's got through! He's done it!"

"He's got away!"

"Who's got away?" I asked one of them.

"Musgrove! He stowed away disguised in a Foreign Legion uniform."

Gradually we all went back to the barrack room and I learned the whole story of Musgrove and of the situation at Fort Saint-Jean. Of course, Musgrove was not his real name. I have forgotten his real name. In fact, I have forgotten many of the names from Fort Saint-Jean, so I will give these men fictitious names – but if any of them ever read this, they will surely know who they are.

I gathered from the conversation at the fort that escaping to England was about the hardest thing on Earth. It wasn't that it was hard to get out of the fort, for you could walk out any time after 6.00 in the evening. The catch was getting out of Vichy France. There was not much object in escaping the fort unless you could leave the country.

All the known exits had been tried. Switzerland? There was no point in going there according to one chap who had tried it; the frontier was too well guarded. Italy was out of the question. Spain? Many appeared to have tried this way but usually the gendarmes picked them up before they even reached the Spanish border. Only one had actually succeeded in crossing the border but he had been turned back by the Spanish Civil Guard. Another, nicknamed

"Bluey", had tried to reach Spain by way of Andorra but had found the mountains impassable. There were two men, "Blondie" Garbett and Williams, with whom I later joined forces, who had been caught trying to reach Spain. They had been put into a concentration camp at Saint-Cyprien before being returned to Fort Saint-Jean.[133] Everybody at Fort Saint-Jean had by now firmly decided the only way out was by sea – hence Musgrove's daring escape in a Foreign Legion uniform. It was the subject of conversation for many days; in fact, "Escape" was virtually the sole topic of conversation at Fort Saint-Jean.

I went up to Padre Caskie's that night to collect my belongings and next morning fell into the strange routine at Fort Saint-Jean. This started with breakfast at an unearthly hour but we were not obliged to get up. It was not much of a breakfast as all it consisted of was a cup of black coffee and a tiny square of chocolate. On these rations I often wondered if the legionnaires still thought they were in the desert. It didn't worry us though. We just dashed out for coffee and dashed back to bed again.

About eight o'clock we would parade on the square. There were about thirty of us when we were rounded up. We would stand to attention while the bugle was played and the French flag hoisted. A good many of the boys did not like this business of standing to attention to the French flag. Among these was Barron. He hated the French army because of the big let-down at St Valery – and in a way I sympathised with him.

As soon as the flag-hoisting ceremony was over, a sergeant of the Foreign Legion would take a roll call. On the first day this was very amusing. In the first place, he could hardly pronounce the English names and he had even greater difficulty with the Scottish ones. Unwittingly, he caused many a laugh. I listened as he went through the roll, each man answering "Sergeant!" – until he called Musgrove's name. There was a deadly silence, then someone in the rear rank shouted, "Départ Angleterre!"

The poor sergeant went up in the air at this, while everybody laughed their heads off – but soon he saw the funny side himself and laughed with us. Then he handed us over to our own Sergeant Major Allan – a London man, I believe. Sergeant Major Allan looked after our interests in general.

During the morning I discovered my bed was next to those of Hills and Caldecott of motor boat fame. I asked them about their escapade and they told me exactly what I had heard from Inspector Gallibourne. They also told me how they came to set sail in a storm. Hills told me they had selected this boat because of its seaworthy appearance. They had discovered a dump of petrol drums and their plan was to take the motor launch and load it with petrol. Night after night they had lain in wait for an opportunity but there had always been someone near either the petrol dump or the boat – until one night when it was very rough and stormy. This was their opportunity. They knew they were taking a grave risk with a heavily laden boat in such a sea but they were tired of waiting. The unfortunate result of this I had heard from Inspector Gallibourne.

A few days later, when I had got the lie of the land around the docks, I approached Hills and Caldecott with the idea of a repeat performance. They were all for it. After a great deal of planning and discussion, we made a series of reconnaissance trips around the dock areas of Marseilles. First we tried the Vieux Port where there were a considerable number of yachts, launches and small diesel trawlers. But we had to rule out this part of the dock. We discovered that, carefully concealed under our own drawbridge at Fort Saint-Jean, at the entrance to the Vieux Port, a police boat was permanently stationed. We watched the police boat – but it had no set habits. Sometimes it went for a little cruise but it was never gone for more than a few minutes – so not even a sailing boat on the blackest night could be stolen from the Vieux Port.

On the other side of the fort were the docks used by the big ships. Now though, the docks were mostly used by the French Military Line, the only ships that left Marseilles. Beyond these was a maze of smaller docks, housing tramp steamers and other miscellaneous vessels, which never went anywhere. Further still, stretching to the village of Estaque, was a long, zigzag breakwater behind which lay many small boats. A great many of these were equipped with petrol motors and used mainly for fishing. Among them were also several big launches – and so it was to Estaque that we made our way.

It was a good five kilometres to Estaque and we were soon tired due to the hot sun and the hot streets, for we went in the afternoon. Strictly speaking, we were not supposed to be out before six pm. but it happened like this; we did our usual fatigue for the Foreign Legion, bringing up the rations from the street to the top of the fort. This was a daily job (volunteers only) which never took long. On this particular day though, as soon as we reached the street, we did a bunk. This suited our purposes better than waiting until six o'clock.

We were rather disappointed with our trip to Estaque. We found surprisingly few suitable boats among the hundreds that lay behind the breakwater. By elimination we sorted the good from the bad, until we had one boat left. This was a fine, white painted, cabin cruiser. The other boats were either too big, too small or were moored in positions that did not encourage piracy. Our luck must have been out that afternoon though, for a closer examination revealed that the boat was moored just out of reach. Without a boat-hook it was impossible to reach it without falling into the Mediterranean. Very disappointed, we decided to abandon our effort until some later date. We had tried every likely quarter of the docks by now so we adjourned to Padre Caskie's for tea.

I think it was the next night (time does not matter in a place like that), when we were all sitting around talking in the barrack-room. One of our sergeants burst into the room. He stated – rather mysteriously – that he was going to mention no names. He wanted to tip off a certain group of blokes who intended stealing a motor boat, saying the police were wise to them and were only waiting to catch them red-handed. The man they had intended buying the petrol from had turned informer.

Having brought this strange news, he disappeared. I wondered how he came to be so well informed. I thought of Inspector Gallibourne and his half English nationality. Of course, it was obvious the sergeant did not mean Hills, Caldecott or myself, for we were not the type to buy petrol when we could steal it. Later in the evening Barron, Williams and Blondie Garbett admitted it was them.

By this, I learned something of this boat-stealing business that I did not know before. Barron claimed that he and one of his friends had borrowed a small rowing boat and had rowed out into the bay to examine the "boom". I had never even heard of a boom before. It was said to be a kind of submarine net about three miles from the shore, stretching from the mainland at one end of the bay to the island of Ratonneau near the Château d'If on the other end.[134] According to Barron, the boom consisted of buoys connected by steel hawsers, which supported chains. He said it was impossible to pass. To prove it, he pointed out that no ships went that way. They all sailed through the narrow channel next to the Château d'If where they were checked in and out by the authorities (this was quite correct). Some of the boys who, like myself, had not heard of the boom, ridiculed him. He told them if they went to the top of the "synagogue" on a clear day they would see it for themselves.

Next morning, out of curiosity, I decided to try this. I made my way to the synagogue – a slang name we had given to the tall tower that stood high above the rest of the fort. Finding a door at the bottom of the tower, I went in. The place was unused. Between the walls, I found a narrow spiral staircase. Down the centre of the tower, built one above the other, lighthouse fashion, were several prison cells with iron-barred doors. The tower looks very pretty and picturesque – but I can assure you that to be imprisoned in one of those tiny cells in the olden days must have been a perfect hell.

I went up the staircase. The stone steps were so worn that in the darkness I stumbled. The only light that came in was through the tiny slits placed at intervals in the outer wall. Reaching the top, I found a small square opening in the side of the dome and stepping out on to the precarious two foot six ledge that ran around the top, I sat down and looked out to sea. This tower dominates the entrance to Marseilles from the sea. I stared hard but saw nothing. Then, as my eyes became more accustomed to the bright sunshine after the blackness of the tower I saw, near the island of Ratonneau, a long line of dark dots. I traced them with my eye. A straight line stretched across the sea towards the mainland when they disappeared in the distance. There was no doubt about it. It was "the boom".

One morning, when I sat on the western wall of the fort with a chap called Williams, a man from the Royal Engineers, I noticed below us, in the first dock basin, a long white schooner. She was a three-masted vessel and on her side, was painted the Spanish flag and the name, *Cala-Gat*. I remarked to Williams that she was a fine looking boat and he told me of the plot there once had been to steal the *Cala-Gat*.

It seemed that a few of the boys, Williams himself being one of the ringleaders, had thought out a plan to pirate the vessel. They were to go down the walls of the fort into the docks one at a time by means of the "bucket and chain". This was a long chain suspended from the battlements by a pulley. There was a bucket on the end of the chain. Once down, they would seize the boat which only had a crew of half a dozen. Then, they would take the *Cala-Gat* out of the docks by means of her diesel engine.

Personally, I thought it a spectacular and adventurous plan. But like most plans at Fort Saint-Jean, it had a hitch. In the first place Williams could not get enough volunteers. Most of the boys were rather shy of full scale piracy, let alone swinging through space in a little bucket in the middle of the night. Worse still, the authorities, who must have suspected something, decided to take away the bucket and chain. But Williams had plenty of guts. He would try anything. It was quite a long, interesting talk with Williams and we became good friends. He told me most of the boys had come to the conclusion that the only practical way out was to stow away to

North Africa and try their luck there.

Fort Saint-Jean can best be described as an "escape club". The men had divided themselves into small groups, each with our own pet idea of escape from Vichy France. If any had information that might benefit the others though, they always told it. So it was, that Hills, Caldecott and I decided to follow the plan of Williams and Co. to stow away. We arranged to go down to the docks and get what shipping information we could by pumping the native dock labourers. It was not hard to get into the docks during the day when the place was moderately busy. We were able to study the layout of various ships and find out their times of sailing and their destinations. Although nine out of every ten sailed to North Africa, we wanted one going to Oran, as this was so much nearer to Gibraltar.[135]

Either the food at Fort Saint-Jean or the sun did not agree with me for I was soon ill with intense pains in my stomach, usually at night. One day I was lying on my bed – or rather, my two blankets on the concrete floor – feeling very ill when Hills and Caldecott burst into the room. They seemed very excited and told me they had information that a ship was sailing for Oran at four o'clock next morning. This meant getting onboard that night. But I was too ill even to walk down to the docks. When I told them this, they offered to carry me. They were mad enough to try – but I refused knowing full well it would jeopardise their own chances of escape. They agreed. Time was getting short and collecting a few of their belongings, they made their exit. I watched them go and shouted, "Au revoir." But I never saw Hills or Caldecott again.

Shortly after, we all very nearly ended up in the Foreign Legion. The legionnaires at the fort were going back to North Africa and had the idea of taking us with them by enlisting us and kicking us out again when we got to Algiers under the pretence of our being unfit. This was a good idea and would at least have got us out of the country but the German Armistice Commission interfered, saying that the French could not enlist men in unoccupied France.

With the departure of the Foreign Legion, conditions at Fort Saint-Jean took a turn for the worse. We were taken over by some ordinary French troops. Compared with our late command, they were a filthy, undisciplined lot. The first thing they did was to move us out of our barrack room to a smaller one situated above the cookhouse. To make up for lack of space in this smaller room they gave us two-tier bunks to sleep in. This may sound like an improvement but they were wooden bunks and alive with bugs. One night I actually found a live scorpion under my pillow. It was about three inches long. After that, whenever the weather permitted and until I got used to these things, I slept outside in the little rock garden that ran along the side of the north wall. The food also deteriorated. With the Foreign Legion it wasn't any too good but now it was ten times worse. We used to get a tin cup full of fairly good red wine with our dinner. Now even this was bad. It tasted like vinegar.

While I was at Fort Saint-Jean I enquired if anyone had seen any Kensingtons on their travels but many of them had never even heard of the Kensingtons, except for one man. He claimed to have met one of my Kensington comrades in Paris. I was surprised at this. I could hardly imagine a man of my own regiment in Paris, of all places. However, this information was soon confirmed. A few days later, there arrived at Fort Saint-Jean, one Freddie Ford of Finchley. He had a pal with him and according to his story he had got away a couple of days before I did, during a rush for some food which was being given away by the French people. I knew Freddie fairly well. He had been called up at Mill Hill the same day as I had. But Freddie must have had a strain of gypsy in him; three or four days later, as quietly as they had arrived, he and his pal left again.[136]

The French soldiers who had taken over kept a negligent watch and we were able to walk out of the fort at almost any time of the day. About the same time as Freddie Ford's departure another man, Adams, also disappeared. Unlike Freddie Ford, Adams came back. He had a strange story to tell. He had tried to stow away. He had succeeded in getting aboard a ship but had been caught trying to hide in a lifeboat. There was nothing terrible in that but on being searched, he had been found in possession of forged papers of some kind. Whether they were identity papers or not, I don't know. The police didn't like that though, and they threw him in prison for a few days.

He gave a terrible, detailed account of his stay in the French prison. I have no wish to tell all of it, except that he was imprisoned in a cell with several other men. Their lavatory was a stinking, stagnant circular hole in the middle of the floor. In this place, they lived, ate and slept – or rather, slept as best they could, for all night big insects crept out of the hole and crawled over their bodies. But that is all you will want to know of Adams's awful story.

A slightly more successful attempt at stowing away was made by a chap whom I only knew as "Titch". He and his two pals got into the docks at night by the ingenious method of going up the passenger gangway which passed over the road outside the docks. The entrance to the gangway was on the opposite side of the road and was barricaded because it was not in use. But they made short work of that and, taking off their boots to avoid noise, they walked up the concrete floor of the gangway until they reached the top floor of a hangar inside the docks. It was from here, in peacetime, that the first class passengers embarked on to the upper decks of the big liners. But now there were no big liners, so Titch's problem was to get down to ground level. This they did by climbing down the leg of a crane.

Taking off their boots again, they crept up the ship's gangplank, passing the ship's night-watchman who, according to Titch was snoring loudly in his chair. Reaching the hatch of the engine room and finding it open, they climbed down into the engine room. Then, to make it even more certain they would not be discovered, all three crawled down the tunnel through which ran the propeller shaft.

Here they felt reasonably safe and expected next time they saw daylight they would be well on their way to Morocco. I think they deserved success – but luck was against them, for half an hour before the ship was due to sail, a greaser came crawling along the shaft, examining it. Of course, he discovered them. This was very unfortunate, for the greaser was the only conscientious member of the crew. The others were quite sympathetic towards the stowaways but the greaser reported them to the captain. That complicated matters. Here again, they were unfortunate for the captain had turned vigorously anti-British since his son had been killed on the battleship *Dunkerque* during the Oran incident.[137] He was not quite as bad as he might have been however. He did not hand them over to the police but gave them a vehement lecture against British war policy. Then he kicked them off the ship, thus ending Titch's gallant attempt to escape.

The next man to arrive at Fort Saint-Jean was a chap called Ritchie. He was fairly well dressed when he arrived. He had lived in a shack on the Somme, where his father went duck shooting in peacetime. Here he had quite a supply of tinned food. As the place was camouflaged for the purpose of shooting duck and being on an island, he had not been disturbed by any Germans.

There were also two men at the fort who, travelling across France together, had reached a river they had to cross but there was no bridge. Finding a boat, they tried to row across. They had just pulled away when two German officers appeared on the bank and called them back. They thought this was the end. Seeing it was useless trying to escape, they rowed back. Then, they discovered that all the German officers wanted – for they suspected nothing – was to be ferried across the river. This they did. Then to add to this gigantic bluff, to make things more realistic, they charged the German officers two francs![138]

There were four officers at Marseilles: a major whom I never saw but only heard of from Williams; a Captain Besley of the Northumberland Fusiliers; a young subaltern whom we called "Doc"; and a Pilot Officer from the RAF. These officers were not obliged to live at the fort, so I saw little of them, Even so, two of them proved to be a nuisance and hindered my final plans to escape.

One of them, the pilot officer, was a nuisance all the time but he ultimately got his desserts. His name was Charles de Clary Scott, a French-Canadian. Since the French army had taken over from the Foreign Legion, he was around more than usual, acting as an interpreter.[139]

Now, as it happened, many of the boys who did not mind doing a few fatigues for the Legion, were dead against working for the ordinary French soldiery. As I have said, the French troops were a filthy lot and left the parade ground and courtyards in a terrible mess. Also, the boys were embittered – as I had been – because of what had happened at St Valery and several other places where the French had let down the B.E.F.. Some who felt like this flatly refused to work. The ringleader was Barron. The day previous to Barron's downright refusal to clean up the filth left by the French army, he got into hot water with Pilot Officer de Clary Scott.

Barron had become involved in some quarrel with a French soldier at tea-time. Even on his way back from the mess room, he was still calling the Frenchman all the ill-mannered names he could think of. As he crossed the square, still chewing a piece of bread and cursing between mouthfuls, he was overheard by de Clary Scott who instantly pounced on him. There then followed the vicious argument. Quite a crowd collected and although Barron's speech was very rough, he was perfectly correct in what he said. On the other hand, de Clary Scott was right, under the circumstances, in curbing Barron's tongue. But de Clary Scott's line of talk showed him definitely to be pro-Vichy. This not only raised a great deal of feeling against him but labelled him with suspicion. Before many days had passed, it became generally believed at Fort Saint-Jean that Pilot Officer Charles de Clary Scott knew very little about aeroplanes and was not really a pilot officer at all.

Not having much interest in the case, I took little notice of this. When Barron refused to work for the French however, de Clary Scott had him put in a cell along with two of his friends. For a time it looked like civil war but it died down. Personally, I kept out of the way but de Clary Scott was a bad penny – and like all bad pennies, he was scheduled to turn up again.

After this purge, I came to the conclusion that Fort Saint-Jean was no place for me. With three companions, I once more decided to try the stowing away business. We were an odd assortment. First there was "Pop". Pop was a middle-aged Scot and was as round as a barrel. Then there was "Bluey", who was thin; and McIver, who was well over six feet tall. McIver was not his real name. It was the name he used because he had been the army twice. He was like that.

For the past few days, we had been scrounging around the docks and had chosen our ship. She was the *General Chansey* bound for Bizerte and then to Algiers, carrying a cargo of heavy truck tyres.[140] We made our way down to the docks about ten o'clock on the chosen night, dropping into a café opposite the gates to pass away the time, for as yet it was too early. These gates were always open but through them one could only gain access to one particular basin of the docks. It was rare any suitable ship came in there – but in our case we were lucky for that was where the *General Chansey* was docked.

Time passed quickly in the café. We ordered beers and discussed things in general. First Pop bought the beers, then Bluey, then McIver and then me. We met a Swede. He bought beers too. We had a right old time. We pumped the Swede, who was a sailor, for any shipping information until a woman came into the café and we lost our friend the Swede to her. A little later he came back and Pop pulled his leg about the woman. The Swede admitted having slept with her for 50 francs. "Never again," he said, shaking his head. Pop screwed up his face in horror. But Pop was a Scotsman and was probably thinking about the 50 francs.

The time came for us to go and we left the café. But the beer was taking effect. I knew that on this particular escapade, I had lost the stealth and alertness I had learned in the forest at Bouzonville. Entering the dock gates without being challenged, we made our way in single file along the quay, to where the *General Chansey* lay. We had to exercise great care as we neared the ship. The hangar she was moored alongside was lit up so we were compelled to keep to the shadows. A big hulk loomed up on our left. We made our way along her side until we reached the gangplank.

Suddenly Pop came rushing up from the rear of the file saying something about night-watchmen. We all stopped and looked around. Two men had come out of the open door of the hangar. Almost at the same moment as we saw them, they saw us. They came towards us and shouted something. Bluey shouted, "Run!"

We ran like hell. We did a good hundred yards down the jetty but there was no way out that way except by jumping into the sea. We dodged behind a pile of barrels and for some time we watched the watchmen looking around for us, shining their torches here and there. We sat still, hardly daring to breathe. But it was only a matter of time before they found us. It was a fair cop. There was no escape, for one of them pulled a pistol from his back pocket. They led us back to the dock gates. As we neared the gates, the watchman who had the pistol put it back in his pocket. This gave the impression that all they were going to do was sling us out of the docks. But just to make sure, I whispered to McIver, "Let's make a run for it!"

Once more, we ran like hell. The watchmen started yelling at the tops of their voices as we raced out of the docks and across the cobbled streets with them in hot pursuit. As bad luck would have it, coming up the street on a bicycle was a gendarme. Hearing the noise of the watchmen – who yelled as though they were being murdered – and seeing four fugitive figures dashing across the street – the gendarme instantly gave chase.

We tore past the café we had not long ago left. The proprietor who stood in the doorway scratched his head as we whizzed by. We turned down a street with me well in the lead. Now I knew why the Germans never caught up with me! The din of the chase was terrific! The watchmen were still screaming their heads off and the gendarme started blowing his whistle. Bedroom windows were thrown open as people craned their necks out to see what was going on. The street we had turned down was a very long one without any side turnings to dodge into. I realised that behind me my companions were been caught one by one – and the gendarme on the bicycle was gradually overtaking me. It is impossible to race a man on a bicycle so I dodged into a doorway.

I cursed his bicycle. I cursed all bicycles. Bicycles had been my salvation but now they were to be my doom. I thought the gendarme might pass me by but he spotted me. With my companions, I was dragged off to the police post on the docks. It was a tiny place but once inside I realised that one of us was missing. It was Pop. We were searched. That is, they flapped their hands up and down our clothes, evidently to see if we were armed, just as they do in American gangster films.

The watchmen started burbling the evidence. Bluey, who could speak French, butted in. At the same time, he was giving us a running commentary on what was going on and what excuses he was making. He said that we were British soldiers and on our way back to Fort Saint-Jean. Not knowing the way we were following the tram-lines but by mistake had followed the lines that turned off into the docks. A furious argument between Bluey and the watchmen followed. The police stood by not showing any inclination to charge us. Finally everyone cooled down. The watchmen had probably learned our real intention, for Bluey told us they said that if we had said we were English, they might have been able to help us.

That settled, the police let us go, pointing the way back to the fort so we would not "get lost" again. On leaving, we wished the watchmen "Bonsoir" and everybody was happy. When we reached the fort, we found Pop already there. When he saw us he burst out laughing. He said it was impossible for a man of his age and shape to run, so on reaching the dock gates, he had started walking. We had all dashed past him as he strolled calmly down the street. Pop was a cool customer!

Chapter 15: Joe Gugeleme – and a plan is made

A couple of days later Pop was off on a boat stealing expedition at some fishing village further up the coast (although this expedition was also a failure and he later returned). During his absence I palled up with Jock. Jock Monaghan[141] was his full name and he came from Stevenston[142], a place somewhere near Glasgow. I got on quite well with Jock. At first it started as an ordinary friendship for the purposes of going to cinema shows and cafés but it later developed into a successful escaping expedition. I think our friendship started at Padre Caskie's when Jock asked me to play billiards. I'd never played billiards before, so he started to teach me. But it was pretty hopeless so we went to the pictures, to the Alcatraf.

The film was called "The Sea Hawk" or something like that and was a story of Elizabeth's time when England was threatened by invasion. I could not help but smile at this, especially when a big Union Jack floated across the screen and an excited murmur went up from the audience. A few words appeared across the Union Jack as a sort of introduction to the film. This was followed by a man on horseback who had sighted the Armada and was galloping post-haste TO WARN ENGLAND OF THE INVASION. Loud cries and cheers went up from the audience when they saw this. I sat surprised and amazed at what was going on around me. Here were these so-called "corrupt" Vichy French actually cheering the Union Jack.[143]

Jock's favourite café was quite a modern place. For the sake of a name, we will call it the *Café Bleu* but its real name was much more up-to-date. Here, we would usually go for a beer as did many men from the fort – but there was more to be had at the Café Bleu than beer. This café, situated in a busy part of the Rue de la République was an outpost of General de Gaulle. From here was issued Gaullist propaganda. This was in the form of numerous small slips of paper with sticky backs so that they could be licked and stuck anywhere. They carried, printed in neat black type, a legend, usually mentioning de Gaulle but more often than not, they reminded people that France had fallen while Britain fought on alone. They usually ended with, *Pourqoui Vive La France? Vive l'Angleterre!!!* We plastered them everywhere.

Jock had some Corsican friends in Marseilles and he introduced me to them. First, there was the woman who sold ice cream on the corner. She always had information of some sort. But the most valuable of Jock's Corsican friends was Joe Gugeleme.[144] Joe was about seventeen but could speak excellent English – better than I could ever hope to speak French. His father had a small electrical shop and we would often go there at six o'clock in the evening to hear the BBC news bulletin. I soon became a firm friend of Joe Gugeleme. He would sometimes also take us to his home and often the three of us would go around town together.

It was during one of our first visits to Joe's home that Jock's and my great secret came out. After a nice quiet cup of tea in the afternoon, Joe showed Jock and I some of his paintings. Painting was a hobby of his. Then came his magnificent collection of picture postcards. I think there must have been several hundred of these, scenes from all over Europe and the French Empire. We looked them all over with interest until quite unexpectedly we came across three or four mountain scenes that intrigued us. We forgot about the others. We forgot about Joe. We forgot everything and held a tense, half-whispered discussion about these few pictures.

Joe sensed a mystery and came nearer. He asked us why we were so interested in these particular pictures. So we told him. We were planning to go to Lisbon – but one great barrier stood in our way and that was the Pyrenees mountain range. That was why we were so interested in these pictures of the Pyrenees. Joe was staggered. It was such a long way to Lisbon.[145] He marvelled at anyone having the nerve to attempt it. But then he showed his real worth. He wanted to help us. At first I failed to see how he could but we explained the difficulties to him just the same.

Our main problem, next to keeping out of trouble (difficult enough in itself) was to find our way once we had crossed the frontier. We had already bought maps of France that would take us to the frontier. The maps were of the sectional type and of a good scale. We had purchased them one at a time and had all the sections from Marseilles to Perpignan and the Spanish border. But we couldn't find any maps of Spain. If we succeeded in getting there we would be lost.

Here, Joe was able to help us. The next day he took us to a large public library and led us into one of its many rooms. From the shelves he began pulling out huge atlases, annoying everyone with the noise he made. He opened one at a large contoured map of Spain, which we scrutinised, trying to pick out a route and simplify the task of remembering it. Joe produced a pencil and paper, and copied the names of the towns we would have to pass through. Later, I copied them into a notebook, in which I intended to keep a record of our journey.[146] Joe himself chose most of the route but we approved of it. It was almost a straight line across Spain and Portugal without crossing unnecessary mountain ranges. However, it had one drawback. His route started at Portbou right on the coast but we had no intention of crossing the frontier anywhere near the coast as it was too dangerous. We said nothing though, not wishing to dampen Joe's enthusiasm – we could always cross further inland and pick up Joe's route further south. This was what Joe wrote. The crosses mean crossroads and the dashes mean keep straight ahead until you reach the next town mentioned. I copied it exactly as Joe had written it:[147]

Port-Vendres – Banyuls-sur-Mer – Portbou[148] *– San Miquel de Colera – Llançà – Perelada –*
Figueres – Siurana – Vilaür – Flaçà –
Girona – Caldes de Malavella X Malgrat de Mar – Arenys de Mar – Mataró –
Badalona – Sant Martí – Barcelona

On the coast:
Vilanova i la Geltrú – Tarragona
Towards Zaragoza
Reus – (follow the river Ebro) – Móra d'Ebre – Fabara – Caspe – Zaragoza
Alagón (take the Plasencia de Jalón road) –
Morata de Jalón – Calatayud – Guadalajara X Madrid
Toledo (follow Targe river) –
Talavera – Garrovillas de Alconétar – Alcántara

Alcántara was the last town in Spain. Beyond that it was just a matter of crossing the Portuguese border and following the river to Lisbon.

While Jock was talking to Joe Gugeleme I sat down and glanced through a few books at random. I had been occupied for several minutes when I noticed someone was sitting beside me. He was a young man, though a bit older than myself. Out of curiosity I glanced over his shoulder to see what he was reading. I was very surprised to see it was a work by Dickens printed in English. What manner of man was this, I thought, who could sit calmly amid this turmoil, quietly reading Dickens. He must have read my thoughts for he turned and spoke.

"Are you English?" he asked.

That infernal question again! I nodded my head.

"A soldier?"

"Yes."

"Have you been in Marseilles long?"

"Three weeks. How did you know I was English?"

"Heard you talking to the French boy."

Here the conversation seemed to lag and he played nervously with his watch chain which looked strangely out of place on so young a man.

"Do you know any English people here?" he asked.

"There's some at Padre Caskie's," I replied, "and some soldiers at Fort Saint-Jean."

He shook his head. These were evidently not what he was looking for. He sat quietly for a few seconds then suddenly, he asked, "Have you seen this before?" He held a queer-shaped medallion attached to his watch chain.

I shook my head. "What is it?" I asked.

"I wanted to get in touch with some English people here," he said. "I'm er… a pilot."

I still failed to see what the medallion had to do with him being a pilot but I never found out for he simply closed up and avoided conversation. A queer place, I thought, Marseilles. And such queer people. I went over to talk to Jock but still kept an eye on him. Maybe he was waiting for somebody – although I watched him for some time, he still sat reading but never appeared to make any headway with the book.

We strolled back through the town to the Vieux Port where we left Joe and returned to Fort Saint-Jean. During the last week that Jock and I stayed at the fort, each man received a grant through the Consul to buy clothes, for by now we were nearly all in rags. This grant was mainly due to Padre Caskie's efforts. He tended his flock well – but he saw that the money was spent on clothing and nothing else. There wasn't enough money for complete rig-out but I managed to get a second-hand suit, a second-hand pair of shoes, as well as socks, and other odds and ends.

This – as far as I was concerned – started the spending habit and during the last week I changed most of my English money into francs. The system of exchange was bare-faced robbery. I received 100 francs to the pound. The lady who conducted the Bureau de Change explained that to her, all English money was a dead loss unless England won the war – which seemed to her doubtful. It was a case of "take it or leave it". I took it.

We made our final preparations and planned to depart on the following Saturday. I bought a small haversack and a new compass in the Rue de la République. Also, a badly needed new razor and a stock of blades. The other boys at Fort Saint-Jean soon learned of our ambitious bid to get home. They marvelled at anyone having the nerve to try and walk all the way to Lisbon, considering the difficulties every man knew lay by the way: starvation by the roadside; pneumonia through sleeping in ditches; and the ever present threat of imprisonment in every town we passed. What puzzled them though, was that we talked of it as though we were going for a walk around Hyde Park. They did not know that we had planned it down to the last detail. We talked freely and dreamed of a voyage to England and spending Christmas in front of our own fire-sides. We gave ourselves plenty of time – it was three months to Christmas…

Before we left Fort Saint-Jean, we became a trio, being joined by Blondie Garbett who was interested in our plans and wanted to come along. We didn't mind taking Garbett for he was a good chap to have around, despite the fact that he had recently been ill. Besides, we did not like the idea of leaving behind anyone who wanted to come. Living at the fort had now become almost unbearable. Strange to say, this was due to our own officers – they did not want us to escape!

I think I have mentioned a little of the officers before. First there was the Major who rarely visited the fort but lurked somewhere in the background. The boys called him the "Mad Major" because – they said – he wanted to pirate a full size steamship. It sounds incredible I know – but all the boys told the same story. He didn't seem to realise that it took those French tubs five or six hours to get steam up – enough time for a destroyer to arrive from Toulon!

Next came Captain Besley, then Pilot Officer de Clary Scott and "Doc", a subaltern. Doc was the only good man in the whole shower, while Besley and de Clary-Scott were the two bad apples that threatened to turn the whole barrel rotten. They did not want anybody to leave Fort Saint-Jean! Why? No man knows!

They started by telling us there was some secret scheme by which we would all be able to escape Fort Saint-Jean. Then later, when we grew restless as to how the plan was going they told us they had abandoned it, saying it was impossible to assemble so many men together at one spot without the police getting to know.[149] Then, when the boys reverted once more to their individual escape plans, they would come round saying, "Don't do anything before Monday as there's still a chance." Then, "Don't do anything before Wednesday." Then later, "Don't do anything before Friday."

This is only an example of what went on for some time. At first I believed them. They were officers after all, and I thought they were really trying to do something for us. But it soon became obvious that their sole object was to detain us at the fort for as long as possible. They would come round at the most ungodly hours of the night with their pestiferous phrase, "Don't do anything before…" I think this was to create a more dramatic effect. I remember once about eleven o'clock at night, being awakened by the voice of de Clary Scott. He was talking to Corporal Newton in the next bunk. In a dramatic voice he said, "…there's something on, don't do anything before seven o'clock in the morning." That shook me – but undaunted by any of these diversions, Jock, Blondie and I continued with our plans for escape. Strange to say, after de Clary Scott's midnight visit, the officers at Fort Saint-Jean were never seen there again. Some said they had gone to Marignane Airport to steal a plane! They were mad! mad! mad!

On the evening of the last Friday we spent at Fort Saint-Jean, we took our kit up to Padre Caskie's where we could collect it the following afternoon when we crept out of Fort Saint-Jean for the last time. At twelve o'clock noon the next day, on Saturday 28th of September, we crossed the drawbridge of Fort Saint-Jean and made our way to the Sailors' Club where, after collecting our belongings we shook hands and said goodbye to Padre Caskie and some of the men there.

While searching for friends to bid goodbye, I found myself in a small room alone. With a pang of regret I took out my identity card for the last time. It was no good to me now. I must complete the journey as an Englishman, for now the Sûreté had a record of me. With a heavy sigh, I folded the card and placed it on the table. With a little ingenuity, someone else might be able to use it. I took care the name "Pas-de-Calais" stood uppermost for that was a place I could never forget. I knew that although I had a long journey in front of me, it would never end until one day I returned there. In the Pas-de-Calais I had something to pay back. A debt so great that, had I inherited a million pounds on the spot, I would still have remained a poor man.

Leaving the Sailors' Club, we walked up the hill that formed the Rue de Forbin. I remembered when I had once walked down that hill and the first time I had knocked so timidly on the door of number 36. At the end of the street we caught a tram to the outskirts of town. This was by far the best method of getting there without arousing suspicion. Three men, obviously foreigners – two with blue eyes, one with a mass of brilliant blonde hair – would have aroused the curiosity of even a Marseilles gendarme. This was especially because I carried a haversack, Blondie a small bundle and Jock had an uncovered loaf under his arm. A tram to the edge of town got over this difficulty and gave us a good start. At the fort, this was popularly known as "getting off one's mark". We de-trammed without incident and another hundred yards took us over the city boundary. Walking up the hills behind Marseilles, we took a last look back over the town. I thought of the Consul's words:

"…to do this, you will have to go through Spain and Portugal. You may be interned in either of these two countries."

I shrugged my shoulders. Once more, I turned towards Spain.

Chapter 16: The road to Perpignan

We passed through the village of Les Pennes-Mirabeau without encountering the local gendarme and by dusk arrived on the eastern edge of the Étang de Berre. Jock started talking about Serrano Suñer, the Spanish Foreign Minister, and the reason for his visit to Berlin.[150] I had heard all about it myself, for he had held the front page of *Le Petit Marseillais* now for over a week[151] but I had never thought anything of it. Jock's theory was that Spain was about to enter the war on the side of the Axis. I dreaded the thought. An enemy Spain would be harder to get through than a neutral one – and not even the most calculating escaper takes international politics into consideration.

Blondie didn't think Spain would enter the war. At least, he hoped Spain would not, for at Padre Caskie's, Blondie had heard a rumour. We had all all heard it for that matter. It was that any British soldier on reaching Spain would, when caught, serve a short term of imprisonment before being handed over to the British authorities for deportation. Jock argued that by getting caught, we could save ourselves a long journey across Spain – but the question arose as to what the Spanish meant by "a short term of imprisonment".

We slept that night by the side of the lake but during the night Blondie became ill again, for it was bitterly cold. He had been ill on and off for some time so, in the morning, he decided to go back to Marseilles until he was feeling fitter. He told Jock and I to go on as he did not want to spoil our chances. We were sorry to see him go but he said he would follow with Williams and Brown when they set out.

We had a glass of beer and a sandwich at a lonely roadside café before he left us, then we watched him until he disappeared from view. Before we had gone very far that morning we passed a small barn. We both remarked about it because had we marched a little further the night before and had a warm barn to sleep in, we might still have had Blondie with us. As things turned out though, he didn't do too bad for, strangely enough, he reached Spain before we did.

I made a little diary of the notebook I had bought and recorded that after marching eight kilometres, we tried a little hitch-hiking.[152] We were successful enough to get a lift as far as Salon-de-Provence where we struck westwards as far as Saint-Martin-de-Crau. We covered a distance of 40 kilometres that day. We measured it on the map and were very pleased, for we had intended to do an average 30 kilometres a day. We were ahead of schedule.

At St Martin we found a haystack to sleep in but we discovered a courting couple on the other side so we had to evacuate! Strolling into the village, we saw a barn. One must live rough to appreciate the values of various types of barn. This one was ideal. It was full of hay and had a convenient ladder up to the open door of the loft. It was still daylight so we had a coffee and rum in a nearby café to pass the time. The coffee and rum was so good that we agreed, whenever possible, to have one every night before we slept out.

Making our way back to the barn, we reached the bottom of the ladder but were greeted by a little dog which barked loudly and made a devil of a noise unless, as I discovered, you stroked it continually. Eventually it went back to its kennel and lay down so we crept up the ladder and crawling among the soft hay, snuggled down for the night.

The next day, September 30th, we covered 36 kilometres, through Arles, as far as Saint-Gilles, then we began looking for someplace to sleep again. We marched a further two kilometres without finding anywhere, not even a respectable haystack – just miles and miles of vineyards with not a grape on them (for it was the time of the grape harvest). Then about half a mile away in the vineyards we saw a few sheds dotted about so we waded through the vine bushes. The first we came to proved to be a flimsy shelter, the floor of which was covered with dung. The next was a derelict stone building with a roof but no doors or windows, however we made it do and slept as we were on the stone floor. It was damnably cold.

Early next morning we got up and walked until we found a haystack where we sat and rested in the sun, for we had had little sleep. Also, my feet were beginning to feel rather sore. As I nursed my feet, Jock went up to the farmhouse to fill the water bottle for this hiking was thirsty work. When he got back, it was not water that he brought but a bottle full of red wine. This we enjoyed, for it was not the cheap variety they issued at Fort Saint-Jean.

The following night we did not find anywhere at all to sleep. We walked – or hobbled, for my feet were getting worse – all night. We tried, here and there, to sleep but without success. It was agony. For us, a night march had many advantages but my feet became worse and worse. Each step made the night a night of torture. We sat down somewhere near Luenl-Viel but had to stand up again when we became cramped and stiff. We went on until dawn broke. Consequently, the next day's march was a slow, tedious affair. Considered all round though, we had made satisfactory progress.

It was necessary to bypass Montpellier. To do this we left Vendargues, the last village on the main road, and and took a smaller road to Clapiers hoping to heaven our map was accurate. Our fears were unfounded for that chap Michelin who had made our map had done a good job of work. The scenery was very pretty as we made our way to the next village of Montferrier-sur Lez. I remember stopping on a bridge to watch the fish in the river below. On reaching Montferrier we both felt like a cup of coffee and rum. We found a café there, ever such a tiny place – but this was one of France's liquorless days.[153] By coaxing the woman however, we managed to get rum in our coffee. It began to rain when we left Montferrier-sur-Lez, not much at first but by the time we crossed the rough moorland to the tiny hamlet of Bel-Air, it was coming down by the bucketful. Although it was still light, we were already keeping our eyes peeled for shelter for the night. The rain showed no sign of stopping and by now we were well soaked. However, we found nothing, for Bel-Air was devoid of accessible barns.

Jock saw a door with a sign above it. It said something about beer so we went in to have one. Of course we didn't really want the beer. That was only an excuse to get in and try to buy ourselves a bed for the night. The place was run by two old women, obviously spinsters and therefore prejudiced against all men, which put us at a disadvantage from the start. Hope springs eternal though, so Jock started a conversation. He had told them we were British soldiers and they didn't seem perturbed by that. He started talking about the war but they didn't express any interest in that either. I joined in here and there in an effort to stimulate proceedings but without success. Finally we both ran out of things to say and one of the old women said something to the other about us talking "patois". Other than that they never said a single word the whole time. Determined not to be beaten and to save time, Jock asked them outright if we could stay there for the night. They shook their heads vigorously.

Of course, we did speak "patois". We had learned what little French we knew in Pas-de-Calais and the Somme where the people were kind-hearted and generous, and knew well the cruel ravages of war. But these witches of the south had never seen the war. I doubt they had even heard of it. There was nothing to be done except leave. Jock went. I followed him, more in disgust than disappointment.

For two kilometres we trudged through the pouring rain until we came across a small, empty brick shed. Inside we found a large door standing up against the wall. By making piles of bricks and placing the door on top of them we made ourselves a bed. It was a very hard one but at least it was up out of the draught and off the cold stone floor. As it was cold and wet we lit a fire and had a good warm-through before going to bed – but even so, we were freezing cold when we woke next morning (it was by now October – the 3rd to be precise). We took good care to have a rum at the next village we came to, Saint-Paul-et-Valmalle, for we did not relish the idea of pneumonia. Bad feet were enough trouble!

The road became rough and stony, so much so that my feet became worse. About midday, since the weather was now warm and sunny, we decided to rest for the rest of the day. We needed the sleep for we were both weary and fatigued. Finding a quiet spot by a stream we bathed our feet and socks, and sans boots, we lay in the sun and slept.

We must have lain there for about 3 hours when Jock began to get restless and wanted to be on the move again. I did not want to move off so soon but I got up, and off we went down the road. Rounding a bend, I discovered, much to my annoyance, that we were being followed by a little black and white dog. It made a nuisance of itself by running around us in circles and barking. I was a little fuzzy from sleep and soon developed a temper. I called the little dog a lot of horrible names and threw stones at it but the persistent little thing continued its antics. Deciding a change of tactics was necessary, I began stroking the dog, hoping to make friends with it and send it back the other way. Just at that moment around the bend came a horse and cart. The cart was loaded with grapes.

The man driving this grape cart was evidently the dog's owner for he began whistling it. Jock and I waited, hoping to obtain a lift. It is a sad state of affairs when one has to hitch-hike by horse and cart. The cart stopped when it drew abreast of us and the driver, a young man, asked us where we were going. Jokingly, I replied, "Espagne."

"Espagne?"

He asked us if we were going to Le Pouget, which we knew was the next village. We said yes. He offered to take us there. We both climbed up and shared his seat. Unlike the two women of Bel-Air, he was full of conversation. The driver told us all about himself. He had been a soldier but had been demobilised after the armisitice. This information kind of thawed us out. After that, we regarded him as a friend and were able to speak freely. He wanted to know as much about us as we could tell him. Jock sat nearer to him and it fell to him to answer all the questions.

Jock took out his pipe and began filling it up but the Frenchman stopped him, insisting that we try his tobacco. He told us that it was Corsican tobacco which had been smuggled into the country. He explained there was a lot of tobacco smuggling in that part of France. We both filled our pipes with this contraband tobacco and he watched intently, waiting for the result. We both nodded our heads and puffed with satisfaction. As the cart jogged along to Le Pouget, he spoke of the qualities of his horse. He said he had several more like it. His eyes sparkled when he talked of his horses. He had bought them cheap from the French army. In return we told him we were soldiers – British soldiers – who had quite recently escaped from a German prison camp.

He became interested and once more asked us where we were going. Jock told him; "Béziers, Narbonne, Perpignan – Espagne!"

He sat thoughtful for a little while, then he brightened and began talking but we could not understand him. Realising this, he took out a piece of paper on which he wrote the letters "N.T.". Pointing to it he repeated, "*Camions* [trucks] – Clermont-l'Hérault – *partir* [depart] – Perpignan – *demain* [tomorrow]."

Jock guessed it first. All trucks with "N.T." in their number came from Perpignan. Bit by bit, the Frenchman made himself understood. It appeared that during the grape harvest, trucks came from Perpignan to collect the local grapes and he knew one of the drivers who, he said, would be able to give us a lift to Perpignan. We were delighted at this. It was something better than we had ever dared to dream of. It would save us many days of marching.

We could hardly restrain ourselves until we arrived at Le Pouget where the Frenchman took us to his home. We went into a kind of store-room which was part of the house. It was stacked with baskets of grapes. On our arrival he introduced us to an older man whom I took to be his father. He was a very amiable old gentleman who no sooner shook hands with us than he dashed away and returned with a bottle of wine and a couple of glasses. We had hardly drained our glasses when a truck arrived outside and – unlike most of the people we had met – the driver was not in the least excited about us going to Spain. He merely said he would pick us up in the village square half an hour later.

It was a rather rambling kind of village but we soon found the square and a café where we had a beer – it was the safe thing to do. Presently the truck arrived. We watched it collect baskets of grapes from different points and we went outside to wait, for we nursed a secret fear that the driver might forget us. But this was not the case for when the truck was loaded, he went into the café and had a beer himself. He was accompanied by an exceedingly pretty woman whose job it seemed was to handle the money. As the baskets of grapes were put on the truck, she would count them (the baskets, not the grapes) and pay people for them from a large bundle of notes.

The driver then told us he would take us to the nearby town of Clermont-l'Hérault where he was staying for the night and where, at eight o'clock next morning, he would pick us up and give us a lift to Perpignan. I was a little disappointed at not being able to set off at once. That was silly really but the spectre of spending another night out loomed horribly in front of me. We found Clermont-l'Hérault quite a nice town. That is to say, there were no gendarmes. A prominent sign said Clermont-l'Hérault was famous for its raisins.

We were pleased with our good luck so we decided to buy ourselves a good meal – and perhaps even a real bed for the night. We made our way to the Hotel Le Louvre, which was in the main street. Here we had a slap-up feed which seemed to last forever and was really more than I could manage. We approached the management with the idea of getting a bed for the night. They regretted however, that there was no accommodation. Instead we found a derelict lorry by the wayside and into the cab we climbed to make a night of it. It had no windscreen and no glass in the side windows. A draught came in through a hole in the back and up through a hole in the floor where the gearbox had been. It was these things that caused us to rise early the next morning.

We were up with the lark and we wandered around until about seven o'clock – then we made our way to where we had left the driver and his truck. We were continually having doubts about whether or not he would slip away and leave us behind. When we arrived at the spot, there was no truck to be seen. My heart sank like a stone but there was still an hour to go before the appointed time, so we strolled around again, returning at eight o'clock. There, true to his word, was the driver with his truck. He and an older man were reloading the vehicle. We offered to help but he waved us aside, telling us he would not be going until nine o'clock and would pick us up near the café on the corner. Once more little doubts crept into our minds but we went away as he suggested. As we did so I took out my notebook and jotted down the name of the street, the name of the truck's owner as it appeared on the side of the vehicle, and the truck's number. I was taking no chances! We couldn't afford to miss it:

Rue Jules Boissière.

Paul Potu (Expediteaux) [Shipping] *Rue Jean Baptiste Lulli, Perpignan.*

NTI 6052.

Finding a water pump in one of the nearby side streets I decided to have a wash and a shave. Jock was rather shocked at shaving in the street but as there was no one about, he followed my example. We felt refreshed after this, one of our periodic shaves. Then, according to the arrangement, we made our way to the café on the corner. Buying a beer each, we sat down sipping it slowly to make it last. An hour is a long time to wait. The first beers finished, we had purchased more. It was safer to sit in the café them to parade in the streets. Even so, at the sound of any motor approaching we dashed out to see if it was the truck. At first the proprietor was alarmed at the sight of two strange men suddenly dashing out of his café, beer in hand, every time a motor went past – but he got used to it.

Eventually the truck did arrive. It pulled up outside the café. The driver clambered out and we went over to meet him but to our immense surprise, he ushered us back into the café and stood us a beer each. I was beginning to wonder if this was a trip to Perpignan or a bottle party!

It proved to be a "quick one" however and we were soon on our way through Pézenas and Béziers. Once we had passed Béziers – a danger spot, where we were likely to be stopped – Jock went off to sleep. Not so myself. I took out my map and studied the route. We were approaching Narbonne. This was where Blondie had been caught on his first attempt to reach Spain. I was glad therefore when the driver avoided the town and went around a kind of bypass. But I soon had a shock. We were suddenly confronted by a gendarme standing in the centre of the road with his hand outstretched. The truck slowed down. So near and yet so far, I thought.

No sooner had the truck come to a standstill than the gendarme went round to the driver's side of the cab (strange to say, it was right-hand drive like an English truck). I watched the driver get down and fumble in his pockets bringing out papers and such-like while the gendarme asked him questions. The gendarme wrote down the number of the truck and walked around the back where he began inspecting our cargo, poking his hand here and there among the baskets of grapes. I imagined he was looking for the smuggled tobacco we had heard about. Satisfying himself there was nothing wrong he came back to the front again. Then he spotted us. Poking his head through the window he asked us where we were going. I decided it was time for a bold stroke so I said in a determined manner, "Nous allons a Perpignan à voir le Consul ..."

Suddenly Jock thrust himself forward and shouted.

"...Américain!"

Good old Jock! He had saved the day. Almost by force of habit, I was going to say "Britannique". We were saved by Jock's quick intervention.

Fortunately the gendarme did not notice this – or else he was not looking for aliens at that particular time. He just grunted something and went to talk to the driver. I could not hear what they said but they were evidently talking about us. Jock was able to pick up a few words. They connected us with the words "work", "Perpignan" and "telephone".

Regarding the word "work" we guessed the driver had told the gendarme we were working for him – but our statement about going to see the American Consul had put the tin hat on that. The words "Perpignan" and "telephone" we could not make head nor tail of. Then finally the driver nodded his head to the gendarme who left and we continued on our way. The driver seemed rather peeved and was not interested in conversation. It was necessary to get him out of this mood for we wanted to be dropped off at a point before we reached Perpignan and so avoid going into the town. I took out the map and told Jock, who showed him the place. The driver nodded.

We were now crossing some low, flat country next to the coast. On my left I could see what appeared to be the sea – but it was actually one of the big coastal lakes common in that part of France. There were miles and miles of flat, marshy beaches. I regarded the scene with awe for I knew somewhere over there lay Saint-Cyprien with its dreaded prison camp. Ahead seemed to lie a range of mountains. We asked the driver if these were the Pyrenees but he shook his head. On approaching, we discovered them to be just a range of rocky hills. A little way in front, a snake crawled onto the road. The driver swerved to run it over but the snake, to my surprise, was much too quick for him.

When we reached the summit of the hills, the driver pointed ahead. Miles away I saw an endless range of jagged blue peaks. He was showing us the Pyrenees. As we approached Perpignan we reminded the driver we were coming to the spot where we wanted to be dropped. He said nothing but on reaching the particular fork in the road, instead of stopping, he put his foot down and belted the last three miles into Perpignan. We tried to tell him we wanted to get out but it was no good. He pretended he did not understand. We could have grabbed the handbrake – and would have done – but at the speed we were travelling the truck would have skidded into the ditch. All we could do was hang on and hope for the best once we reached Perpignan.

Presently houses began to appear and in the early afternoon we ran into the town over a small bridge. We turned suddenly right and came to a standstill. The driver pointed across the road to a little café where he suggested we should get a drink and he would meet us later. For a full five minutes we sat sipping a coffee, wondering why he had taken such a sudden interest in our activities; then we realised the awful significance of the words "Perpignan" and "telephone". The horrible truth dawned on us. There could only be one meaning. He was deliberately trying to detain us at the café while he telephoned the police. He was probably not that kind of man by nature – but he would certainly have to account to the gendarmerie for our presence in his truck.

No sooner did this possibility flash across our minds then we made a beeline for the door. I knocked over a couple of chairs in my attempt to get out quickly but we regained the street and walked as quickly as we dared without attracting attention. I thanked heaven I had studied my map well beforehand. I knew what road to take. Westwards we went, to a small village called Le Soler. Here we left the main road and took a smaller road south. Gradually this deteriorated into a cart track, which suited our purpose even better.

We covered about thirteen kilometres before dark and were approaching the village of Pontiella when we lay down by the side of the road. Sleep was impossible and we were glad when the sky began to lighten the following morning. It was October 5th. We had been on the road for just over a week.

Chapter 17: "Frontier hoppers"

As soon as it was light enough for us to follow our map we continued on our way.* We were now climbing the foothills of the Pyrenees. Beyond the village of Fourques we found a vineyard. It was the only one we had found since we passed Montpellier in which the grapes had not been harvested. We had been short of bread and so, needless to say, we tarried by the wayside and had a good gorge. These grapes were not of the same quality as those grown between Montpellier and Marseilles. Many had withered to the size of raisins – but we were hungry.

At Llauro, a small hamlet, we succeeded in buying a loaf of bread with the last of our bread coupons. We went into a tiny boulangerie and were served by a fat woman who was in an inquisitive frame of mind. She wanted to know what nationality we were. She insisted on knowing. This brought me to the conclusion that 50% of the French population spend their time guessing other people's nationalities. We discouraged her from conversation and made a quick retreat.

Pressing on to reach the frontier as soon as possible, we came to a fork in the road. We turned south, calculating we were now sufficiently far inland to try crossing the frontier. In front of us was a high range which we thought could not possibly be as well guarded as the lower land at the coast. The going became very rough and winding. The country around was covered with forest. It was beautiful scenery. On our right rose a sheer face of rock. On the left was a steep downward slope covered with bushes and trees.

---

* As Ray and Jock set out to cross the Pyrenees. It is worth reflecting on the difficulty of their circumstances. Although the days in this region are still relatively warm in early autumn, night-time temperatures higher in the mountains are often very cold. They are carrying no bedding and are wearing only cheap town clothes, including street shoes that are hopelessly inadequate for scrambling up and down the steep mountainsides. While they are in the mountains, they will only have food if they can find it.

A small vehicle approached. It looked like a small shooting brake and was travelling at a good speed. As it passed, I noticed it was full of gendarmes. One of them in the back got up from his seat and craned his neck to get a better view of us, just as it rounded a bend. Fearing he was suspicious and might come back, we both dashed across the road and down the steep slope. We lay hiding in the bushes straining our ears for the sound of a car engine. Fortunately they did not come back and after hiding a little longer to make sure, we continued on our way.

Owing to this little incident, we decided the best thing to do was to get off the road altogether, so we followed a small track which led downwards into the forest. Eventually we came upon a dried-up riverbed. This seemed the ideal route for us, as it led south to the valley of the river Tech, the last river before the frontier. We followed this dried-up watercourse for a good distance, taking advantage of a pool to fill our water bottle and have a wash. Then the riverbed changed its course so instead, we cut across country following tracks and small paths, always going south by our compass. A lady came to the door of a small cottage we were passing, pointed in the direction we were going and shouted something about *Espagne*. We both nodded our heads and shouted "Oui Madame!" – and then "Sí señora!" just to be sure.

By this time the second-hand shoes I had bought in Marseilles were wearing thin. Holes had begun to appear in the soles but I did not worry. I still had my first pair in my pack. As for Jock's shoes, they never seemed to wear. They were quite an expensive pair. He had spent almost his entire clothing allowance on them.

At the river Tech, we were confronted with another problem. We found ourselves standing on the edge of a steep cliff about seventy feet above the swiftly flowing river. We had the option of climbing down and wading across, or crossing by the bridge two kilometres away at Céret. But Céret was a frontier village and we thought the bridge might be watched or even guarded. It was a place to be avoided.

Jock decided we should climb down the cliff. I gazed with horror at the rocks and the river at the bottom. Jock went first, telling me about the mountains in Scotland. I followed, gingerly lowering myself by the roots and tufts of grass that grew from the side. Many times these would give way and my haversack unbalanced me, threatening to throw me headlong into the river. I did lose my grip about twelve feet from the bottom. I nearly fell into the water but a clump of bushes saved me and I was unhurt.

The current was faster than we anticipated and it was necessary to get hold of a stout pole each before we could wade across. The pressure of the river – which came up to our thighs – was terrific and threatened to sweep us off our feet. I kept my shoes on to protect my feet from the sharp stones. Once across the river I threw my shoes away – for they were worn out – and put on my second pair. We continued to follow our route as per the plan. We struck a road and turned west. It was dark now and we had not yet even started climbing the mountains proper. According to our map we had to pass under a railway bridge and turn sharp left to Reynès, the last village in France.

Jock suggested we find an estaminet and have a drink before doing our frontier-hopping act. I agreed. We passed several scattered buildings in the darkness. One of them had a lighted doorway. We tried it but discovered to our embarrassment it was a private house. We did find an estaminet but it was a queer place. I think we went up some wooden steps to get to it. It was dimly lit and the tables were occupied by dark, swarthy men who continually looked us up and down but never spoke, not even among themselves. We ordered a beer each but stayed only as long as it took to drink it among these strange, silent men.

Travelling still further along the dark road I began to wonder when on earth we would pass under the bridge. It seemed an age before we eventually found it and turned up the narrow road to Reynès. My feet were very sore and I was tired but I didn't mind – we were on our way to Spain. As for my companion, he was tireless.

Like the Exide Battery as advertised, he could still keep going when the rest had stopped.[154]

We began exercising great caution. It would be hard to take to get caught so near the frontier. I know it sounds silly but we almost tiptoed along that road. It climbed steadily upwards and after half a mile we were fagged out. We sat down to rest. I think we must have fallen asleep for when we rose we were both stiff and cramped. We decided to plod on and if we must sleep, to find a more comfortable spot. Presently we came to a fork in the road which was not marked on the map. We took the right fork and luckily found Reynès a little further on. It was only a hamlet with a few houses, a couple of farms and a white church that looked like it had been transplanted from Mexico. We found a pile of hay in a barn and were soon in a deep sleep.

As usual we were up early next morning, October 6th, a Sunday. We had to be up early, for even in the Pyrenees, farmers are early risers. As it happened, we met the farmer outside the barn anyway – but he simply wished us "Bonjour", which was very considerate of him. There were no roads out of Reynès. It was at the end of the road – so we followed tiny tracks and dry watercourses. Following these was the only way to get through the undergrowth, which was very thick.

We were climbing steadily up the mountain which appeared to be a spur of the main range, when below us, we heard footsteps. We could see no-one because of the bushes but by the sound, they were following the same track as us, and moving faster. We dived into some bushes, for sooner or later they were bound to overtake us. Three men came stumbling up the track. I watched them go by. Although I could not see their faces, I noticed each man carried a small bundle. As they disappeared up the side of the mountain, I wondered who they were and where they were going – but by their little bundles I guessed they were probably at the same game that we were.

We continued following these small tracks until midday when

we found ourselves on top of the spur. We were confronted by an impenetrable wall of forest through which we could not possibly force our way. We seemed to have come to a dead end. Further progress in that direction was impossible. From our elevated position we viewed the scenery. It was beautiful. But our object was to memorise, not to admire. On our left was a steep slope leading down into a valley which cut into the mountains. At the bottom of the valley, according to my map, flowed a stream – but from where we were, the stream was hidden by the trees. The valley sloped upwards towards a series of steep, grassy slopes, the summit of which was high above us. We decided this was the top of the range – and therefore, the border between France and Spain.

We followed the only way open to us. We descended the steep slope into the valley. I had one or two anxious moments as I lowered myself down by holding the branches of trees. Jock was well ahead. I had given up pointing out the difficulties to him for it always ended with him telling me what the mountains were like in Scotland. About halfway down we found a path which went in the right direction so we followed it. We had not gone far when the forest cleared and we came upon a small house perched on a mound. Closer examination revealed it to be a tiny farmstead, completely deserted. I found it hard to imagine anyone trying to farm here – there wasn't an inch of flat land for miles.[155] What annoyed me though was the fact that from this house, halfway up the mountain, there was a path that ran right down to the bottom of the valley. A path we could have come up. We had climbed unnecessarily up the steepest place and tortured ourselves trying to force our way through the thick forest!

We decided to explore the house. It had a small garden surrounded by a high wall. The sole entrance was a double gate. Unfortunately, this was locked, bolted and barred. The only other door led into a stable. Walking around the wall, I found a crack and peered through into the garden. I gave an exclamation of surprise at what I saw. There were two apple trees and a row of tomato plants.

The ground was covered with yellow, fallen apples. The tomato plants were red with tomatoes. We were famished so we wasted no time in finding a place where the wall was low enough to climb over – and over we went. We were two very hungry mountain climbers!

We ate what we could and filled our pockets and haversacks before we continued following the path. We discovered that it led still further up the valley. We were among the trees again when a couple of men came down in the opposite direction. We had no time to hide or to get out of the way so we kept going. They both carried little parcels. Everyone in the Pyrenees seemed to carry a little parcel of some sort. I could see they would just as surprised to see us as we were to see them. As they passed, one of them said, "Bonjour Messieurs." But his accent was certainly not French.

A little further on, the path crossed the stream to the other side of the valley and went back in the opposite direction. This started a discussion. We could follow the path and try to climb up the other side of the valley which, from the bottom, looked pretty formidable. Or we could go straight ahead, through some more forest. But in this latter direction, we could see the outline of a building among the trees. It was not much further ahead but was about fifty feet above us. We regarded this building with suspicion.[156] We were on dangerous ground now. We decided to avoid the building and see where the path went.

For a little way the path went back down the valley, then it turned and climbed steeply up the mountainside. Steeper and steeper it went; up and up and up until at last it petered out and we found ourselves in front of a wooden gate. Beyond the gates was shack with a little garden. In front of the shack sat a couple of old men who jabbered to each other unceasingly. They did not see us and we made our way back down to the stream again.

The only way now left was to get past the building we regarded with so much suspicion and try our skill on the slopes beyond. As quietly as possible we crept up through the trees to a low wall. Cautiously we peered over the top and discovered – to our disgust –

that the building was only a tumbledown barn. We laughed at our own fears but then lost no time in attacking the steep slopes behind the building. With the aid of our hands we could crawl up without any great difficulty – but it was much further to the top than we had previously realised. After much huffing and sweating, and many rests, we finally reached the top. It was some gradient!

A rare sight met our eyes – at least, rare to me. We were in a world of mountains. To the west the scene looked like an aerial view of the Himalayas. In front of us lay a longer valley, the bottom of which was studded with little farms. They were tiny dots in the distance. At once, I labelled this as Spain for a few hundred yards to our left stood the peak of *Puig de la Pourasse*, and beyond that, the Roc de France. We knew by our map that the Roc de France marked the frontier. As we were standing in the same chain as these two peaks, this valley in front of us must surely be Spain. To make completely sure however, we decided to cross the frontier at the Roc de France. We rounded the *Puig de la Pourasse* without difficulty but between the two mountains was an enormous gap which was impossible to cross. This gap of a hundred yards separated us from our goal. Darkness began to fall and put an end to our activities for the day.[157]

Making our way back to the *Puig de la Pourasse* we sat down, sheltered by some low bushes. We witnessed a glorious sunset among the mountains but my thoughts were elsewhere. We both hated the idea of sleeping out on a mountain top so near the frontier – that is, if we actually were near the frontier. If we were, I wondered why there were no frontier guards. I thought and thought but could not puzzle it out. We decided that the next morning would go down to one of the farms in the valley which we had a hazy idea was in Spain. There we would find out our exact position.

And so we spent a cold night in the Pyrenees. I was first to wake next morning, which was unusual. I gathered a few sticks and abandoning all caution, I lit a fire to thaw out our frozen limbs. I didn't disturb Jock but the heat of the fire woke him and after warming ourselves, we ate the last of our tomatoes and descended into the valley. About a hundred yards down we found a track. It was a tiny track only about six inches wide but it was a track that was good enough for us. Following it down the valley for a mile, we came upon a farm. We passed a young man digging up potatoes.

I said to Jock that I was sure this man was definitely Spanish and we went straight up to the farmhouse. It was quiet and there was not a soul in sight. We hollered out and made a noise to attract someone's attention. Onto the veranda of the farmhouse came tottering a very old woman. We asked her in French if she had anything to eat. She remained silent. Fearing she was deaf I asked her again but she did not understand. She began talking in a strange language. I recognised it as Spanish.[158]

Our hopes soared to heaven. We must be in Spain! The old lady was very hospitable. She summoned the young man we had seen digging potatoes and we found that he could speak French. I told him we were very hungry, not having had anything to eat for several days. I said we would like a meal and had plenty of money. I showed him our money and said we were willing to pay. He wanted to know if we had ration cards. I said no – that was why we had not eaten for several days. He looked rather sorry for us and ushered us along the verandah and into the house. He was a very capable person, for he immediately seized a frying pan and began cooking.

While he was occupied I had a talk with Jock. A difficulty had arisen. I had promised to pay for the meal but if we were in Spain, I had no Spanish money. On the other hand when I had showed the young man French money he had not said a dickie bird. That meant we were probably in France although the old lady spoke nothing but Spanish. It was quite a puzzle. I spoke to the young man rather delicately and approached the question of where we were. He told us we were still in France. This shook us. We had not known for sure of course but – both being optimists – we had more or less assumed he would say "Spain".

The meal he provided proved to be one of the best. The omelette was the biggest and most delicious omelette I ever tasted. He made me laugh when he talked about bread being rationed, yet continually brought out plate after plate of it. He brought it as fast as we ate it. It was the same with the red wine. He would fill our glasses as soon as they became empty. In the end he gave up and stuck the whole bottle on the table.

After dinner I asked the young Spaniard (I will call him a Spaniard, for he spoke more Spanish than French), exactly where the frontier was. In reply he took us out to the veranda and pointed up the valley to the Roc de France. This was not much in the way of information for we already knew the frontier lay on that mountain, so we told him we could not reach it because of a big gap in the mountains. This was rather difficult to explain – we did it by signs more than anything but when he understood he laughed at us. He told us to follow the path we had just come down but to follow it all the way and it would take us to the top. Of course we had to take his word for this. We thanked him and I gave him fifty francs for the dinner. He insisted on giving me ten francs change when we left.

Being unused to full stomachs – let alone overloaded ones – we found the going very hard indeed. By the time we reached the spot where we had first found the path during our descent into the valley we were well out of breath and sweat was running in rivulets down our faces. We found a mountain spring and cooled off. We sluiced ourselves down and filled the water bottle. Jock spoke well of the qualities of the water. I complained of the queer taste, only to be informed I wasn't used to spring water.

The trail began to wear very thin. Sometimes it disappeared altogether and we had to take pot luck in finding it again. Once it ran across a boulder strewn slope and was only marked by splashes of red paint at intervals. These splashes of paint intrigued me. I wondered what their purpose was and who on earth had gone to the trouble of marking out a track across the slope. Nearer the top, the gradient flattened out and the rocks gave way to heather. About three hundred yards further on we could see the peak, a rough, conical-shaped rock jutting upwards. As we drew nearer, we could see something was painted on the side. In our excitement we ran. Puffing and panting we stood before it looking at the French flag painted on the rock. I looked at Jock.

"This is the frontier!" I said. My nerves were tingling. "I'll bet the Spanish flag is painted on the other side."

Instantly we both doubled round to the other side. Then we both stopped dead in our tracks. I fell back and sat on my behind. I passed my hand across my forehead. I think I almost swooned. There in front of us, instead of the Spanish flag or even barbed wire was what seemed to be a bottomless precipice! Now we knew why they did not bother to guard this part of the border.

We sat down and had a smoke. A brisk, chilly wind was blowing from Spain. We had a bird's eye view of the place. Far below us we could see the village of Maçanet and in the distance the town of Figueres, which we knew was about 25 miles away. To the east we could see the sea, for our elevated position was nearly 5,000 feet above sea level. Even Jock had to admit that this was a bit higher than Ben Nevis.[159]

It was decided we would get nowhere by merely sitting around and talking about it. Jock wanted to climb down the precipice. We could see one or two footholds but the very thought made me feel dizzy. Jock did actually go over the side but after climbing down about a yard, he came back again, appreciating my point of view. Even in Scotland they had nothing like that.

Making our way eastwards along the ridge, we found a place where it was not so steep and began climbing down. At this point there had been a landslide and the steep slope was covered with loose rocks and boulders, making footholds very precarious. We had to test each rock before we put our weight on it. By this method we descended about halfway. Here we encountered a stream which went down the mountainside by leaps and bounds. Following the bed of the stream, progress was easier. Every few yards however we would have a six foot jump onto wet rocks covered with moss. It was not always possible to land on one's feet. It was a very wet business indeed.

We got a considerable distance in this manner when the gradient became less steep. We found a path leading off to the left. Following it we went for about 200 yards and lay down in the shelter of a large rock. By now it was almost dark. It was bitter cold. We did not mind that though, for we were only too pleased at having got down such a nasty bit of mountain. Personally I could not take my eyes off the huge mass of rock that towered up into the sky. It was hard to believe we had just climbed down it. It was easy to cross the frontier when you knew how!

And so, 300 yards inside Spain, we lay down to sleep. It was the land where anything could happen…

Part Five

ESCAPE THROUGH SPAIN

This 1930s image of Barcelona shows a corner of the Plaça de Catalunya at bottom left with the Paseo de Gràcia (location of the British Consulate) stretching away into the distance.

Chapter 18: The Spanish Eagle

INTRODUCTORY NOTE

Having successfully crossed the border with France, Ray and Jock are in the far north-eastern corner of Spain, 250 miles (400 kilometres) from their starting point in Marseille. They are exhausted by their journey so far but they still face a trek of almost 900 miles (around 1,400 kilometres) to their intended destination of Lisbon in Portugal where they have hopes of finding a passage home.

The first 750 of those miles must be travelled through Spain. Spain was officially a neutral country during the Second World War. This did not mean however, that it was a safe haven for two escaped British PoWs; far from it, in fact.

The situation in Spain in 1940

After his victory in the Spanish Civil War in 1939, the government of General Franco had quickly established Spain as a totalitarian state. Franco's political ideology naturally inclined his government towards supporting Hitler; indeed, at this period, Spain was even flirting with the idea of joining the Axis Powers in the war. Under such a regime there was no hope of official sympathy for British soldiers attempting to get home and re-join the fight against the Nazis. The arm of the Spanish state that Ray and Jock were most likely to encounter as they travelled across the country, was the *Guardia Civil* or Civil Guard. The Civil Guard was a form of gendarmerie that had primary responsibility for rural policing. It was a long-established agency of law enforcement that had previously enjoyed broad public support. Since the end of the Civil War however, the Civil Guard had become increasingly associated with the enforcement of the Franco government's policies of social control and the repression of opposition.

Foreigners of all sorts who were unlucky enough to encounter the Civil Guard and to be judged undesirable, were likely to find themselves summarily detained in a concentration camp. It is thought that the Civil War had left Spain with a network of perhaps two hundred such camps. These camps had originally been built to house Spanish nationals who had fought on the Republican side. Huge numbers of Republican prisoners were still being detained in them. One of the camps in particular, the *Campo de Miranda* at Miranda De Ebro, about 50 miles (80 kilometres) south of Bilbao, had become the favoured location for the Spanish authorities to hold the small number of escaped British PoWs who had managed, like Ray and Jock, to make their way across the Pyrenees.[160]

Military historians and eye-witnesses agree that inmates at Miranda were held in appalling conditions. The provision of food, water, heating and bedding was hopelessly inadequate and sanitation was non-existent. Disease and malnutrition were common. As in all such camps, the treatment of inmates by guards could be brutal. One Polish soldier who, like Ray and Jock, had escaped to Spain in the aftermath of the fall of France in 1940, described his experiences at Miranda to an interviewer many years later.

In the interviewer's words:

> "He was beaten up on several occasions by the camp functionaries. He was held in solitary confinement for a week for using abusive language against a *cabo* [guard]. He was flogged with a bullwhip ... On another occasion when he was in the camp's canteen he was hit on the face and head with a rifle-butt and a whip. He saw other prisoners being beaten up and abused for minor infringements of camp regulations. For instance, if a *cabo* found a louse or a bedbug on a prisoner, he would force him to wash in urine."[161]

The consolation for the small number of British PoWs who ended up at Miranda at this time was that their release was negotiated on a regular basis by British diplomatic staff. Because of Spain's official position as a neutral country, this meant that once British prisoners had been handed over to British officials they could legitimately be repatriated through the diplomatic process. This usually happened via British military bases in Gibraltar.

Great personal anxiety however lay in not knowing how long it would take for one's own release to be agreed. Ray referred sardonically to this matter in Chapter 16 as he, Jock and Blondie discussed rumours that escaped PoWs captured in Spain need only serve a "short term of imprisonment" before they were released to the British authorities. As Ray observed at the time: "...the question arose as to what the Spanish meant by 'a short term of imprisonment.'"

The area of northern Spain through which Ray and Jock must travel on the first leg of their journey (from the French border towards Barcelona) was well known as the most strongly anti-Franco part of the country. That meant there was greater potential for sympathy and fellow feeling for Ray and Jock in this region than there might be elsewhere. Rather less encouragingly though, it also ensured that the security machinery of the Franco-ist state – in the form of the Civil Guard and the police – was a visible and threatening presence wherever they went.

The Spanish Eagle

The path led eventually eastwards until it came to a group of trees among which we could see a building. On the map, it was marked as "Las Salinas", a church of some kind.[162] As we approached the church we heard voices so we cut across an intervening piece of land to reach a narrow road leading down to the village of Maçanet de Cabrenys. What a road! It twisted and turned about the mountainside like no other road I have never seen. It covered about ten miles in a distance of three. Maçanet was a poky little village with narrow, squalid streets full with the noise of mothers shouting and kids squalling. We soon left it behind.

By now both Jock and I were very weary. We had made up our mind that our best plan, when we got to Barcelona, was to attempt to find the British Consul who might be able to help us before we tried to reach Lisbon.

Beyond Maçanet my French maps were useless but Jock produced a tattered fragment of a map showing this corner of Spain, from the frontier as far as Girona. It showed only the main and secondary roads but it was better than nothing. From Maçanet the road was dry and very dusty. For the best part of the way it was wooded either side by forests of cork trees. The trees were marked by broad rings of bark cut from the trunks and stacked in piles to dry. The road took twists and turns for no apparent reason. In places it was littered with cartridges and empty cartridge cases – relics of the Civil War. Wrecked tanks lay rusting in the fields; reminders of a war we had only heard about.

Feeling rather hungry – for it was a good 24 hours since our meal at the farmhouse in the mountains – we went up to a ramshackle farm, just off the road. Our excuse at first was to fill our water bottle from the well but we gradually worked round to the subject of food. The farmer did not understand a word we said but we conveyed the idea by signs. He took us up some rickety steps to where the family lived. It was dinner time and his wife and children were sitting at the table. A few words to his wife and she supplied us both with a large plate of mashed potatoes which we ate heartily. I was surprised to note that all the family ate themselves was plain mashed potatoes and bread. I did not know the conditions that existed in Spain at that time.

We only met two people before we reached the main road to Barcelona. They came along pushing bicycles. Jock started to chat with them trying out his French. He thought they were Spaniards who might know a little of the language. To his surprise they spoke better French than he did, actually being Frenchmen! During the course of the conversation – such as it was – we learned that one of them at least, was a truck driver whose run was between France and Spain. He showed us his permit which entitled him to roam about in the "Zone Fronterizo" [Border Zone]. Having learned this much we told him who we were. He asked us if we had any papers and was horrified when we told him "no". He warned us to beware of the Spanish police; the "Guardia de Civil", as he called them. He told us quite a lot about these Civil Guards. Most of it we didn't understand – but we gathered we had to keep out of their way.

We reached the main Barcelona road at a point where it crossed the river. We sat down on the banks to rest. My feet were badly blistered. On the side of the bridge I could see the words, "Viva France" – but as I nursed my feet, I damned France! Jock had wondered what had happened when Serrano Suñer visited Berlin.[163] Obviously, his mission had been a flop and as *Le Petit Marseillais* had suggested, Spain was not going to enter the war. It was a pleasant thought – but a large blue and white sign saying "Barcelona 159 kilometres" made me think of our own troubles. We were hardly in any condition to march another 159 kilometres – and we had no idea how long a Spanish kilometre was.

Darkness began to fall about seven kilometres from Figueres. We stopped at a house by the roadside. You couldn't call it a farm – it was just a house with a bit of land attached to it and a haystack in what appeared to be the back garden. Going up to the gate we called out to a young Spaniard about our own age who was drawing water from a well. He looked up but evidently he did not understand. We pushed open the garden gate and walked up to him. Experience had taught us that when in doubt, it was best to be brazen. Already I had my water bottle in my hand. We always had the convenient excuse of wanting it filled. This served to start a conversation which we could work around to the more important things such as food or a place to sleep for the night. Unfortunately the Spaniard was not much of a linguist so we had to resort to sign language. This was mostly Jock's department. He was better at it than I. In the meantime I filled the water bottle.

Jock appeared to be getting on quite well with the young Spaniard, whose mother and father had arrived on the scene. They listened with rapt attention to what Jock had to say. The result was that we were led to a shed at the back of the house. This was to be our sleeping quarters. It didn't look too promising at first, for the young Spaniard disappeared inside and began dragging out odds and ends of timber and farm machinery. The old man then put a tarpaulin on the floor. Quite an improvement, I thought. But that was not the end of it. They began talking among themselves and presently the young man ran off. I heard him go into the house and run upstairs. The bedroom window squeaked open. A couple of blankets came sailing down, followed by two pillows and a first class eiderdown.

These things made a handsome bed. The eiderdown gave it a civvy street touch. A last smoke before we went to sleep brought the young Spaniard back. It was plain he wanted to talk to us. In his hand he carried a small atlas. I remembered Jock having told him about our march from France and he wanted Jock to show him on the map where we had been. I went on sucking my pipe in the fading light but I soon became aware that they were no longer discussing our march from France. They were discussing the war. The young Spaniard kept constantly referring to the USSR. I whispered, "They're reds. Anti-Franco-ists."[164]

Jock – thinking it would help matters – developed communist sympathies on the spot. He demonstrated on the map how Britain and Germany would fight until they exhausted themselves, then the USSR who had not yet entered the war, would step in and take control of all Europe. It was nonsense really but it pleased the Spaniard. He took us into the house and gave us a terrific supper of fried sprats, beans and wine, which went down very well indeed.

The next morning we said farewell to our communist friends and set off once more on our way to Barcelona. My feet were terribly blistered. I hoped to heaven we would find a British Consulate there and so avoid the long trek to Lisbon. Then, on entering the village of Pont de Molins, on our way to Figueres, we discovered its only street to be full of men in strange uniforms. At once, we decided these must be Civil Guards, so we beat a hasty retreat up to a cart track, hoping to detour the village. Meeting a farmer with a horse and cart, we asked him how we could get to Figueres but he told us to go down to the road we had just left. We told him we couldn't do that as there were Civil Guards in the village. He understood. He indicated we should follow the cart track and bear right, then we would find the road again. We thanked him and before we left, Jock succeeded in borrowing enough tobacco for half a pipe each – that morning we had run out of tobacco.

The cart-track proved to be longer than we expected and included crossing a river by doing a tightrope act on a weir. By the time we reached the road my feet were in a terrible state and I could only hobble along. A little hitch-hiking eased the situation. Two men in a cart going to Figueres were only too pleased to give us a lift. Of course, being only human, they wanted to know our business. We told them we were going to Barcelona to see the Consul – the British Consul. The driver, on hearing this, raised his eyebrows and wanted to know why we should go all the way to Barcelona, when there was a consulate at Figueres. Of course, he wasn't sure what nationality the Consul was but he was fairly certain he was English. He said we would find the Consul's office at the Hotel Paris.

I had quite a shock as we rode into Figueres, for out of a concealed sentry box sprang a military looking gent in a grey uniform. I thought at first he was German. His uniform seemed of German design and on his peaked cap he wore a spread eagle. A closer examination however, revealed this to be of the Spanish Falangist variety.[165] No sooner did the guard appear than the cart stopped. Frankly, I thought we were for it – but in this case all that happened was that the driver dived into his trouser pocket and pulled out a coin. The man in the spread eagle cap gave him a ticket.

When we were out of earshot I asked the driver about it. In reply he told us more or less that because of his horse and cart he had to pay a tax before he could enter a Fascist town. I had wondered why Spanish carts carried a number plate. We now found ourselves in a town – the one thing we had wanted to avoid – but we saw no harm in trying to find the Hotel Paris and enquiring if there really was a British Consul there. We found ourselves in a broad street decorated at intervals with armed men wearing queer triangular hats. These were the Civil Guards. We passed a bookstall displaying German newspapers. Many swastika flags were hanging about, making the town resemble Munich on the Führer's birthday. We could not find the Hotel Paris so I asked directions from a woman who passed me in the street. I asked her in French and to my surprise, she answered in French – good French. Acting on her instructions we soon found what we were looking for.

We went to one door and on enquiring for the Consul were politely told to go in by another door. Here we found ourselves in a small deserted hall which appeared to lead nowhere except upstairs. Upstairs we went. On the first landing we asked a page-boy where the Consul was, thanking heaven that "Consul" sounds the same in any language. The page-boy indicated a door. I knocked.

Presently a little grille opened and a face appeared. It was a hard face with steely grey eyes and close cropped hair.

"Is this the British Consulate?" I asked

He frowned but said nothing. I did not know that he had been struck speechless. I tried again.

"Est-ce que le Consulat Britannique?" I hoped that if it wasn't, he would tell me where the British Consulate was.

The man behind the grille appeared to choke. He was red in the face but at least he found his voice.

"Nein! Nein! Das ist das Deutsche Konsulat! C'est le Consulat Allemand!" He was raving.

I turned to Jock, "My God! It's the German Consulate!"

We turned to go. The German was still shouting. We told him what we thought of him and dashed downstairs.

We got out of Figueres as quickly as possible. We walked as fast as my feet would allow. I tried not to limp, for even a small thing such as that attracts attention. We passed another uniformed man in a sentry box but he took no notice of us. When we reached the last house outside the town, I could walk no further. The blisters on my feet had burst and every step was agony. We sat down. I saw a man on a horse and cart approaching. I suggested we should try hitch-hiking our way to Girona, which was the next town. Jock agreed, so we hailed the man as he went by. He proved to be a very dull-witted Spaniard indeed, for when we asked him if he was going towards Girona, he just pointed down the road and told us how many kilometres it was. Jock tried to point out that we knew where Girona was – and only too well, did we know how many kilometres it was – but what we wanted was a lift. Even a few hundred yards would help us if it was in the direction of Girona. Again he pointed down the road and repeated how far it was.

This repeated conversation went on for some time. It got bad-tempered and developed into an argument with raised voices. A little crowd collected, mostly old men and girls who were working in the fields. Whenever we spoke, the girls giggled, making me feel embarrassed. The man in the cart took advantage of this and also laughed, jabbering a lot of heathen words at us. Then a strange thing happened. A woman elbowed her way through the crowd and whispered in my ear.

"Guardia de Civil!"

Jock heard her too and as quick as a flash, before anyone realised what was going on, we dived after her through the crowd. She ushered us across the road and into a house. No sooner were we inside than she closed the door, and locked and bolted it. She peered through a crack in the woodwork and motioned us to keep quiet. We said nothing. We just looked at each other. Anything might happen now.

For some minutes the woman knelt, staring through the crack in the door, then she rose, led us up a passage and out into the back garden. She indicated we should sit down and wait. She said there were still Civil Guards outside. I wondered who this woman was and why she had gone out of her way to hide us from the Civil Guards. We hadn't seen the guards approach and would certainly have been caught.

Half an hour elapsed before the woman returned. She led us back into the house where we both sat down to a plate of chips. Very tasty! We had just finished this welcome meal when her daughter arrived. At last we were able to hold a conversation, for the daughter could speak French. She acted as interpreter for the woman, who had a sad story to tell.

She had a son. During the Spanish Civil War, like most of the men in Catalonia he had fought against Franco. As a punishment for this when Catalonia fell, he had been sent to a concentration camp. The poor woman was visibly distressed when she described how she only saw him now at rare intervals and how life in the concentration camp had reduced him almost to a skeleton. She complained bitterly of conditions under the Franco regime. They got little food and had to exist mainly on potatoes. She said they could not get proper food for her daughter's baby, not even milk. I could see for myself how thin and puny the child was.

She advised us to stay until nightfall. I didn't mind that as it gave my feet a rest. During the afternoon we helped her to peel some figs that her daughter had brought in. We talked as we helped her and continued talking until about six o'clock when the daughter's husband arrived. We all had a bowl of potato soup and we told him that we wanted to get to Barcelona. He wanted to help us and advised us to go there by following the railway line at night. It was good advice. I think anyone could probably walk right across Spain unchallenged by following railway lines. The roads are a different matter.

When darkness had fallen, the daughter's husband took us out and showed us the railway line. He told us to to take cover every time a train approached. We followed the line for a little distance but my feet grew worse as we stumbled over the wooden sleepers. Progress in this manner was impossible. We called a halt and slept out for the night. The next morning we cut across country to reach the coast.

It was now the 10th of October, the thirteenth day of our trek from Marseilles.[166] We found several fig trees and spent a good deal of time eating the figs. They were delicious. Figs formed a substantial part of our diet for the next few days although we found that eating them in quantity made our mouths sore and gave us cracked lips.

While crossing some open fields during the afternoon, we ran into a heavy rainstorm and before we had gone a hundred yards we were soaked to the skin. We were forced to go on for another three miles before we found shelter in the form of a haystack. Luckily, the hay was fairly loose and we were able to burrow our way under the stack. We blocked the entrance with sheaves of dried reeds. Our clothes were soaking. My shirt was clinging to my back but we fell asleep and our clothes dried on our bodies.

The next morning I was a sorry sight. My second-hand suit had shrunk and was wrinkled with a million creases. It was devoid of any shape whatever. The day was uneventful. We scrounged and begged at the isolated farms we passed. Sometimes we were lucky and got a crust of bread. Once we got a handful of nuts. At one place we got a useless ten centime piece that a woman threw to us from an upstairs window. We ended the day in a barn at the village of Vilamalla.[167]

We discovered a pile of onions in the corner – large onions about five inches in diameter. We devoured them while the tears streamed down our cheeks. Then we lay down on a pile of strange dried weeds. We tried to smoke some of these weeds but without success.

The next day was very similar – and the one after that, except that that night we slept at a farm where they were generous enough to fry us a pancake for supper. We reached the coast at the town of Sant Feliu de Guíxols. In Sant Feliu, we hugged the back-streets for safety but even so, we passed close to the local prison and had to dodge behind a wall when the door opened and a Civil Guard walked out. It was a formidable prison with grey stone walls and thick iron bars.

Once on the coast road, we decided to put as great a distance as possible between ourselves and the prison. This coast road was a convenient one, for it led all the way to Barcelona. Few people used it as it was a very dangerous highway. On one side there was a sheer drop into the sea, while on the other was a steep mountainside. The road wriggled and curled along the ragged cliff edge and was never straight for more than a few yards at a time. It crossed gullies by bridges but these had been damaged during the Civil War and not yet rebuilt. These broken bridges were forewarned by the sign "¡PELIGRO!" [DANGER!].

At sundown, we lay down under some low trees. The road was completely deserted. I could not help thinking of all that had happened since I embarked at Southampton. I wondered what had happened to my old pal Gus. He would probably be in Poland by now or was being paraded through the streets of Berlin.

I didn't know it but the next day I was scheduled to lose another pal, in the form of Jock Monaghan.

Chapter 19: The road to Barcelona

October 15th turned out to be a tough day. Exhausted and hungry, Jock and I were plodding along the dusty coastal road towards Barcelona.* Sitting down on the edge of the cliffs for a breather, I took out my water bottle for a drink. I was in the act of handing it to Jock when, to my horror, I saw a Civil Guard approaching. He was walking up the slope pushing a bicycle. It was too late to take cover, for he had already seen us; anyway immediately on one side of us were the cliffs down to the sea, on the other side rising high above us was the steep hillside, completely unclimbable. We decided to stay put and just stare out to sea.

It was quite a warm day and out of the corner of my eye, I could see the guard puffing and blowing as he approached. We continued to stare out to sea, pretending we hadn't seen him. I could hear him now though, very near. Then he was level with us. He began to walk past. I had another swig at the water bottle and squinted out of the corner of my other eye. He was still out of breath and making hard work of it. I saw him stop, mop his brow and look around. He shouted something. We turned to face him but said nothing. He spoke again and by the gesture of his hand we guessed he wanted a drink of water. Not understanding the language though, we were unable to reply. He came over to us. I rose and handed him the water bottle. He drank deeply. But it was too late. His curiosity had been aroused.

He said something in Spanish. Seeing we did not comprehend,

---

* The coast road was winding and undulating, rising to over 2,000 feet (650 metres) at some points. It was cut into a shelf in the rocky hillside for much of its length, with steep slopes – some almost sheer – falling towards the sea on the right hand side. Similar steep slopes rose high above the road on the left hand side. The road had been badly damaged in places during the Spanish Civil War and consequently there was little traffic on it.

he decided we were foreigners – and therefore objects of suspicion. There was nothing to be gained by remaining dumb so we spoke a few words in French. He asked us – still in Spanish – where we had crossed the frontier. This we could understand but we vehemently denied having crossed any frontier. This baffled him and, as we could not understand very much of what he said, he tried speaking in French – but we could no more understand his French than his Spanish. He must have been very proud of his French for he became annoyed when we could not understand.

He asked us again, what nationality where we? More to see what would happen than anything else, we said we were British. The Civil Guard's eyes sparkled at this and he asked us if we had any papers. Our reply of course was in the negative. Pondering for a moment he dived into his pocket and produced a packet of cigarettes – or rather, twists of cigarette tobacco rolled in paper. He handed one to Jock and one to me. I was surprised at this unexpected gift. It was welcome but immediately put me on my guard. Instead of rolling a cigarette I stuffed the tobacco into my pipe. I kept one eye on my pipe and the other on him. Most probably he was off duty I thought, for I noticed he was unarmed. Certainly he had the power to arrest us both and throw us into a concentration camp though. He should really have arrested us on the spot but he was a thought-reader. He was in an awkward position. He was unarmed and there were two of us. No matter how he tried to manoeuvre himself during the conversation he always found himself back in the same spot – between us and the edge of the cliff! I wondered what would happen next.

I didn't have long to wait. By signs and a few French words that we could understand, he told us he was going to Sant Feliu and if we went with him he would take us to a man who could speak English. I didn't doubt him in the least! He could probably take us where there were a few men who could speak English – but they would be where the dogs couldn't bite them.[168] I should have expected something like this. He was trying to arrest us by means of the

"Chamberlain Method" – that is to say, by trying to carry out his duty without resorting to force.[169]

I laughed out loud when the guard told us of the man who could speak English. I told him then that we were really Germans on our way to Barcelona. This turn of events seemed to puzzle him quite a lot. Here were two men, he must have thought, that both spoke French but also spoke English and professed to be German – and looked as if they might belong to any nationality. The Civil Guard turned the problem over in his mind. He started to speak but hesitated. Finally, he asked us if we had any money. I took out some of the German notes that Madame Benoit had given me at Acheville. I showed them arrogantly, pointing out the swastikas. Having made myself a member of the Axis I had hoped for a little co-operation but he screwed up his face at the German money.

He told us to wait where we were until he returned from Sant Feliu. He told us he would take us on to Tossa de Mar where he would introduce us to a young German woman. To get rid of him we agreed to wait. We said we would be glad to meet a Fraulein from the Fatherland. Then he went. No sooner had he gone than we held a council of war. Our chances of escape were slight. He would return on his bicycle, armed – and in all probability with reinforcements. We would be caught long before we reached the town of Tossa.

Jock suggested that we should allow ourselves to be caught, relying on the Marseilles rumour that British soldiers caught in Spain would suffer only a short term of imprisonment for illegal entry. After that they would be handed over to the British authorities. Needless to say, I was dead against this. Even though I knew they would eventually hand us over to the British authorities, I had serious doubts about the Spanish idea of a short term of imprisonment. I didn't trust these Spaniards.

We discussed and argued over and over for a good half hour. It was a heated argument at times. Jock was set on the imprisonment idea. I think hunger and exhaustion caused him to make this decision. I was just about beat myself as well. It was only a little spark – a very little spark – that kept me going. In the end, even after much talking, we reached deadlock. The only thing to do was to part company. The guard might return any minute. To argue any longer would jeopardise my own chance of escape – assuming there was any chance of escape.

We parted on the best of terms, each thinking his own way was the best. I left Jock sitting by the side of the road waiting for the return of the guard and walked slowly away. Somehow I thought he was doing the right thing – but I refused to admit it. It seemed too much like surrender. He was saving himself from further marching and from hunting for food. In a strange sort of way I envied him. But stubbornly I kept going.

After a little way I selected a spot and started to scoot up the steep hillside. There were few footholds and only the bushes and shrubs to hold on to. It seemed a long time before I climbed any distance at all but eventually I came to a small road that was invisible from the road below. I followed it. It wound steeply uphill, each kilometre marked by a neat little stone. I passed five in all before I reached the top. I found before me nothing, absolutely nothing except a little church and a couple of fig trees. Beyond that there was only forest and crags. The road led nowhere.

The only thing to do was to go back down again; not right down to the road but to an overhanging ledge where I hid among the bushes to wait for darkness. While I waited, I worked out the distance it would be to Barcelona. I reckoned it was 96 kilometres. I must have dozed, for I fancied I heard someone shouting my name. I leaned forward and look down at the road. Most of it was hidden by trees but I thought it must have been Jock calling me. As loud as I could, I yelled, "JOCK MON-AG-HAN! JOCK MON-AG-HAN!" But there was no response, not even an echo. I wondered what had happened to Jock.

About half an hour before sunset, I climbed down to the road and continued my way, hoping to pass Tossa de Mar under cover of darkness. I had however, made a miscalculation. It was still twilight when I reached the hill overlooking the town. I risked it anyway and pressed on towards Barcelona.

I wondered why I was going to Barcelona anyway. My destination was Lisbon. At Barcelona there was only a consulate (if I could find it). But there had also been a consulate at Marseilles and that had been no help. Things didn't seem promising but something kept me going. I could visualise many difficulties now. My shoes were wearing out. A small, neat hole had appeared in each sole. They would not last many more miles, yet somehow I had to conserve them for this last lap into Barcelona. Barcelona was a big city and I would probably have a great deal of walking to do before I found the British Consulate. One simply can't walk around big cities in bare feet – not even in Spain.

Beyond Tossa de Mar, I once more found night marching a very trying business. Very tired I lay in a hedge-bottom and tried to sleep but odd raindrops began to fall on my face so I pushed on again, keeping my eyes open for somewhere to shelter. I tried some allotment gardens in which I could see several small huts but on investigation they all proved to be strongly locked. Lying on the ground though, I found a pair of wooden clogs. Taking off my holed shoes I tried marching in them. They were about ten sizes too big but they gave my feet protection. For two days I clumped along in them, drawing attention wherever I passed. Curious eyes un-nerved me so I took to walking by night again and sleeping during the daytime. The clogs made a terrible noise in the night. I continued to wear them though. I had to save what was left of my shoes somehow. I was soaked through and completely fatigued.

I passed through one small town beyond Tossa where a Civil Guard stood outside a sentry box with a rifle and fixed bayonet. He did not attempt to stop me but he gave me a good looking over as I went by. Eventually the clogs began to chafe my ankles. It was bad enough having blisters on the bottoms of my feet without getting them on the top as well so, finally I abandoned them. Later I saw some peasants walking in bare feet. I tried to follow their example but my feet just wouldn't let me. I put on my shoes again, patching them up with cardboard.

Reaching the main Barcelona road where it joined the coast road, I sat down on a low wall for a breather. Opposite me was a sign post: "BARCELONA 64 kilos". A man and a woman with two children went by. They were pushing a handcart with a bundle in it. It reminded me of the refugees at Foucarmont. A little girl also went past, carrying a fish in a piece of paper. She looked at me as if she were going to say something but had changed her mind.

I got to my feet and pushed on. I overtook the little girl but then the cardboard in my shoe became uncomfortable. I stopped to adjust it and the little girl caught up with me. She stopped and said something – probably about my footwear – but I didn't understand her. I fixed my shoe and went on. The little girl walked by my side, still chatting away. Suddenly she realised that I hardly understood a word she was saying. Then she wanted to know who I was and where I was going. Very natural I thought – most people seemed to want to know that. As best I could I told her I had come from France and was on my way to Barcelona.

She was only a child. She couldn't really do much harm. I told her I was English. She wanted to know if I was a soldier and if I had been in the war; yes, I was a soldier and yes, I had been in the war. This puzzled her. She wanted to know where my *camaradas* were. I could not easily tell her, even in sign language, that most of them were in Poland and that a few others were locked up in Marseilles. However, I did my best. This gave her much food for thought and I chuckled at what she must have been turning over in her little mind.

Then I looked up and immediately saw two Civil Guards coming down the road, one on either side. They carried rifles and had their bayonets fixed. A cold fear possessed me. I could see a cart track just ahead on the right, leading off the road. But the little girl gripped my sleeve. It was as though she'd read my thoughts and was preventing me from taking to my heels. She jabbered something that I couldn't understand but by her actions I gathered she was saying that the civil guards must not see me trying to dodge them. So I continued to walk straight on.

A man passed us on a bicycle and the Civil Guards stopped him. He began taking out his papers. As one of the guards examined them, the other stepped back on to the pavement, just where I had to pass. The little girl began to talk more loudly. She laughed frivolously, almost as if she was acting. I took my cue and laughed with her, pretending that I understood every word she said. As we drew nearer to the guards, I remembered my old formula which had been so successful with the Germans. Be brazen. I called myself a fool for not having thought of it before. The more brazen the better, I thought. I walked on towards the Civil Guard on the pavement and passed him so close that I brushed against him. I almost trod on his toes! The little girl was chattering loudly. We lengthened our stride and soon left them behind. I was greatly relieved.

We passed several villages and seemed to walk for miles but the little girl continued to walk by my side. I wondered where she was going. I also wondered why it was always a female who appeared when I was in difficulties. First there was Madame Benoit who fed and clothed me, and hid me from the Germans. Then "Jacqueline" who provided the all-important identity card. There was the woman on the bridge in Rouen, the woman at Le Mans, the old lady outside the Consulate in Marseilles and the anti-Franco mother who bustled us into her house in Figueres.

Six total strangers, all women, who had gone out of their way to help me, who had turned up whenever there was trouble in the offing. Now there was this little Spanish girl, without whose presence, I could never have got past those Civil Guards. I turned to thank her. But when I looked around, my little friend had disappeared.

At dusk, I ran into a shower of rain. I kept plodding on as there was nowhere to sleep when everything was wet. The shower passed as I went through the town of Calella in the darkness. Through the glass door of a baker's shop I could see some newly baked loaves.

They reminded me that I was hungry, as well as cold and wet. When I reached the outskirts of the town it started raining again. The wind blew until it became a storm. The road led back to the coast. Just ahead I could see a lighthouse. Very cautiously I approached it, moving only a few yards at a time but there was really no need for such caution. No one could see or hear me. The night was black as pitch. The howling wind and the noise of the sea breaking on the beach drowned out all other sound. Once beyond the lighthouse, I realised further progress was impossible. I tried to sleep under a bush but that was also impossible. I tramped on again.

I went under some weeping willows for shelter but by then I was already soaked. In the darkness I saw a little path, which I followed, more or less just to see where it went. It led to some allotments. I roamed about looking for something to eat. I had eaten nothing since I left St Feliu, nearly thirty miles back. I found some tomatoes and devoured them, ripe ones and green ones alike. In the blackness I stumbled against a wooden hut. It was a toolshed. It was padlocked but I needed a place to sleep and was in no mood to abide by the laws of the land. Already, in the space of six months, I had broken everything from Company Orders to international law. I thought a little shed-breaking would not harm matters much more.

I seized an iron bar that was nearby, thrust it through the padlock chain and levered it. My fingers were wet and numb but I increased the pressure and the lock suddenly broke. I fancied the noise would have been heard miles away but then I laughed at my fears. I could have fired a cannon in that storm and no one would have heard it. Closing the door behind me I struck a match. It was a tiny place. On a shelf I found a stub of a candle and lit it. Sitting down in a broken chair I surveyed the place. There were a few spades and rakes and such-like. Hanging on the wall were a couple of old coats – one of them a Spanish soldier's coat. I saw a pair of clogs in a corner but – like the pair I had before – they were too large.

I began hunting around in case there was another pair that might fit me. In doing so, I stumbled over something. Shielding the candle flame, I looked down. There were boots! Two pairs of them. I could see the first pair was too large for me but the other pair showed more promise. They were in good condition, had rubber soles and fitted me perfectly. I laced them up quickly and scanned the shed for more loot. Seeing two umbrellas, I grabbed the biggest one. It could be useful but I wondered if it would be full of holes. I half opened it then stopped. Opening an umbrella indoors is unlucky. I closed it and stepped outside to examine it. There were no holes. I looked up at the black sky. Now it could rain in torrents if it liked. I had an umbrella to keep me dry and a new pair of boots on my feet. These were gifts from heaven.[170]

Automatically I looked towards the road. "Why not?" I asked myself. A tattered figure with a fine umbrella looked rather odd. But once more, I began walking onwards.

Chapter 20: And so, home

All through the night I walked. I passed through small towns and villages. The night grew into dawn and the dawn into morning. Still it rained and still I had nothing to eat. I stole a few tomatoes from a garden and went on again, manoeuvring my umbrella to prevent the wind from turning it inside out. Villages began to appear with greater regularity until they formed a continuous string and I knew I was nearing Barcelona. I noted their names and ticked them off on the route I had in my notebook: Malgrat de Mar; Arenys de Mar; Mataró (where I saw some old pill-boxes – relics of the Civil War – standing right on the edge of the sea); Badalona; Sant Marti.

At Sant Marti, I stopped. This was the last village I would pass and was really part of Barcelona itself. Somewhere, I would have to sleep for the night. I had been marching all day and it was growing dark again. There was no object in tramping round the streets of Barcelona all night – that would be inviting trouble. I sheltered against a house but I could see no place to sleep. The road ahead was clustered with houses.

I retraced my footsteps five miles back to the pill-boxes. I crossed a railway line to reach them. I found the first one blocked up. I had better luck with the second one. I pushed open the steel door and went in. There was a concrete gun platform covered with hay. "Ideal", I thought. I stuffed up the only open gun slit to keep out the wind and the sea, which broke against the walls of the pill-box. Only one thing was needed to make it complete and that was something to eat. I remembered a field of tomatoes and other vegetables nearby so, taking off my haversack I went out and helped myself. They had been spoiled by the rain but I took as many as I could and went back to the pill-box. Barricading the door with a piece of wood, I sat on the gun platform and dined.

Before long I heard footsteps outside and the noise of someone trying to open the door. I waited for them to go away then peered outside – but I could see no one. I knew it could not have been the police or anyone else from the authorities for they would have made a more determined effort to open the door. Probably it was someone, like myself, seeking shelter so I removed the piece of wood that barricaded the entrance.

Using my haversack as a pillow I lay down to sleep. It was uncomfortable in my wet clothes. Presently there was a noise at the door again and two men entered. They were tramps. They were very familiar with the place and evidently lived there but they did not resent my presence in the least. They merely nodded to me, as much as to say, "How do you do?" After that they took no notice of me whatsoever.

In the morning the rain had stopped but the roads were covered with pools of water and in places, the countryside was flooded. It was 22 kilometres to Barcelona and there were more people on the roads. I hung the crook of my umbrella on the strap of my haversack and set off. I was hungry – damnably hungry! I had lost count of how many days it was since I had eaten anything substantial. After parting from Jock, my luck as far as food was concerned had deserted me. We had had wild figs before but on the coast there was nothing. It was useless begging for food, for the people hadn't enough for themselves. Since I had been on my own, all I had had to eat were the tomatoes in the pill-box. There was a hollow, gnawing feeling where my stomach had once been. I was weak and my walking was automatic.

Anxiously I looked for signposts. Barcelona was getting nearer – but oh, so very slowly – while I became weaker and weaker. Eventually I could hardly walk more than a couple of hundred yards at a time without having to sit down and rest. Very slowly and with great effort I would get up again and plod onwards. In the afternoon I found tram-lines and I knew I was there. In a park with big ornamental gates a woman was sitting on a seat. I knew a dozen words of Spanish. I also knew the fact that the Consul's place was somewhere off the Plaça de Catalunya. I went up to the woman.

"Señora," I began. "¿Dónde está la Plaça de Catalunya?"

She shook her head. She didn't know.

I walked around the streets. The pavements and roads were strangely uneven. They had been bombed and never properly relaid. Very noisy tramcars went up and down. I looked at their destination boards and saw one going to the Plaça de Catalunya. I followed it until it was lost from view, then I waited for the next one and followed that and thus I found my way to the Plaça de Catalunya. It was quite a large square with trees and a fountain in the centre. I walked around it several times but failed to find the British Consulate, neither there nor in any of the streets that converged upon it.

Feeling very weak, I sat down in one of the seats next to the fountain. A woman came along and sat next to me. Out of a paper bag she took crumbs to feed the pigeons. How I envied those pigeons! They were at least being fed. I could only recollect about four meals since crossing the Pyrenees ten days before. Lisbon was now out of the question unless I found several good dinners in the near future. I rose to my feet. I must find that consulate.

I walked around the square again in case I had missed it but it was nowhere to be found. The American Consulate was there and so, right next door, was the German Consulate. I was disappointed. Crossing the road I heard a voice shout and, looking around, I saw it was a policeman on point duty. He was shouting because it appeared I had not crossed the road by a pedestrian crossing. I decided to ask him where the British Consulate was. After all, I argued to myself, it was the Civil Guards, not the ordinary police, who threw people into prison. I also reasoned that a policeman on point duty would be too busy to be suspicious and anyway, he had to stay put. If anything happened, I could bolt and he could not follow me.

He proved to be a very obliging policeman. I asked him, "¿Dónde está el Consulado Británico?"

"Ah! Cónsul Inglés," he replied, smiling as though the Consul was a great pal of his. He told me the address but I could not understand him. I produced my notebook and he wrote it down: Paseo de Gràcia No. 37.[171]

Actually, it was number 36 but I found it alright. Two policemen stood at the entrance, one of them armed with a submachine gun. I walked quickly past them and up the stairs to the first floor, where the Consulate was. A door and a brass plate confronted me, stating office hours were from 9:00 a.m. – 1:00 p.m. and from 4:00 p.m. – 5:30 p.m. It was all very brief but I turned and walked down the stairs again. It was only half past three.

I returned at four o'clock. It was a much nicer place than the Consulate at Marseilles. I was asked to tell the Consul my story. To my great surprise he told me that he was getting used to escaped prisoners. Other soldiers had passed that way and he had begun to get things organised for the repatriation of escaped Tommies. To my joy, he assured me that soon I would be back in England. He was very trusting, as I didn't have any identity card or discs – but I did tell him my regiment, my service number and where I lived in England.[172]

The Consul took me in to meet the Vice Consul. He measured me for clothes and sent a clerk out to buy me a new outfit. We swapped stories. He told me he had been an artillery officer but had been sent to Spain as a Vice Consul at a moment's notice. I was given a new suit, a pair of shoes, a shirt and socks.

The Vice Consul went out and a young woman, his wife, took over. She adopted a most motherly attitude, speaking in Spanish, French and English with equal fluency. She asked me for a photograph of myself. I told her I had only two passport photos – but she needed three. However, with one of the photographs she made out an emergency certificate to show that I was a British subject. She said I would have to get more photographs taken but in the meantime she gave me the certificate. She told me I would be taken to a hotel where I could stay the night. She gave me a packet of cigarettes and then I was taken to a hotel where I had a good night's rest – after a damned fine feed!

Next morning, I returned to the Consulate where, with the Vice Consul and his wife, I was taken in the grey Vauxhall around Barcelona. We visited a photographer's and the Portuguese Consulate en route. We returned to the British Consulate where my certificate had a Portuguese visa attached to it. The Vice Consul's wife also gave me 50 pesetas and my instructions. The following morning, October 20th, I was to go on the nine o'clock train to Madrid. I was told to contact the British Consul once I got there. I was given a train ticket and told I would be driven to the Estación de Francia.

I thought my troubles were over – but then the final words of the Vice Consul's wife changed my opinion. She told me that I had had a pretty rough time of it already but that I still had a hard time in front of me. The last group had failed to reach Madrid. She explained that the certificate I had was not actually in order in Spain, as it had no Spanish visa. I would be travelling third class – with the peasants – so that I would not be questioned as much. An hour after leaving Barcelona there would be an identity inspection on the train by the police. There would be another approximately one hour before the train arrived at Madrid. She explained that the peasants make a devil of a noise when asked for their papers. That would be my cue to leave my seat and go to the lavatory, so as to avoid the police. At the end she lightened matters slightly by saying that once I got to Portugal I would be safe!*

At nine o'clock the next day I was on the train leaving Barcelona. It was jammed and it was uncomfortable sitting on the wooden seats, six or seven to a seat. Still, it was a luxury for me. I kept listening for the noise to break out and got rather worried when nothing happened. Then, suddenly, into the dooway to the

---

* Given later events, it is not clear why the consulate in Barcelona seems initially to have advised that the best thing for Ray to do was to travel to Portugal and make his way back to England from there. The most likely explanation is perhaps that this was still very early in the war and very few escaped British PoWs had so far made it to Spain. There presumably was not yet a clearly established system to deal with them.

compartment stepped a burly gent. He pulled open the lapel of his coat to display a brilliantly coloured badge, about three inches in diameter.

I was thoroughly shaken!

The third class passengers immediately got out their identity cards and showed them to this detective. What was I to do? I noticed the peasants all shoved their cards out at the same time so that there was a mass of cards in front of him. I pulled out my certificate as well and hoped for the best. After he had seen a few, the passengers folded their cards and put them back. I did likewise before he had seen mine. He didn't notice and turned to go. Then suddenly he stopped and turned back. He saw me putting my certificate away and asked for it.

Blimey! I gave it to him. He took it outside, examined it and took every word down in his notebook. He then handed it back, said nothing and went on his way. This thorough inspection worried me. I figured he would probably be waiting for me when I got off the train.

The second predicted inspection of identity cards an hour before reaching Madrid didn't happen, so I arrived in the capital without any further incident. I got off the train alright and into the station. In the station however, several policemen were swinging their truncheons menacingly with one hand and checking parcels belonging to the peasants with the other. I managed to get past them without inspection though and with great relief, got into a taxi (I had been told to take a taxi straight to the British Consulate). The streets of Madrid were lined with policemen in new uniforms, grey with vivid red trimmings. I arrived at the Consulate, 23 Monte Esquinza but to my disgust, it was closed! It was Sunday!

A fat Spanish woman was in charge of the Consulate. She was the caretaker. She pointed to a brass plate that said in cases of emergency to go to 10 Marqués de Riscal, the Consul's private address. It was just up the road, so I walked up and found that the Consul was not at home! A second fat Spanish woman, who was washing the steps, suggested I ring up the Consulate, as she thought the Consul was there. There was a phone in the porch, so I asked the woman to dial the number. I got someone who jabbered in Spanish. I tried French, the person went off the phone, then a French voice came on, telling me the Consul was not there. He was at home. Now I had the mystery of the missing British Consul to deal with!

At this point, the woman at my side got back on the phone and began to tell the person at the other end a thing or two in Spanish. This commotion brought upon the scene a well-dressed lady, who had turned out to be the Consul's wife. The Spanish woman's flow of speech stopped immediately and she put the receiver down. The Consul's wife, who was English, told me her husband was away. I told her I had come from Barcelona and had been told to report to the Consul. She took me inside and asked me if I had had anything to eat. She gave me a good dinner and also a packet of cigarettes. She apologised for the cigarettes as they were Spanish.

The Consul's wife phoned the British Embassy and a young man came up for me. He took me to the Embassy in his car. He told me that the Spanish police would be outside the Embassy door. When he stopped the car I was to get out and go straight through the nearby iron gates – at all costs, without being stopped.[173] As it happened though, there were no police at the Embassy door so we went in by the front entrance. In a beautifully furnished waiting room I met two more British soldiers. These were Cpl Burr of the Royal Signals and Pte Jones of the Green Howards who had both travelled from Toulouse. Later de Clary Scott, the RAF officer from Fort Saint-Jean arrived, unsoiled.

It was a very dull life at the Embassy, with nothing to do. But we were fed on the fat of the land. A bottle of beer with every meal, chicken most of the time and bags of fruit. But, as the days went by, I was getting worried about my progress. We couldn't leave the embassy of course and news about the possibility of escape was scarce. The Spanish government wouldn't grant exit visas and it was quite a distance to Portugal, where our visas would become valid.

There was another possibility. We were told that there were some English soldiers in a Spanish concentration camp for political prisoners. The Embassy was trying to secure their release. If these prisoners were released, they would be brought to Madrid and then sent to Gibraltar for deportation. We were told that if that happened we might be shoved in with them and sent off to Gib.*

For three weeks we waited[174] and then the news came that the British soldiers had been released from the concentration camp at Miranda. They were on their way to Madrid and we were to be ready to leave. The released men were put up in the Hotel National and we were taken there in a taxi. When we got to the hotel, some of the boys from Fort Saint-Jean were there. They had all had their heads shaved. They all wore little skull caps and were dressed in convict uniforms with a black letter "P" painted on them. "P" stood for political prisoner. They had all been caught at the border. All except one, that is. That was my old pal Jock Monaghan who I had left on the seaside road a few weeks before.

Jock told me that after I had left him he had decided, after all, to follow me, rather than wait by the roadside to be arrested – but he had been picked up by Civil Guards after about 30 kilometres anyway. He had been imprisoned at the Castillo de San Fernando in Figueres[175] and later taken to the concentration camp at Miranda. There he met up with the rest of the boys, including Garbett, who had started out with us. We found that Garbett, despite the fact that he had gone back and started again, had got into Spain before we did by doing a bit of train-hopping to Perpignan. He was caught on the frontier, crossing nearer the coast.

Apparently, there were a few German deserters in the concentration camp as well as themselves and the Spanish "Reds".

---

* This is a crucial point for understanding what happens next. The British prisoners in the concentration camp will be released on deportation orders i.e. they are to be handed over to British Embassy officials who must arrange for their removal from Spain. The idea seems to be that the four escaped PoWs living at the embassy can be "smuggled out" with this larger group from the concentration camp without the Spanish authorities noticing.

Every day, they reported, a few of the Reds were shot. Another inmate was an American gangster who was wanted for murder back in America. He had left America, finding life there a bit too exciting for his liking. Only one person, a German, had escaped from Miranda. Before every meal in the camp, the inmates had to sing the Spanish national anthem and give the Franco salute. The food was terrible. One day the jaw bone of a dog was in the soup bowl. Dog soup! They slept in a tiny huts. They were so close together they overlapped. Every day they had a debugging parade.

We left Madrid by train, accompanied, as far as Algeciras[176], by two Spanish detectives. At Algeciras we got into a bus and were driven round the bay, through the Spanish customs and the neutral zone, past the maze of tank traps and the big iron gates – and into Gibraltar! We were on British soil!

The party was split up and billeted with different regiments in bases on the island. I went to the 4th Devons. I was issued with personal kit, uniform, new pay book (I got a good bit of back pay) and everything I needed. We stayed in Gib for five days awaiting the convoy to take us back to England. We had all our time to ourselves and I took the opportunity of seeing the island and its wonderful surroundings. Then suddenly we were warned to get ready to sail. We went down to the docks where we were taken onboard a boat. The Governor of Gibraltar wished us "God speed" and hoped we had had a good time in Gib.

The convoy left that night. For fourteen days we travelled towards England. There were no thrills. No submarines. No dive-bombers. Nothing. We arrived at Liverpool in great excitement. We were home. All our troubles, our risks, our discomforts had been worth it. We were home again.

* * *

After we landed we travelled by rail to London and were taken to a reception station for troops at the Hotel Grand Central. The next morning, we were interrogated by an MI9 officer.[177] In a moment, with his words, I'll end this story of my escape.

First however, let me tell you that I reported back to Mill Hill with a letter for the C.O., saying that I was entitled to seven days' leave on the authority of the War Office. Colonel Browne added seven days privilege leave – so home I went to Dunstable for fourteen days. My parents naturally were overjoyed to see me back safe and sound. They never seemed to tire of my story, bringing in friends from far and wide to hear it until I was tired of hearing it myself.

I have been back now five months and I am still being asked to tell my tale. In fact, if I'd known I had to tell it so often I think I would have stayed at the fort in Marseilles!

Also, there is one thing I should like to ask the British government to do. Please put a flag at your foreign consulates! All other countries make it easy to find their consulate because they hang their national flags outside. Not only would the Union Jack help us in finding the place, it looks better than any of the other flags hanging out on the continent just now.

And my ambition? It is to go back to France soon, to help drive out the Germans. I want to see the Benoit family, Padre Caskie and the other friends I made. Until I can do that, thank you all for your help.

* * *

Now, back to the intelligence officer who interviewed me at the Hotel Grand Central. He asked me, "Did you have a lecture called 'What to do if taken prisoner?', in which some hints on how to escape are included?"

"No," I said.

"Are you sure?" he asked, "because, if you didn't, you must have been dodging."

He leaned forward, smiling. "You see, I happened to give that lecture to the Kensingtons at Ilminster myself."[178]

Part Five

AFTERWORD

Snapshot found among Ray's papers.
Ray (presumed), at second right.

Afterword: Italy, 1943-44

Ray rejoined his regiment sometime in December 1940 following his honorary leave. He was awarded a Certificate of Gallantry by his Commander-in-Chief in recognition of his escape (as also was Pte Freddie Ford). According to a letter that was among the papers in the original box bought at auction, Ray was also rewarded by promotion to Lance Corporal. Perhaps unsurprisingly however, this latter honour does not appear to have encouraged him to take soldiering more seriously. Before long, for reasons unrecorded, he was demoted to become, once again, mere Private R. Bailey.

For over two and a half years or so following Ray's return, the 1st Battalion Kensingtons were deployed exclusively on home defence duties, mostly at coastal locations in the south of England. Towards the end of April 1943 however, the battalion, at that point stationed in Dorchester in Dorset, was placed on notice that later in the year it would be sent to join the Allied Forces in North Africa.

An overseas posting was often preceded by a period of leave, intended to give soldiers the opportunity to say goodbye to family and friends. For both sentimental and practical reasons, soldiers who were engaged to be married, sometimes arranged for their wedding to take place during such times. On May 4th 1943, Ray married his fiancée Cynthia at the Register Office in Dorchester. Cynthia lived in Dorchester at the time but the newly-weds would nevertheless have had very limited time together during their early married days. Ray would of course have been required to return to the Dorchester barracks as soon as his leave was over.

Once all the preparations had been made and final orders received, the 1st Battalion left Dorset for Liverpool where they boarded the troopship, H.M.T. *Samaria* and sailed for Algeria. On arrival at their destination ten days later, the Kensingtons became part of the 78th Division (often called the "Battleaxe" Division), one of the divisions making up General Montgomery's Eighth Army. Algeria was largely peaceful at this time, having been taken by Allied forces the previous year. Initially the Kensingtons were stationed just outside the capital, Algiers, receiving new equipment and familiarising themselves with its use (two companies of the battalion had recently been re-designated as heavy mortar units). After just a couple of weeks, the battalion was relocated to Hammamet in Tunisia. Like Algeria, Tunisia was already in Allied hands.

Again, the battalion was in a fixed location for only a short period. Within weeks, the expected call came and the 78th Division was called into action in Sicily, a day's voyage away across the Mediterranean. This was of course, the first active service the Kensingtons had seen since the Battle of France three years earlier in 1940. Ray and his comrades now found themselves in the thick of the Italian Campaign, first in Sicily and later, on the Italian mainland (Italy itself had surrendered once Sicily had fallen but the large concentrations of German forces in the country fought on). The Kensingtons were involved in the weeks of running battles that took Allied troops northwards, through Bari, Foggia and Termoli. In late November 1943 they fought in the Battle of the Sangro River, one of the most important engagements of the whole Italian Campaign.

Not long after the Battle of the Sangro River, in mid-December, one unit of the Kensingtons, B Group, was ordered to join other Allied troops over three thousand feet (1,000 metres) up in the Appennini Mountains. The extremely challenging mountain terrain and the harsh winter weather now stood firmly in the way of the Allied advance. What had previously been good progress came to a near standstill, and was to remain so for several months. B Group's HQ was at the tiny village of Forli del Sannio. Across the mountains they faced German troops who were higher up and some miles away at Monte Greco. In the immediate vicinity of B Group's position, German patrols and raiding parties were a constant danger.

Meanwhile, the rest of the 1st Kensingtons, including D Group of which Ray was a member, were greatly more fortunate. They travelled to the small, picturesque city of Campobasso, well behind the lines, where almost the entire 78th Division had been placed on rest. According to the regimental history, the Kensingtons celebrated Christmas Day in Campobasso "in great style"; the Quartermaster and his staff had "worked wonders transforming a dingy hall into a banquet-room ... with proper tables, chairs and decorations". They had also "scrounged enough turkeys for the whole battalion" and managed to include "all the traditional ingredients" of a Christmas dinner.[179]

Immediately after Christmas, D Group, including Ray, was ordered to join B Group in the mountains. They arrived there on December 27th and were dispersed as platoons into smaller camps around the local area. The winter weather at that time was brutal. The following day the 1st Battalion Kensington Regiment's war diary, kept by Lieutenant Colonel F. C. Parker, recorded that:

> "Severe weather continues across the whole front alternating between driving rain and snow which, with a high wind behind, assumes a blizzard intensity, blotting out all observation and causing deep drifts of snow over the roads."[180]

The war diary also noted that on that same day, two of the newly arrived D Group men were unloading a truck when a second truck – perhaps skidding on the snow and ice – crashed into them and their vehicle. One of the two men, Lance Corporal Harry Harvey, was killed instantly. The second man was seriously injured. That second man was Ray Bailey.

The war diary does not record what happened to Ray next. Under normal circumstances, he would probably have been taken to the nearest field hospital or at least to the nearest HQ, where conditions would have been better. With local roads impassable by the following day however – and remaining so for many days afterwards – it seems almost certain that this would not have been possible.

Conditions for the Kensingtons at the time of Ray's accident were unimaginably tough. Rations could only be sent up intermittently by mule, so food supplies were constantly low. Virtually no winter kit had yet been issued to the men and despite the extreme cold, some platoons were having to live under canvas because so many buildings in nearby villages had been destroyed in fighting. The situation was so bad that the regimental history of the Second World War later observed that "...there were times when the icy winds sapped the vitality almost completely". It goes on to describe men feeling an irrational desire "to fall on the inviting snow and sleep".

No further record of Ray's situation appears in the war diary until a week later on January 4th when Lieutenant Colonel Parker wrote:

> "The road to Carovilli was today finally re-opened, although long stretches remain covered with ice and only permit one way traffic. The snow has now become solid without any sign of a thaw and has to be cleared in solid lumps of ice. Pte Bailey R., injured in a motor accident, died today."[181]

* * *

The 270 or so men of the 1st Battalion Kensington Regiment who were taken prisoner at St Valery in 1940 lived through an experience unimaginably dreadful to most of us today. They were deprived of their liberty for five years, and their living conditions throughout the whole period were extremely poor. Disease was common in the PoW camps, food was often scarce and punishments could be vicious. For much of their incarceration they would have been forced to labour for long hours, often in harsh, unsafe conditions. In the winter of 1944 – 45, as the war was inching towards its close, many of them would have had to endure one final brutal and degrading ordeal. They would have been among the tens of thousands of PoWs forced by their captors to march hundreds of miles westwards across Poland, Germany and Czechoslovakia to keep them distant from the approaching Allied Forces and thus delay their liberation and potential return to military service.

A few of those comrades taken prisoner alongside Ray in 1940 would not live through the trials of their captivity or the barely credible inhumanity of those final forced marches. Others would have suffered long-term damage to their physical and mental health. By escaping when he did, Ray avoided all of this. On the other hand, almost all of those Kensingtons who were captured and incarcerated at St Valery survived the war.

Ray's story therefore raises some existentially challenging questions. Here was a young man whose sheer, irrepressible human spirit drove him to risk an escape. He was determined to be no-one's captive. The fraction of a second it took to leap that hedgerow in northern France in 1940 depended at least as much on the nerve to seize the moment as it did on physical bravery. It was this same repeated willingness to chance everything on one throw of the dice that enabled Ray to make it back to Britain.

In making the choice he made in the moment he made it, Ray regained his freedom. He also ensured that he would return to the battlefield and fight again. And we should acknowledge, by the way, that returning to the action was something he wanted to do. Despite his apparent ambivalence to military life, Ray comes across in his memoir as a patriot and a man of duty. He clearly felt a personal responsibility to re-join his nation's fight against totalitarianism.

We cannot fail, however, to see that Ray's leap for freedom led directly to his early death. The great majority of his captured Kensington Regiment comrades would experience the joy of homecoming. In time, they would heal from the physical and mental damage of their captivity. They would live the rest of their lives largely in a time of peace. They would marry and raise families; they would work and have careers; they would have friendships, indulge their interests and enjoy the increasing prosperity of the 1950s and 1960s.

Ray would have none of these things. His courage and sense of duty saved him from five grim years in a PoW camp but cost him several decades of life. Back in England, his mum and dad lost a son. Eighteen year old Harry lost his elder brother. After eight months of marriage and almost no time alone with her husband, his young wife was a widow.

Ray Bailey was one of around 120 men of the Kensington Regiment who gave their lives during World War II. Like most of the others who were killed, his passing is noted briefly in the official war history of the regiment. Because of his exploits earlier in the war, he is also granted a modest personal acknowledgement – something that most of the other rank and file deaths do not receive. The author writes:

> "Pte R. Bailey...will be particularly remembered for his daring escape from France in 1940".[182]

The means of Ray's remembrance – his manuscript account of his adventures – has remained unknown to the public record for more than eighty years. Now the manuscript is rediscovered, 6205182 Pte R. Bailey of the 1st Battalion Princess Louise's Kensington Regiment stands before us. So too, does cheerful, young Ray Bailey, apprentice lathe operator from Dunstable, son of William and Margaret, brother of Harry, and newly wed husband of Cynthia.

* * *

Ray Bailey is buried in the Sangro River War Cemetery in Italy. He is commemorated on both the Dunstable War Memorial and the Vauxhall Motors War Memorial in Luton. Formal commemorations such as these are extremely important – but they have their limitations. A name on a monument is not a story. Even the most dramatic episodes in a family's collective memory fade away as the years and decades go by.

Ray Bailey was an ordinary lad who did two extraordinary things. The first was to escape his captors and – against all odds – make his way safely home. The second was to use his facility with words to write down what happened to him.

Ray did not survive the war but his words did. In pencil, in Ray's neat handwriting, on the pages of his notebooks, Ray's words lived on, unchanging and patient, through the decades that Ray himself would never see. Then the words were discovered and now Ray's story is told. Ray Bailey is, at last, "particularly remembered".

Part Six

THE STORY BEHIND THE BOOK

Some of Ray's original notebooks and journals

Raymond Bailey's manuscript

The cardboard box

Ray Bailey's adventures took place over the course of fourteen months, between October 1939 and December 1940. But this book embodies another story besides Ray's. This second story – explaining how the first story came to be told – happens more slowly. It has taken eighty years for that story to unfold.

The first sign of this second story appeared on my computer screen in the summer of 2019. I was browsing an online auction, when I spotted an interesting lot. A couple of photographs showed a bunch of old spiral-bound notebooks and some loose papers spread out on a table. A few sentences had been added by way of description. Here, the seller said, was a box of documents that related to a British soldier of the Second World War. The soldier seemed to have been taken prisoner by the Germans and it looked like he had made it home.

That wasn't very much information to go on but it was intriguing. I've been buying old diaries, collections of letters, photo albums and so on in auction salerooms for decades. I began buying online as well when the first online auction platforms appeared in the early 2000s. I like the idea of rescuing people's forgotten stories. It is amazing what is still out there asking to be found. In this case, the online seller's scant description suggested that he knew relatively little about the collection of material he had listed. That probably meant these were not documents from his own family. Perhaps the collection was being sold by a house clearance firm – or maybe it had been purchased speculatively at a live auction for re-sale online. It was impossible to know for sure whether the seller had understood the collection accurately. Neither of the photos gave many clues either. It would be a bit of a gamble to bid. The collection could easily have turned out to be not very interesting. But that's part of the fun. If you don't buy a ticket, you can't win the raffle.

In online auctions it is possible to leave one's bid confidentially, days in advance of the end-time. This I did. I left a bid rather less than the collection might have made if it had been properly described and in a specialist sale of military artefacts but nevertheless high enough – so I thought – to secure the lot. I was wrong. I did not win. When I checked back after the close of bidding, I found I was the "under-bidder" (the prospective buyer whose bid was the next highest to that of the winning bidder).

It is annoying to be the under-bidder. It's like being the losing finalist in a sports tournament. The root of this feeling is the nagging question of whether bidding just a few pounds more would have made the difference. But this of course, is a question that can never be answered. It is futile even to think about it. I put the box of notebooks out of my mind and moved on.

That seemed to be the end of the matter. Except that several weeks later I was browsing the same site again when – entirely by chance – I came across exactly the same lot with exactly the same description, being sold by the original seller. I emailed the obvious question and received the obvious answer. Had the previous sale fallen through? Yes it had. The winning bidder had turned out to be overseas and this seller had not wanted the trouble of posting a large package to another country. I explained that I had been the under-bidder on the previous occasion and was still keen on the lot. I offered to match the amount of the earlier winning bid. The seller emailed back suggesting another five pounds would make my offer more appealing. For an extra fiver I wasn't going to miss this same opportunity again. And so the deal was done.

It seemed to me then – as it still does now – that fate had intervened to direct this collection of material into my possession. I know that will sound fanciful to many people but it is worth reflecting that if the collection had gone overseas, as it very nearly did, the story that you have just read would almost certainly have been lost to the British social and military historical record forever.

A few days after my email conversation with the seller, an

unexpectedly heavy, rather untidily wrapped parcel arrived at my house. I pulled off the sticky tape, tore away the brown paper and lifted the flaps on the cardboard box inside. The first things visible were some loose items – a few tatty old envelopes with George VI stamps, some yellowed newspaper clippings and a few old photographs, including one of a soldier in uniform. These are familiar items in any box of old family papers. Beneath these things was the collection of notebooks I had seen in the seller's listing. There were a couple of dozen of them altogether. This was maybe twice as many had been shown in the images online and was, I suppose, the first tangible indication that this might turn out to be a good find.

The notebooks had more pages than I had expected and each was filled from the front page to the back with pencilled handwriting. It was obvious at a glance that there were many tens of thousands of words. I arranged the notebooks on the floor and had a preliminary go at making sense of them. They seemed to belong in two different sets. The first set consisted of around half a dozen exercise books with lots of loose sheets of paper tucked between the pages. This set was some kind of rough draft. It had sections crossed out and notes in the margins. Arrows and asterisks indicated chunks of text that needed to be moved elsewhere.

The second set was made up of sixteen cheap note-pads of the kind widely used in the middle of the last century for writing informal letters to family and friends. Each was numbered on the front cover. I placed them on the floor in numerical order, praying that there were none missing. There weren't. Laid out like this, the notebooks had a satisfying look of organisation and completeness. Inside the pads, it was the same. The handwriting was neat. There were barely any additions or changes. This was a finished manuscript, tidied up and painstakingly copied from the exercise books – a whole story that had been put together with serious intent.

I had glanced at the contents of the notebooks as I sorted them out but only to check that each followed on from the previous one. Even so, I had easily been able to confirm that this really was a first person account of a PoW escape. But, very frustratingly, that was where I had to leave it for the time being. By bad luck, the parcel had arrived only an hour or so before I had to leave home and catch a train. I had a commitment that involved an overnight stay. It would be late the following evening before I got back. Luckily though, the following day was a Friday, so I would have the whole of the coming weekend to read through the notebooks and examine the various other items that were in the box.

As I had unwrapped the parcel, I had noticed that the box had a sticky label with an auction lot number. The label had the name of a firm of auctioneers but not the firm's address. That evening in my hotel room I did a bit of research online and found that the auction house was situated in a small market town in north west England. Not all auction houses leave their previous catalogues online but as good luck would have it, this one did. Since I had the lot number it was fairly easy to search though the previous catalogues one by one until I found the box of notebooks. The collection turned out to have been sold over a year previously at a general sale. General sales are usually no-frills affairs where prices tend to be relatively modest. Over the course of the day, hundreds of lots will be sold, including anything from modern electrical goods to potentially decent antique pieces needing restoration or further research. It is not uncommon for boxes of old family papers to crop up in such sales.

I had hoped that the live auctioneer's catalogue description might have more information about the history of the material in the box than the subsequent online seller had provided – but it did not. It seems most likely that the person who bought the collection at the live auction was the person who subsequently sold it to me. Why they had bought it and why they sold it again is a mystery though, not least because I could see that the price they had paid at auction was more than the price for which they had sold it to me. This was the end of the road in terms of finding out the history of the collection though – or at least of doing so quickly.

When I arrived home from my night away, I was able to inspect the collection more thoroughly. In addition to the sets of notepads, there was a photo of the author and another of one of his army mates. There were also a few family letters; some French, Spanish and German bank-notes of the wartime period; a couple of military badges; two or three wartime newspapers; some newspaper cuttings; and a tiny pocket notebook half-filled with handwriting so miniscule as to be almost illegible. Rather incongruously, there was also a hardback notebook containing what appeared to be the first four chapters of a crime novel – but more of that later. In due course every item in the box would take its place in Raymond Bailey's story.

A rough count revealed that the sixteen notepads that made up Ray's final account of his experiences contained over 80,000 words. Writing that many words is no easy task; 80,000 words is the length of a medium-sized novel. But this was no work of fiction. Over the next week or so, I read through the whole manuscript twice. I was perhaps the first person to do so for many years or even some decades. I encountered Ray Bailey's story exactly as you have just encountered it, except that I had no way of knowing at that point who Ray Bailey was.

In due course I was to discover more about the history of Ray's memoir by searching for and contacting later generations of his family. All I could know at that early stage however, was that at some point after the event he had written this dramatic and engaging true-life account of his experiences. Beyond that I could only wonder how the manuscript ended up being sold among the boxes of crockery, the shelves of old books, the costume jewellery, the battered furniture and the faded watercolours of a general auction sale.

Once I had read the whole story though, I did know something for sure – and that was that I had stumbled on something very good indeed. But even so, it was to be a considerable time yet before I realised just how special this collection of material was.

What does it take to make a successful escape?

If Ray's story was a novel it would be a page-turner. The central character is a young, inexperienced, working class lad who almost certainly had no formal education beyond the age of fourteen. He has never been outside of his native country before boarding a troopship to France. He speaks no language other than English. He has no access to information about the state of the war or the wider political situation. He knows nothing of the laws, customs and behaviours of either France or Spain, the two countries through which he must travel to get home. For much of the time he has no money. Apart from when he steals a bicycle he has no means of transport. For most of the time he has no map. He is unarmed. He is alone.

And yet 21 year-old Ray succeeds in making a journey of over 2,000 miles in circumstances that mean he must be constantly alert to the risk of discovery. He knows that in some areas, if he is found, there is a realistic possibility he will be shot. He slogs much of this huge distance on foot. There are times when he feels safe only to travel after darkness has fallen. He has had only rudimentary military training but he must learn how to survive without shelter. He goes without food for days on end. He is often exhausted. At times his feet are red raw but he has no choice but to drag himself onwards. He has unnerving encounters with the German military authorities in Occupied France, the Gendarmerie in Vichy France and with the Fascist Civil Guard in Spain. Every day he must think and plan, and decide and act. And, perhaps most challengingly of all – young and inexperienced as he is – he must do all this largely without support or advice.

But whether or not he intended it to be so, Ray's story is something more than a series of exploits and perils; more than a tale of grim survival. It speaks to us about the importance of comradeship and the sense of having a loyalty to something greater than oneself. It shows us that humour can be a powerful force in coping with adversity. It gives us insight into what it is to be completely alone in the face of darkness and fear. It does not wholly shirk the inhumanity of war but it prefers to recall the expressions of human goodness that Ray encounters on his journey. He is sheltered, fed and clothed (and on one occasion, actively rescued) by ordinary French and Spanish working people – people like himself, and his mum and dad. These people have little enough to spare and expect never to see Ray again, yet they treat him with warmth and affection. It took no small degree of courage to assist an escaped British PoW in Spain or occupied France in 1940; even in unoccupied France it could attract attention from the authorities. Without the decency and humanity of these people, Ray might very well not have made it home.

For an escaped prisoner of war, there is no turning back. Once he has cast the die, he must go forward. Sunshine or storm, Ray wanders on, mostly (but by no means always) in the right direction. He has good luck, he has bad luck. He gets into scrapes and has so many near misses that he seems sometimes to be leading a charmed life. Not that he ever seems to notice. Ray doesn't ask any big questions about why things happen as they do. His coping strategy can be summed up in one word, "pragmatism". He takes each incident as it comes and looks no further than the next day; sometimes he looks no further than the next couple of hours.

What makes a hero?

Ray's memoir challenges perceptions. Many, if not most of us, would regard a man who escapes a PoW column and makes it home against all odds, as a hero. But there is nothing obviously of the hero in Ray's appearance – and not really, by the sound of it, in his general demeanour either. Ray tells us good-humouredly and more than once, that he is just a "little fellow". In the two photographs of him that we have he looks slight and boyish. By his own account, he is no great shakes as a soldier. As he says himself, he is regarded by his superiors as "generally a spare man" – someone not thought capable of being useful in any particular way. He is no stranger to disciplinary action for minor misdemeanours. In brief, he seems a reluctant soldier who does not readily accept the need just to buckle down and get on with it.

In these and other ways, Ray sounds perhaps a recognisable "type"; something of a flippant character, possibly rather immature, and defiant of authority for no good reason. Yet there are elements of his nature that seem at odds with these outwardly juvenile tendencies. At times he seems rather naive and unworldly; he is repeatedly shocked by the bad language of his fellow soldiers for example and he seems over-awed by those who are tougher than him. And as we already know, he has an unexpectedly serious, hard-working and conscientious side to his personality. The evidence for that is in your hand.

Ray therefore lacks almost all the physical and personal qualities that are generally thought of as crucial to heroism, particularly in the military context. He is not a commanding or physically imposing figure. He would not immediately inspire respect from a stranger. He hasn't the steady self-discipline and worldly confidence of a regular soldier. He can't fall back on the self-assurance and social graces that might help a young, privately educated officer out of a tight spot. So what was it about Ray that enabled him to escape from captivity and make it all the way home?

Well, undoubtedly, his default setting is "cheerful". He knows how to look on the bright side. When, despite his ragged, half-starved condition, he takes time to admire the sunshine and scenery of southern France, you could be forgiven for thinking you were reading a holiday journal rather than the story of a fugitive's gruelling trek to escape a ruthless enemy. Often Ray seems to have the luck of the devil – and that is perhaps because he has the cheek of the devil too. When there is a choice between brazening out a situation or slipping away to think things through, he will almost always choose the former.

But then, you feel Ray deserves all the luck that comes his way. He never gives up. His resilience is extraordinary. He almost always believes that eventually things will turn out alright. Perhaps most importantly, he has the reckless impulsivity of youth and the ability to screw his nerve to maximum tightness whenever he needs to take a risk. This combination of qualities may not have the purity of courage or the nobility of heroism. But at that time, in those circumstances, it could deliver much the same results.

Writing the memoir

After the fact of its sheer physical survival for eighty years, perhaps the most surprising thing about Ray Bailey's memoir is that it was written at all. As we have seen, Ray was from a working class family and probably had only the most basic level of secondary education. Before joining the army he was a manual worker in a car factory. Of course, none of these factors precludes his having the ability to write well. It is however, true to say that that the overwhelming majority of young men from a similar background during that period, would not have been able to do the same.

I have already mentioned that Ray's original manuscript has 80,000 words and was twice written out in full – once as a rough draft and once as a finished text. An enormous amount of self discipline was needed to complete such a lenghty piece of writing. It would have been extremely difficult for any active, twenty one year-old lad to stick at such a task. It must have been even more so for a serving soldier. Ray had a stroke of luck here; he was undoubtedly helped by the fact that, after its tour of duty in France, the 1st Battalion, Kensington Regiment was based on home soil for almost three years.

During this period the Kensingtons were stationed at a number of locations in the South-East and South-West of England as part of the home defence force. For much of this time they were housed in relative comfort in purpose-built barracks or requisitioned buildings. This prolonged break from overseas service would have given Ray the time and space he needed to work on his memoir.

Ray mentions at one point towards the end of the manuscript that he is writing five months after his return to England following his escape. That suggests the first draft was well under way by the summer of 1941 and possibly therefore fully complete by the end of that year. If Ray carried straight on to work on the final draft, then that would perhaps have been finished comfortably by the end of 1942, and perhaps a good deal earlier. Certainly, we can be sure that the manuscript was in its finished form and stored safely at home by the time Ray and the 1st Battalion of the Kensingtons embarked for once more for active service overseas in 1943.

This narrow timescale highlights a particularly interesting aspect of Ray's memoir. This is the fact that it was written so close in time to the events it describes. The great majority of eye-witness wartime memoirs were written and published decades later, largely between the 1960s and 1980s. It is easy to see why this was so. It is widely documented in interviews with ex-servicemen that in the years immediately after the war, many did not want to recall their experiences on active service. After all, they had forfeited their youth; witnessed death, destruction and misery; and survived chaos on the grand scale. Many had had terrible experiences they could never hope to forget. When the war was over they wanted the luxurious ordinariness of family life, home, friendships and a steady job.

This is all perfectly understandable – but in terms of the written record, it means that when veterans did come to write, their recollections were filtered through the lens of memory and mediated by their later life experiences. What you read in this book on the other hand, was written by a young man who was recalling events of only a few months earlier. Ray was still the same person to whom the events had happened. He had had no experiences in the meantime that might have changed the way he looked back. He could easily recall the physical reality of what happened – and as he wrote, he must surely have felt again the emotions that he had felt at the time.

I should stress that I do not for a moment suggest that any of this makes Ray's account "better" than memoirs written decades later. It is simply that it offers a different perspective. If I had to summarise what that means in practice, I would say that Ray's account of his experiences, with its informal style, its episodic format and its liberal mixing of the light-hearted with the serious, is in some ways, nearer in style to a contemporary blog than it is to the considered and reflective memoirs with which we are more familiar.

In discussing Ray's memoir from the point of view of the historical record though, there are two factors associated with its writing that make it both important and unique. The first is – as described above – that Ray wrote his memoir so soon after the events described and that those events happened within the first fourteen months of the war. It is highly likely therefore that this book contains the earliest long-form, eye-witness account of active service in the Second World War to have been written by a British soldier. Second, given that Ray was aged only 21 or 22 when he wrote his memoir it is probable that he is now the youngest soldier ever to have published an account of his wartime experiences. These are the two remarkable aspects of my auction buy that I mentioned in the opening section of this essay and whose great significance I failed initially to recognise.

Soldier as writer

The only item in the original box of Ray's papers that was not related to his time in the Kensingtons was a hardback notebook, just a little smaller than A4 size. The first 68 pages of the notebook contain more than 10,000 words in Ray's usual tidy script. These are the first four chapters of what Ray clearly intended to be a full length novel. The notebook is undated but it seems most likely that these chapters were written before Ray's call up, probably therefore when he was in his late teens.

The central character of Ray's embryonic novel – or at least of these early chapters – is a lively, cheerful, independent young woman, Valerie Howard. Valerie is a shorthand typist, originally from a "village in Bedfordshire" but now living alone in London (both her parents are deceased). She has been looking for work in the city without any success, so she decides instead to apply for a job in the countryside. She is absolutely delighted when her first interview, at the Bluebird Flying Club, results in her appointment. The club is situated in an expensively furnished, ultra-modern building in landscaped grounds. Shiny modern aircraft are to be seen on the airfield and the clientele of the club are people of the "wealthy classes". Valerie is thrilled to have landed a job in such a sophisticated setting.

What Valerie does not realise however, is that the Bluebird Flying Club is a front for a criminal organisation involved in both counterfeiting British banknotes and smuggling illicit goods to and from mainland Europe. Interestingly, the brains behind this underworld operation, Zoë Faulkner, is also a woman. In addition to introducing

Valerie and the Bluebird Flying Club, Ray also fits into these early chapters, a dramatic armed robbery from a security van and the arrest of a criminal by Detective Bradley of Scotland Yard. It is probably safe to assume therefore that Ray had already sketched out a plot for the book in which these various narrative threads would eventually come together.

The existence of these four chapters, slight as they are, suggests not only that Ray had an inherent drive to write but that he was capable of sticking at the process. He may very well have written other lengthy pieces in his teens – indeed, there might once have been other notebooks continuing Valerie Howard's story to the end. Ray, it seems, liked writing.

But of course, this does not necessarily mean that Ray could write well. The starting point of preparing his memoir for publication therefore was to consider the quality of the content. There were enough words to fill a book – but would that book merit publication?

Assuming you are reading this essay after reading the book, you will know that the answer to this question was a pretty clear "yes". It would be misleading to present Ray's memoir as a work of literature but it has genuine narrative force and for the reasons given earlier, it has a sense of immediacy that is rarely found. This is so much the case, that it is easy to get lost in the story and overlook the competence of the writing. Ray does nothing fancy. He describes events simply, succinctly and in the order that they happened. He does this very well, in nicely constructed sentences and with a natural feel for the rhythm of language. For the kind of story he is telling, this is the perfect approach.

This straightforwardness does not mean however, that the memoir lacks depth or detail. Quite often Ray steps aside from the narrative to zoom in, in sharp focus, on some small incident occurring within the bigger picture. From the reader's point of view, this feels similar to the way that human memory can often recreate the feeling of a complex experience by recalling one vivid moment of it. Sometimes the incidents that Ray chooses to share with us in this way are grim or frightening. Sometimes they are full of hope. Sometimes they may even seem banal. But that is misleading. We learn what it is like to get up one morning, bleary eyed and dopey, and discover immediately at gunpoint that you are no longer a free man. We find out how it feels to cook rotten turnips in a rusty petrol can when you are desperately hungry – and then discover the result is inedible. Ray also occasionally takes juvenile pleasure in describing the mishaps and mistakes of others. Here, his tone is exactly that of young men everywhere, when refusing to take serious matters seriously is a last ditch attempt to stave off the looming threat of adulthood. Each of these little anecdotal sidetracks bring us a few steps closer to understanding Ray's day-to-day experience of military life and the madness of war.

One significant and perhaps surprising aspect of Ray's memoir is that, even though the Kensingtons are in the thick of the action during the retreat to St Valery, he offers relatively little description of the fighting and its aftermath. Other published descriptions of the same events – both eye-witness accounts and detailed studies by military historians – make it plain that, like every other soldier involved, Ray lived through a terrifying experience and must have witnessed sights of unspeakable horror. This was particularly the case in the streets of St Valery itself where there was carnage. It can only have been a deliberate choice on Ray's part not to describe these scenes; scenes which must surely have remained sickeningly vivid in his mind at the time he was writing.

After much thought I decided to include in the book a number of brief descriptions of the fighting at St Valery taken from the accounts of other British soldiers who were present. These accounts are included in the introductory notes to Ray's chapter on St Valery. I recognise, that in doing this, I was inserting imagery that Ray had consciously decided to exclude – and furthermore, that I was adding content that jars with the tone of most of the rest of Ray's memoir. In the end though, I think that if we want to try and understand this period of the war, we should not shy away from the horror of it. And perhaps even more importantly for the purposes of this book, if we are properly to understand Ray and

Ray's story, we need to know what he endured at St Valery.

Of course knowing about St Valery ourselves, leads us to wonder why Ray chose not to describe the experience in more detail himself. We can never really know. It may be that his powers of expression failed him as he stared, appalled, at the flickering screen of his own memories. Or perhaps, by recalling the human aspects of his experiences in more detail than the soldiering, he found solace as he wrote. More prosaically, he may simply have thought it best not to worry his family and friends, who would inevitably have been the first audience for his memoir and who knew that Ray – like all the other young men they cared about – had no alternative but to remain in uniform for the duration of the war.

When all these various characteristics of Ray's writing are brought together, the result is something special. Behind the clamour of the intervening decades, you hear the authentic voice of hundreds of thousands of young British soldiers of the Second World War; young men, many of them barely more than boys, wrenched away from home and family, from work and mates and evenings in the pub, and thrown into a frightening, disorientating world with which they must learn to cope as best they could.

Ray's written story is probably not so very different from the verbal account of his adventures that he gave to numerous visitors invited "from far and wide" by his parents to the family home in Dunstable after Ray's return. Ray had to tell his story again and again until, as he says, "I was tired of hearing it myself". It is this guileless, almost conversational, tone in Ray's writing that gives life to his words. It is as if your amiable young nephew, still in uniform, has slipped into the armchair opposite, poured himself a cup of tea and begun, quietly but keenly, to describe his experiences to you, exactly as if you had particularly asked him to do that.

Entirely a military history?

Ray was a soldier on active service, then a prisoner of war, then an escaped prisoner of war. From start to finish, his story takes place against a background of war. While he is on the run, the ever-present threat to his freedom – and indeed his life – comes from enemy soldiers and the military authorities in France and Spain. His eventual repatriation to the UK is organised through military channels. On his return, after a fortnight's leave spent at home, he rejoins his regiment. Certainly then, this book has many elements of a military history.

But Ray's memoir also evokes a number of universal ideas that extend beyond the boundaries of his wartime experience and take this book into broader territory. The memoir is a story of survival against the odds, not just in the obvious way in relation to Ray's escape from captivity but also – as we have already noted – in relation to the remarkable eighty year survival of the original manuscript. His story is therefore also about chance and the importance of keeping memories alive where that is possible. My dad, like Ray, a working class industrial apprentice, was also conscripted to fight in the Second World War – and like many men of his generation, would never speak of his experiences. I use that word "never" in its literal sense. If asked about the war he would say only that that was a subject he had chosen never to discuss. My dad's late teens and early twenties – his equivalent of my fondly remembered student years – had been shut up in a box marked "never to be opened". At least not in front of anyone else.

My dad's memories went to the grave with him in the 1970s. Ray's memories, captured when they barely had time to qualify as memories at all have, like Ray himself in 1940, been lucky enough to survive a long, lonely journey. Ray made it home in eight months. His memories have remained almost unknown for eighty years – but now, suddenly, Ray can speak directly to us. As the *Dunstable Borough Gazette* pointed out when it celebrated Ray's safe return home, Ray's story is one of resilience and perseverance. These are qualities that flourish in war but are not exclusive to wartime. Ray's is also a story suffused with humanity and – as I have said – of human kindness found amid inhumanity of the grossest kind. Ray accepted the kindnesses that were offered to him – and was deeply grateful for them. I imagine too, that none of those good people ever forgot the young English soldier who passed briefly through their lives. Those people are gone now but their kindness and their bravery are recorded here. Most of us will face our own trek through hostile territory at some point in our lives. The kindness of those who care about us during those times will live with us forever.

This book is also about the importance of words. Ray was an ordinary British lad of unremarkable background. Millions of young men like him served in the Second World War. But Ray did something that very few others did. Evening after evening, wherever he was, in spare moments whenever he could find them, as the bombs fell on Britain and despite his mates taking the mickey (which one can readily imagine was probably the most off-putting thing of all), Ray sat on his barrack room bunk and wrote. Consequently, his story has survived. The enormous majority of other soldiers' stories, shared perhaps with friends and relatives but never written down, have been lost or forgotten. Many other stories – like my dad's for example – never even got told in the first place.

I don't mean to be fanciful but from the moment I was gifted by fate that unexpected second chance to act as custodian of Ray's manuscript, it has seemed my responsibility to make the story public. Ray's words give us a unique insight into an extraordinary experience. They are a rare and precious survival; a lost hoard disturbed from the earth by a turn of the plough. We are lucky to have them.

Editing the manuscript for publication

1. Introduction

Did Ray Bailey himself intend his memoir for publication? I think it is probable that he did. I have already pointed out the huge amount of work he must have done, under extremely difficult circumstances, to get his memoir into its finished state. We know he was a determined character and of course, he must have enjoyed the process of writing or he wouldn't have done it; indeed, as I pointed out in the preceding section, we know that Ray had already begun at least one intended novel before he even joined the army.

Even with this level of commitment though, it must sometimes have been a complete slog to see the memoir through to its finished state. This seems far too much trouble to have gone to for something intended only for the eyes of a few friends and family members. Ray knew his escape was a significant achievement and he was rightly proud of that. It is important to remember that Ray's was one of the earliest escapes of the war. At the time he wrote the memoir, it must have seemed to him that very few others would ever do the same.[183] Surely then, he wanted his account to be read as widely as possible.

2. General editing of the text

I tried to keep to an absolute minimum the editing that was necessary to turn Ray's manuscript into a book. I made no large scale changes at all and changed language, construction or grammar in the fewest places necessary – and then to do no more than "tidy up" the occasional difficult-to-follow sentence or paragraph. In a small number of places I removed sections of text where doing so enabled the narrative to progress more smoothly. I also shortened a fair number of Ray's longer sentences. Ray had a tendency sometimes to describe events in long chains of phrases linked by conjunctions such as "and" or "but". I split sentences of this type into two or three shorter sentences. This inevitably meant that in order to keep the flow, I occasionally had to insert words or short phrases that Ray did not use. I kept these insertions to the minimum possible.

My only aim in making the few changes described above was to improve readability. None of my changes has altered the meaning or mood of Ray's writing in any way. As I have already pointed out, Ray writes extraordinarily well when you take into account his young age, his relatively low level of education and the circumstances in which he worked on the manuscript.

3. Chapters 1 and 2

My "light touch" approach to editing does mean however, that there are a few passages where the use of language is not perfect or where Ray's logic is slightly difficult to follow. In particular, I should mention Chapters 1 and 2, which are rather sketchy and disjointed by comparison with the chapters that follow and are not typical of the book as a whole. I imagine Ray wrote the memoir chronologically and it seems to have taken him a short while to find the right "tone of voice" for himself as narrator. I hope readers will have been forgiving of these first couple of chapters. Despite their shortcomings, they tell us a lot about Ray as a person and without them the rest of the book would be less engaging. Once Ray gets into his stride around the beginning of Chapter 3, the story settles into a rhythm and begins to move forward very nicely. I think most readers will accept, that these few early imperfections of style and content are a small price to pay to hear this young soldier's natural voice speaking to us across a gap of eighty years.

4. Other changes to the text

I ought also to describe two other types of intervention that I have made into the original text. These are both of an entirely practical nature and do not interfere with Ray's original content at all. They concern dates and locations.

Dates

In the entirety of the original manuscript Ray gives only one specific date. I have however been able to establish accurate dates for many of the events he describes by cross-referencing his memoir with several other sources. In the first half of the book (before Ray escapes) the two main sources for these dates are the official history of the Kensington Regiment in the Second World War[184] and the diaries of Lt. Reg Wood of the Kensington Regiment, cited in Robert Gardner's excellent account of the Kensingtons' time with the British Expeditionary Force.[185]

For the dates after Ray's escape, I had the benefit of a tiny pocket notebook kept by Ray himself. This notebook was among the odd extra bits and pieces that came along with the manuscript in the original auction lot. It wouldn't be quite true to say that Ray used this little notebook as a diary – his entries in it are not regular or organised enough for that – but helpfully, it does give dates for some of the events described in the final manuscript. Rather than add complications to the book by putting the dates from these various sources in the end-notes, I have taken the liberty of inserting them directly into Ray's text. On every occasion but one therefore, when you see the phrase "On [specific date]" or similar formulations (e.g. "in late November"), those words are my additions.

Locations

The second group of practical changes relates to place names. In his manuscript, more often than not, Ray misspelled French and Spanish place names. These misspellings are commonplace while Ray is travelling through France and once he gets to Spain, it is barely an exaggeration to say that only "Barcelona" and "Madrid" are spelled correctly in the original manuscript. Sometimes Ray uses rough phonetic approximations. In other cases where he was perhaps more familiar with the place names he spells them almost – but not quite – correctly. Via the magic of Google Maps, I have been able to give each location its proper name, even where it is just a tiny village. For anyone who wants to do so, it is now possible to track Ray's epic journey accurately on a map. Any errors that may remain in the place names are now mine, not Ray's.

5. Sequence of events in Chapters 4 and 5

As I said above, my guiding principle was to make as few changes to the original manuscript as possible. I have not departed from this principle in editing Chapters 4 and 5 but I have adapted it. These chapters describe the retreat to St Valery and the fighting in the town itself. Probably because of the chaos and confusion of events during these terrible days, Ray had not written these two chapters in chronological order, even though he clearly believed he had. Cross-referencing his original text with official sources, I was able to re-order his original. I hesitated for a long time before deciding to amend the text in this way but I am completely confident that the result has been to make Ray's account both easier to follow and more consistent with the established historical record. Note that, apart from adding a few new words and phrases to link the re-ordered sections, I have left the original text precisely as Ray wrote it. It is now simply in a different order.

6. Forms of additional information in the book

As we have seen, Ray completed his memoir before the war was even halfway through. This means that he saw no need to include background information about – for example – military strategy or the political situation in Europe. He presumably took it for granted that whoever read his story would understand the context for the events he described. To take a couple of broad examples, Ray would have assumed that everyone knew that Germany's objective after the fall of France was likely to be the invasion of Britain. Likewise he would have assumed that readers understood the idea of "Vichy France". He would also have expected people to be familiar with the sequence of military events in which he was caught up.

Even if Ray had felt it necessary to add background information, it seems probable in any case that he would not have been able to do so with any degree of accuracy. One of the things that Ray's memoir demonstrates time and again, and with absolute clarity, is that a rank and file soldier on active service during the Second World War was not at all well placed to see the bigger picture. Ray and his comrades rarely know what the overall objectives are or where their own actions are intended to fit in. They are equally in the dark about what is going to happen in the immediate future – and when they try to guess, they are invariably wrong. Events simply whirl around them like leaves whipped up by an autumn gale.

One of my editorial contributions therefore was to write notes on the text. These notes take two forms. The first set are brief scene-setting introductory notes to some of the chapters (where there are no introductory notes it means that the circumstances of the coming chapter are self-explanatory). Where there are introductory notes, the purpose of them is to give the reader sufficient contextual information to follow the story – and thus remain engaged with Ray's narrative – without the need to stop and look things up. In other words, I have added material that Ray would no doubt have added himself, had he written the memoir thirty or forty years later. My introductory notes are presented separately from Ray's original chapters and can easily be skipped if you already have a good understanding of the period and the circumstances. I am not a military historian and it goes without saying that the introductory notes are intended to provide no more than the barest summary of the relevant background events. Those who wish for a better understanding of the military and political context for the Battle of France will easily find excellent sources in any good bookshop or online.

The second set of notes are added as endnotes to each chapter. These endnotes are gathered together at the end of the book and provide background information that is interesting or relevant to what is happening in the story at the time. They also answer factual questions that might arise from a particular passage. Endnotes are indicated in the text with a numeral. Sources and acknowledgements for the information in the endnotes are always given where that is relevant. A handful of the endnotes contain information from primary sources that may not be on the public record elsewhere.

In a very small number of places I have added a footnote at the bottom of a page. These footnotes are used to give information that is of immediate relevance to the story. Footnotes are indicated by an asterisk in the text.

I should add that with both the introductory notes and the endnotes / footnotes, my only aim is to enhance the reader's enjoyment of the book and to point readers in the direction of further information if they want to know more. Like the club secretary who sets up the projector for the guest speaker and arranges the chairs for the audience, my intention is to help with the presentation of Ray's story without intruding into it.

7. Soldiers named in the book

Finally, on a number of occasions, Ray refers by name to other soldiers. In the first part of the book, these soldiers are generally his comrades in the Kensington Regiment. Later, when he is on the run, there are times when he meets men from other regiments. My last contribution to the book has been to put together an appendix, "Soldiers named in the manuscript", which gives details (where that detail is available on the military record) of what happened to these individuals later in the war. Ray was a sociable character who made friends easily. He would be pleased I think, that as we picture in our mind's eye the men with whom he shared experiences, we are giving brief remembrance to their humanity too. As you will see in that appendix (Appendix 1), some of them did not live to tell their own story.

APPENDICES

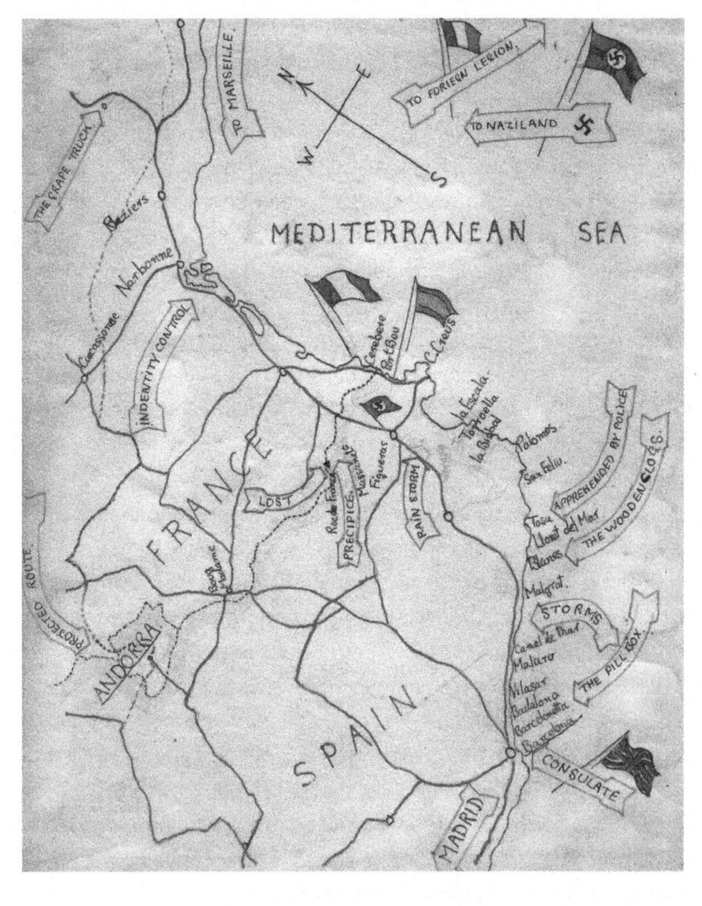

Map, presumably drawn by Ray,
found with his orginal journals

Appendix 1: Soldiers named in the manuscript

About this list

This list includes the name of every soldier mentioned in Ray's memoir for whom it was possible to find further information. If a soldier who is named in the text is not included in the list below, it is for one of three reasons: either no information was available on the military record; or not enough information was given in the text to identify him in the military record; or because Ray could not recall the man's actual name and so gave him a fictitious name instead (this latter applies particularly to the men Ray meets at Fort Saint-Jean).

The majority of those whose names appear below are comrades of Ray in the 1st Battalion, Princess Louise's Kensington Regiment. A soldier's regiment is only given in the list below if it is other than the 1st Kensingtons. Those Kensingtons captured at St Valery on June 12th 1940 were initially listed as "missing" from that date and "missing" is the word that would have been used in official notifications to their nexts-of-kin. For the majority, confirmation of their PoW status was typically not received by the War Office and passed on to their loved ones until August or September 1940.

In the case of some of the captured men, the location of their PoW camp was available on the military record. Where that was the case, the information is included below. PoWs were sometimes moved between camps, so where a camp location is given below, that does not necessarily mean that the man spent the whole period of his captivity there (note that an "Oflag" was a camp for captured officers, a "Stalag" for captured rank and file soldiers). Most PoW camps were liberated in the spring of 1945 as the Allied forces gradually occupied Germany territory. Unless otherwise stated, all the men who became prisoners of war were not freed until this time.

BESLEY, Captain Charles Robert Ingram
Royal Northumberland Fusiliers

Capt Besley was one of the four officers interned at Fort Saint-Jean. He had been a member of the Royal Northumberland Fusiliers since before the war (like the Kensingtons the RNF were a territorial regiment in peacetime). In his civilian life, Capt Besley was a solicitor, practising in Monkseaton near Newcastle upon Tyne. Like Ray, Capt Besley was captured at St Valery and escaped by slipping away from a PoW column just before the Belgian border. Capt Besley was among the men from the Miranda camp who travelled home with the smaller group, of which Ray was a part, who had been living at the British Embassy in Madrid. For his own escape and the support he gave to other escapers, Capt Besley was awarded a Military MBE on his return to the UK

Major Besley (as he had by then become) was killed in action on February 14th 1942 during the battle for Hill 105 in Singapore. A married man, Major Besley was aged 34 at the time of his death. He is buried in Kranji War Cemetery.

BREWSTER, Private F. W. or Private H. O.

There were two Privates Brewster in the 1st Kensingtons. It is not possible to know which of the two Ray mentions. Brewster is not a particularly common name so they were perhaps brothers or cousins. Both Brewsters were taken prisoner at St Valery on June 12th 1940. Pte H. O. Brewster was held for some of the time in Stalag 20B at Marienburg in Poland. There is no record of where Pte F. W. Brewster was held.

BURR, Corporal George
Royal Corps of Signals

"Cpl Burr of the Signals", whom Ray meets at the British Embassy in Madrid, seems almost certain to have been Cpl George Burr. Cpl George Burr was reported missing sometime between May 10th 1940 and June 16th 1940. He was presumably either captured in northern

France at some point between those dates and later escaped, or slipped away to avoid capture following a defeat. Those dates could mean that he went missing at Dunkirk or, like Ray, at St Valery (or of course, in fighting at many other locations). In 1941 after his return to active service, Cpl Burr was awarded the Military Medal for gallantry under fire.

BUTLER, Company Sergeant Major J.

CSM Butler had been a pre-war, Territorial Army member of the Kensingtons. He was CSM to HQ Company when the Kensingtons joined the BEF. In December 1941 he transferred to another regiment.

COOMBS, Private Douglas John

Pte Coombs, a single man, from Hornsey in Middlesex, was among those captured at St Valery on June 12th 1940. He was held for some of the time at Stalag 20A at Thorn (Toruń) Podgorz in Poland. Pte Coombs died in captivity on March 16th 1945, just a few weeks before the end of the war in Europe. This date suggests he may perhaps have died on one of the infamous forced marches of PoWs described at the end of the book. He is buried at the Berlin War Cemetery.

de CLARY SCOTT, Pilot Officer Charles
Royal Air Force

Despite his unusual surname, it was not possible to find any information about Pilot Officer de Clary Scott on the military record (or about his wider family by online searching). In the text, Ray describes de Clary Scott as a French-Canadian but his (Ray's) notebook has an address for de Clary Scott in Salem, West Virginia, USA. Given the disparity in their ranks and the fact that Ray reports a strongly rooted dislike of de Clary Scott in the manuscript, it is both surprising and puzzling to find de Clary Scott's personal contact details in Ray's notebook.

DODGE, Major John Bigelow DSO DSC MC

Maj. Dodge (1894 – 1960), who was known generally as Johnny (sometimes spelled "Johnnie"), was Ray's OC (Officer Commanding) in D Company. He had a most unusual background for a British officer and must have seemed an exotic character to the men in his command. Maj. Dodge was an American, from a high society family. He had moved to Britain, aged 18, in 1912, when his American mother and English step-father decided to re-locate to his step-father's home country (his mother and natural father had divorced in 1903). Maj. Dodge's step-father, Lionel Guest, was a first cousin of Winston Churchill.

Maj. Dodge took British citizenship in 1915. He was a swashbuckling figure who had lived a colourful life even before the Second World War. A distinguished and decorated soldier in the First World War, he had fought at Gallipoli and on the Western Front. By the end of the war he had risen – at a very young age – to the rank of Acting Lieutenant Colonel with the Royal Sussex Regiment. During the early 1920s Maj. Dodge wandered widely in the Middle East, Asia and Russia, ostensibly looking for business opportunities but, according to his family and his biographer, probably also spying for the British intelligence services. He was jailed in Russia on more than one occasion. Later in the 1920s after his return to Britain, he became a stockbroker in London and stood twice (unsuccessfully) for parliament as the Conservative candidate in Mile End, East London. Maj. Dodge married in 1929, and he and his American wife Minerva, lived a gilded life between their house in London and their "cottage" at Ferring on the West Sussex coast. They had numerous wealthy and influential friends, including the Duke of Windsor and Wallis Simpson, who visited their London home on several occasions.

Maj. Dodge joined the Kensington Regiment at the beginning of the Second World War. During the "Phoney War" before the Kensingtons were posted to France, Maj. Dodge was selected as prospective Conservative candidate for Gillingham in Kent. He was captured at St Valery. Over the next five years he escaped from German captivity on no fewer than six occasions but was caught each time. As a result of his troublesome behaviour he was frequently moved between PoW camps. He was twice imprisoned at Stalag Luft III, where, in 1944, he became one of the organisers of what has become known as the "Great Escape". He was one of the 76 men who made it out through the tunnel but among the 70 who were recaptured. He was spared from being among the 50 executed.

Probably because of his personal connection with Churchill, Maj. Dodge was freed by the Germans in February 1945 after he agreed to act as a "peace envoy" carrying an offer of conditional surrender from the Germans military leadership to the British government. Because of the complicated political situation in Germany at that time however, arrangements were not made for Maj. Dodge actually to travel back to Britain until the end of April. By that time, the war in Europe was almost over anyway (Hitler's suicide was on April 30th), so Maj. Dodge's strange diplomatic mission was never needed and it is almost certain that he did not attempt to contact Winston Churchill. After the war, Maj. Dodge was awarded the Military Cross for his bravery as a PoW.[186]

FEATHERS, Private R.E.

Pte Feathers was taken prisoner at St Valery on June 12th 1940. He was held for some of the time at Stalag 344 at Lamsdorf in Poland.

FORD, Private Frederick Davis.

Pte Frederick ("Freddie") Ford was born in East London. He was married to Gladys and lived in Tottenham, North London. Pte Ford was the only other Kensington successfully to escape from German captivity during the Second World War. Like Ray, he was awarded a Commander-in-Chief's Certificate of Gallantry on his return to the UK. He was also Mentioned in Despatches. At some point after his 1940 escape, Pte Ford transferred from the 1st Battalion, Kensington Regiment to the 2nd Battalion. He was killed in action in June 1944 during the Battle of Normandy, at Tessel Wood near Caen in France. He was 25 years old. Pte Ford is buried at Tilly-sur-Seulles War Cemetery.

FORTUNE, Major-General Victor KBE CB DSO DL.
Black Watch (Royal Highlanders) / Seaforth Highlanders

Maj Gen. Fortune (1883 – 1949) was a career soldier who had joined the Black Watch in 1903. He had a distinguished First World War, rising from the rank of lieutenant in 1914 to Lieutenant Colonel and Commander of the 46th Brigade in 1918. He was appointed General Officer Commanding (GOC) of the 51st (Highland) Division in 1937. Maj Gen. Fortune was captured at St Valery on June 12th, 1940 and spent the rest of the war as a prisoner-of-war. He had a stroke while still in captivity in 1944 but declined the option of repatriation. He was knighted very soon after his return to Britain in 1945 "in recognition of valuable services in the interests of British Prisoners of War in Germany".

FRANCIS, Lance Corporal G.

LCpl Francis was taken prisoner at St Valery on June 12th 1940.

FROST, Platoon Sergeant Major Charles W.

PSM Frost had been a pre-war territorial member of the Kensingtons. Before the war he had worked in a department store in Kensington High Street. As Ray records, on May 5th 1940, PSM Frost became the first Kensington Regiment soldier to be killed in action in World War II. During the Kensingtons' time on the Saar Front his platoon came under enemy attack and he was shot by a sniper. He was 28 years old and only recently married.[187]

GARBETT, Sapper Jack R.
Royal Engineers

Ray met Sapper Jack "Blondie" Garbett at Fort Saint-Jean. Before his call up, Sapper Garbett, who was from Belvedere in Kent, had worked as a carpenter. Sapper Garbett, who was also captured at St Valery, had originally escaped from a PoW column in northern France with his friend Sapper J. E. Williams (see below). Sapper Garbett initially accompanied Ray and Jock in their escape from Fort Saint-Jean but illness forced him to turn back to Marseilles on the second day. Not long afterwards he made another escape attempt in company with two other soldiers. The men were captured by Spanish Civil Guards shortly after crossing the Pyrenees. After a spell in the prison at Figueres and the concentration camp at Miranda, Sapper Garbett and his comrades were given into the custody of the British Embassy in Madrid and were subsequently repatriated to the UK.

GAYLER, Private R. J.

Pte Gayler was taken prisoner at St Valery on June 12th 1940.

HAMMOND, Second Lieutenant R.

2/Lt. Hammond – "Ham" – was one of two platoon commanders in D Company. He had been a pre-war, Territorial Army member of the Kensingtons. He was taken prisoner at St Valery. The date given on his record for his capture is June 13th 1940, a day later than the majority of those Kensingtons taken prisoner at St Valery. He may have been among the numbers of men from all regiments who slipped away from the main part of the town during the chaos on the 11th and 12th of June and looked for means of escape further down the beach. The majority of these men were quickly rounded up by the Germans. 2/Lt. Hammond was among a group of 200 officers captured at St Valery (including five Kensingtons) who were initially sent to a "Strafe Lager" – a punishment camp – at Posen in Poland. The group was kept there for a year. Later, 2/Lt Hammond was moved to Oflag 8B at Eichstätt in Germany.

HARVEY, Lance Corporal Harry

LCpl Harvey came from Portsmouth. He was the son of Henry and Harriet Harvey and was married to Gladys. He was killed in an accident while serving with the Kensingtons in Italy in 1943. He was aged 31 when he died.

HUMPHRIES, Private A.

Pte Humphries was taken prisoner at St Valery on June 12th 1940. He was held for some of the time in Stalag 20B at Marienburg in Poland.

JEACOCK, Lance Sergeant A.

LSgt Jeacock was awarded the Territorial Efficiency Medal – for twelve years service – in 1946, so it is safe to assume that he was a member of the Kensington Regiment before the war. He was taken prisoner at St Valery on June 12th 1940. He was held for some of the time at Stalag 383 in Hohenfels, Germany.

JONES, Sergeant T.

Sgt Jones was reported wounded on June 26th 1940, This is a somewhat confusing date since it is after those Kensingtons who had been evacuated via Le Havre had returned to the UK. We know Sgt Jones must have been among this group since he is recorded as having returned to the UK after the fall of France. It is possible perhaps, that his wound was not officially recorded until he was in treatment back in Britain. In October 1943, during the Italian Campaign, Sgt Jones was wounded again. He survived the war.

KENT, Second Lieutenant G.

2/Lt Kent joined the Kensingtons from the Middlesex Regiment on May 9th 1940, as a replacement for PSM Frost (see above). He was later given command of 8 Platoon, B Company. 2/Lt Kent and 2/Lt Shanks, commanding officer of 9 Platoon, B Company, were both Mentioned in Despatches for their role in leading their platoons safely to evacuation from Cherbourg in June 1940.

KING, Lance Corporal W.

LCpl King was taken prisoner at St Valery on June 12th 1940. He was held for some of the time at Stalag 20A at Thorn (Toruń) Podgorz in Poland. Shortly after he was liberated from captivity LCpl King was recorded as a "casualty" but with no further details. This suggests perhaps that he was found to be in need of treatment for illness or injury at the time of his release, perhaps because he had been on one of the forced marches.

MILTON, Captain R. D.

Capt Milton, known as "Tubby" Milton to his men (but as "Tiny" Milton, to his brother officers according to the regimental history) was the 1st Battalion's Motor Transport Officer (MTO). This meant he had senior responsibility for the organisation and maintenance of the battalion's vehicles. Capt Milton had been an officer with the Kensingtons since before the war. At some point in the autumn of 1942 he transferred to the Royal Electrical and Mechanical Engineers (perhaps when the REME was first established in the October of that year).

MONAGHAN, Private Hugh
Gordon Highlanders

Born in Stevenston in Ayrshire, Hugh "Jock" Monaghan is one of the most important figures in Ray's story. He and Ray escaped together from Fort Saint-Jean, although they eventually parted ways in northern Spain. Jock also made it safely home.

MORRIS, Private H.

Private Morris was taken prisoner at St Valery on June 12th 1940. He was held for some of the time in Stalag 20B at Marienburg in Poland.

MULLENDER, Platoon Sergeant Major J. H.

PSM Mullender was in D company. He had been a pre-war, Territorial Army member of the Kensingtons. PSM Mullender was taken prisoner at St Valery on June 12th 1940. He was held for some of the time at Stalag 8B at Teschen in Poland.

MURKIN, Private D.P.

Pte Murkin was taken prisoner at St Valery on June 12th 1940. He was held for some of the time in Stalag 20B at Marienburg in Poland.

PAGAN, Lance Sergeant J. W.

LSgt Pagan was taken prisoner at St Valery on June 12th 1940. He was held for some of the time at Stalag 344 at Lamsdorf in Poland. LSgt Pagan was awarded the Long Service and Good Conduct Medal in 1937, so must have had at least fifteen years service before that date. He was presumably therefore a regular soldier.

PAGE, Lance Corporal L. J.

LCpl Page was taken prisoner at St Valery on June 12th 1940. He was held for some of the time at Stalag 344 at Lamsdorf in Poland.

PEARCE, Private Jim

Jim Pearce was one of two brothers who served with the 1st Kensingtons. Since both brothers had first names beginning with the letter "J", it is not possible to tell from the military record whether Jim was J. H. Pearce or J. J. Pearce. Both Pearce brothers were taken prisoner at St Valery on June 12th 1940. Both were held for some of the time at Stalag 20A, Thorn Podgorz in Poland. J. H. Pearce was also held for a period at Stalag 20B, Marienburg in Poland. Both Pearce brothers were pre-war Territorial Army members of the Kensington Regiment.

(NB: Pte Jim Pearce is not mentioned by Ray but is quoted in this book in consequence of his being interviewed by Sean Longden for his book "Dunkirk: The Men They Left Behind", published in 2008. Before the war, Jim was a porter in a block of flats in Maida Vale, London. He was a committed Christian throughout the war and for the rest of his life.)[188]

SALMON, Captain A. H.

Capt Salmon was second in command of D Company. He was taken prisoner at St Valery. Capt Salmon was held for some of the time at Oflag 9A/H (Spangenburg Castle) in Germany. Major-General Victor Fortune, Commander of the 51st Division was also held at this camp (see above).

SCOTT, Sergeant A. T.

Sgt Scott was taken prisoner at St Valery on June 12th 1940. He seems to have been repatriated in 1943. Under the Geneva Convention those prisoners eligible for repatriation were: members of the medical corps; chaplains; non-combatant troops such as labourers; those who were seriously ill; and those who were seriously wounded. Presumably Sgt Scott fell into one of the latter two categories. Repatriation was uncommon and for obvious reasons, difficult to negotiate and organise. Where it was arranged, it was generally for groups of men on an exchange basis.

STACEY, Company Sergeant Major F. J.
Middlesex Regiment

A regular soldier, CSM Stacey had been awarded the Long Service and Good Conduct Medal in 1938, so must have had at least fifteen years service before that date. He seems not to have seen active service during World War II, so may have remained on training duties on home soil throughout the conflict.

SUTTLE, Private John

John Suttle, nicknamed "Gus", was Ray's best pal in the Kensingtons. Gus's family home was in Kensington, so he seems likely to have been a territorial soldier with the Kensington Regiment before the regiment was embodied in 1939. Gus was taken prisoner at St Valery on June 12th 1940.

TOBIN, Sergeant M. E.

Sgt Tobin was awarded the Long Service and Good Conduct Medal in 1945, so must have had at least fifteen years army service before that date. He does not seem to have seen active service with the 1st Battalion in France but he is mentioned in the official history as having taken part in the Italian Campaign between 1943 and 1945.

WILLIAMS, Sapper J. E.
Royal Engineers

Ray met Sapper Williams at Fort Saint-Jean. Sapper Williams was a regular soldier and had had several years service before the war. He was from Shropshire. Sapper Williams had also been captured at St Valery and originally escaped from a PoW column in company of Sapper Jack Garbett (see above). Sometime after Ray's escape from Fort Saint-Jean, Sapper Williams also escaped, along with two other men. He crossed the Pyrenees on foot alone, having become separated from his companions because of illness. Once in Spain, he gave himself up to local police and was imprisoned at Figueres. He was eventually given into the custody of the British Embassy and repatriated.

WILLIAMSON, Captain Charles Kenneth

Capt Williamson had been a pre-war, Territorial Army member of the Kensingtons. He was a married man from Shepherd's Bush in west London. Capt Williamson was the senior officer of the First Line Reinforcements when the Kensingtons joined the BEF. He left the Kensingtons in October 1940 to join the Middlesex Regiment and was posted to Hong Kong. He was killed in action on Christmas Eve 1941 during the Battle of Hong Kong. (The Battle of Hong Kong followed the Japanese invasion of the colony on December 8th.)

WILLMOTT, Sergeant George Alfred

Sgt Willmott was born in Canada but lived in London. He was shot in the head on May 15th 1940, the day after the German Army launched its full scale attack on the Maginot Line. He died of his wound the following day. He is buried at Choloy War Cemetery.

Appendix 2: Letter from Jock to Ray, March 13th, 1941

3318831 Pte. H. Monaghan,
No. 12 Pln. "B" Coy.,
5/7th Bn. Gordon Highlanders
Hayton Park
Woodside
Aberdeen

13 - 3 - 41

Dear Ray,

I was very pleased to hear from you. I received a letter from Jack Garbett a few weeks ago. I am sending on his address. Well Ray, I received 14 days leave when I arrived in Aberdeen. Like you I have had £20 but I have more to come. I had my story in the paper here, but of course I did not mention Spain. A relative of my father's wrote to him and said my photo and story were in two American papers.

I see by your address that you are a Lance-Corporal. I was before the Company Commander and he told me he is putting me through for a stripe. It seems a dream since we left Marseilles to go to Spain. Do you remember when we rode in the "grape" cart talking to the Frenchman? Also the time we went into the vineyard for the grapes.

One thing I deeply regret Ray, was my impatience at times. Believe me, my friend, I was only trying for the best. I was always afraid we would be caught in the snowstorms in the Pyrenees. I know your feet were very bad and I feel rotten when I think of the times I grumbled at our slow speed. Never mind, we won through to "dear old Blighty".

Well Ray, it's nearly lights-out but before I go and put out the lights I want to add; if you are agreeable to tour the north to the south of France again, I would like to partner you. I have made plenty of friends in France and we could have a good time. Ask Garbett, perhaps he would agree.

Cheerio Ray and write soon.

Ever your pal,

"Jock"

P.S. How do you like the photo?

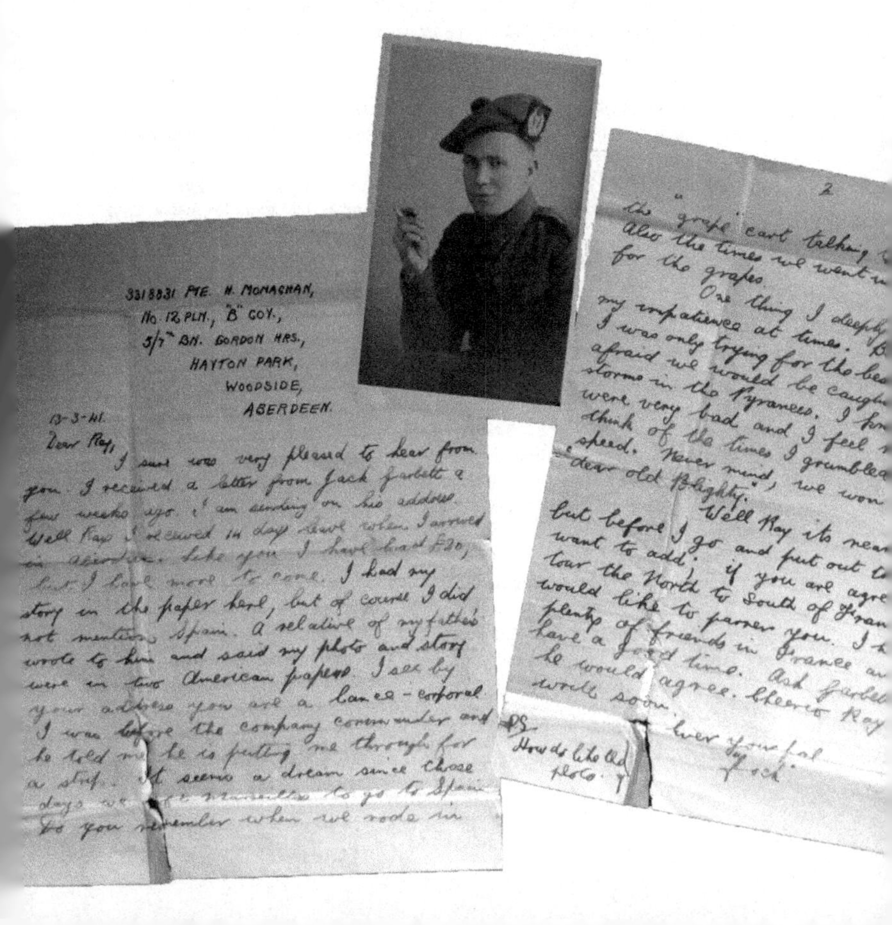
3318831 PTE. H. MONAGHAN,
No. 12 PLN., "B" COY.,
5/7th BN. GORDON HRS.,
HAYTON PARK,
WOODSIDE,
ABERDEEN.

13-3-41.

Dear Ray,

I sure was very pleased to hear from you. I received a letter from Jack Garbett a few weeks ago. I am sending on his address. Well Ray I received 14 days leave when I arrived in Aberdeen. Like you I have had £20, but I have more to come. I had my story in the paper here, but of course I did not mention Spain. A relative of my father's wrote to him and said my photo and story were in two American papers. I see by your address you are a lance-corporal. I was before the company commander and he told me he is putting me through for a stripe. It seems a dream since those days we left Marseilles to go to Spain. Do you remember when we rode in

2

the grape cart talking
Also the times we went
for the grapes.
One thing I deeply
my impatience at times.
I was only trying for the be
afraid we would be caught
storms in the Pyranees. I
were very bad and I feel
think of the times I grumbled
speed. Never mind, we won
"dear old Blighty".
Well Ray its near
but before I go and put out th
want to add; if you are agre
tour the North to South of Fran
would like to parner you. I
plenty of friends in France an
have a good time. Ask Garbet
he would agree. Cheerio Ray
write soon.
Ever your pal
"Jock"

PS. How do you like the photo?

Endnotes

Who was Ray Bailey?

1 Ray gives no information about his background in the memoir. This summary of his family history and pre-war employment has been pieced together from public records such as census data, and birth and marriage records. Information has also been drawn from reports of Ray's escape in wartime issues of the Vauxhall Motors in-house magazine, the *Vauxhall Mirror*, and in his local paper, the *Dunstable Borough Gazette*.

2 Estimates vary significantly. General Fortune, the senior British officer at St Valery, suggested in a signal to the War Office that 24,000 men were present, split roughly equally between French and British. Saul David gives 25,000 in Churchill's *Sacrifice of the Highland Division, France 1940* (London: Brassey's, 1994); Alistair Horne suggests 40,000 in *To Lose a Battle, France 1940* (London: Macmillan, 1969); and Martin Gilbert, 46,000 in *Second World War* (London: Phoenix Press; 2000).

3 The official regimental history of the Kensington Regiment in the Second World War notes that after the Fall of France and the return of the First Battalion to the UK, "7 officers and 267 other ranks were reported missing, most of whom were subsequently reported Prisoners of War".

Harpur B.V.M., Wood B.R., Evans J.J., Jacobson S. Cannon R. J., *The Kensingtons Second World War*. London: Regimental Old Comrades' Association; 1951.

Chapter 1: Becoming a Soldier

4 The date of Ray's journey to Mill Hill is assumed from a dated letter written home to his mum and dad the day after his arrival. His intial impressions were mixed: "It isn't too bad except for the food, which is vile".

5 Navy, Army and Air Force Institutes. An independent agency providing recreational and retail facilities to service personnel.

6 A company is a unit of around 150 men. For operational purposes, a company is often split into smaller units called platoons. Platoons vary in size but during the Second World War might typically consist of around thirty men

7 Bisley, near Woking in Surrey, is still the headquarters of the National Rifle Association and home of the National Shooting Centre. During the Second World War, Bisley's shooting ranges were turned over to the military. "Fire a course" is a standard term used in military and other specialist settings to mean weapons training with live fire, often involving formal assessment of participants' abilities.

8 The Old Diehards" (or "Die Hards") was the nickname of the Middlesex Regiment. The regiment traced its origins back to the 57th (West Middlesex) Regiment of Foot, established in 1755. In 1811, at the Battle of Albuera in Spain, during the Peninsular War, the 57th Foot fought heroically, almost to the last man. They were

driven on by their seriously wounded commanding officer, Colonel William Inglis, with the cry "Die hard 57th, die hard!" "Send away" in the lyrics means simply "send", i.e. send to fight.

9 "Blanco" was a cleaning compound which came in either powder or "cake" form and was standard British army issue. It was used to clean and refresh the colour of webbing (strong, flat, woven cotton used for uniform belts among other things). "Brasses" are buttons, badges and buckles.

10 The former shirt factory in Ilminster is still standing. It has been converted into an office building.

11 At around the same time as the men from the Middlesex Regiment arrived, soldiers from various other regiments also transferred into the Kensingtons. These men were from the King's Royal Rifle Corps, the York & Lancaster Regiment, the East Yorkshire Regiment, the Bedfordshire & Hertfordshire Regiment and the East Lancashire Regiment. At this early point in the war, soldiers aged under twenty were prohibited from service overseas. This influx of new men was necessary to double up for the large number of Kensingtons who were below that age.

12 Compulsory "gargle parade" had been introduced in the First World War and was still practised in some regiments. It involved each man gargling every morning with dilute disinfectant. The idea was to help prevent the spread of infectious diseases – especially diphtheria – among men living so closely together.

13 The word "fatigues" can refer either to a casual form of military uniform worn around the base, or to menial, non-military activities such as routine maintenance or cleaning, in which all soldiers are required to participate. Soldiers whose performance in drill or exercises was not up to scratch were often required to do additional fatigues as punishment.

14 It is clear that Ray does not regard himself as prime soldier material. This is an admirably honest piece of self-assessment and it seems that Ray' superiors agree with him. In particular, Ray's inclusion in the group of thirty men chosen for transfer to the Kensington Regiment looks suspiciously like a sign that his original regiment, the Middlesex, feels it would be no great loss to their fighting strength if he went elsewhere. This decision is also an early example of several twists of fate that eventually contrive to place Ray at the centre of his great adventure.

Chapter 2: To France

15 The Scottish infantry battalions were drawn from five regiments: the Seaforth Highlanders; the Queen's Own Cameron Highlanders; the Black Watch; the Gordon Highlanders; and the Argyll & Sutherland Highlanders.

16 Allcorn W., *The Maginot Line 1928 – 45*. Oxford: Osprey; 2003.

17 The group comprised one officer(2/Lt Kent) and 48 other ranks.
Gardner R., *Kensington to St Valery en Caux: Princess Louise's Kensington Regiment, France and England, Summer 1940*. Stroud: History Press; 2012.

18 Although he doesn't say so, Ray is presumably disappointed to be allocated to a reinforcement company which will be held back from the fighting. The fact that he was held back may be another indication that he is probably not regarded as a particularly accomplished soldier.

19 "Jankers" is British military slang for the official punishment for minor

misdemeanours. Jankers involved being restricted to barracks for a fixed period of up to fourteen days. During that period the soldier would be subject to frequent kit and uniform inspections, and repeatedly assigned to unpleasant work or other irksome tasks around the base (see earlier note on "fatigues").

20 The regimental history concurs with this, noting that "the population [of Ilminster] turned out in force" to say goodbye.

Harpur B.V.M., Wood B.R., Evans J.J., Jacobson S. Cannon R. J., *The Kensingtons Second World War*. London: Regimental Old Comrades' Association; 1951. p.19.

21 SS Amsterdam was later converted into a hospital ship. On August 7th 1944, on her way from France to England, she struck a mine and sank with the loss of 106 lives including crew members, patients, army medics and German prisoners of war captured in the Battle of Normandy. Sister Molly Evershed and Sister Dorothy Field, both nurses from Queen Alexandra's Imperial Military Nursing Service, who were working on the Amsterdam, made repeated returns below decks to save patients trapped on the sinking vessel. They helped the wounded men up to the deck and over the rails into the lifeboats. The ship when down while the two nurses were below decks and both women lost their lives. Sister Evershed and Sister Field were posthumously awarded the King's Commendation for Brave Conduct. Theirs are the only female names among over 22,000 men listed on the Battle of Normandy Memorial.

22 Maconochie's was a tinned soup or stew made by the company of the same name in Aberdeen. It was first issued to British troops in the Boer War, then again during the First World War and was still standard issue at the beginning of the Second World War. It was generally made of carrots, turnips and potatoes. By some accounts it also sometimes included scraps of meat. Maconochie's was made to be eaten either cold or hot (it was heated by boiling the tin in water for half an hour). As a foodstuff it was widely recognised as being of doubtful quality. It was said to be tolerable when hot (depending how hungry you were) but was considered inedible by many servicemen when served cold, as in this case.

23 "Tanner" is a slang word for sixpence (6d) i.e. six pre-decimal pennies, equivalent to 2½ pence in modern coinage.

24 Infantry units move and fight on foot. The 1st Kensingtons are a machine gun unit and as such, are "mechanised" i.e. they have a fleet of vehicles to move men and equipment from place to place. An infantry unit would therefore expect itself to be better at marching.

25 A "picket" is an informal guard, for example at the gate of camp.

26 "Pukka" is British military slang of colonial origin, from the Hindi word for "absolutely sure". The word has now entered everyday.language and is used to mean anything from the "the real thing" to the "very best" but Ray uses it here with its more specific military implication of "first class".

27 A formal salute in which the rifle is held vertically in front of the body and the soldier remains rigidly in position.

28 The term "flaming onions" was widely used in both World Wars to describe bright lights seen in the sky during bombing raids or aerial battles. There is however no consensus about what a "flaming onion" was. Candidates include flares, incendiary bombs, anti-aircraft fire and exploding aircraft. The term may have been used to describe any or all of these things.

29 By "the front" here, Ray means the Franco-Belgian border where almost the entire BEF was stationed. As mentioned in the introductory note to this chapter, he and his comrades in the First Line Reinforcements have no way of knowing at this point that the 1st Kensingtons have become part of the 51st (Highland) Division. Nor do they know that the 51st Division, including the main body of the 1st Kensingtons, has been redeployed from the Belgian border to the Saar region of France, on the Franco-German border.

30 Once it had become clear that the First Line Reinforcements were not headed for the Belgian border it must have been an absolute mystery to them where they were going. As mentioned in the introdutory note to this chapter, It is unlikely they would have been familiar with the ongoing small-scale fighting between the French and Germans in the Saar region. When the French railwayman tells them that they are bound for Metz, the largest city in that area, it seems probable most would not even know where that was, let alone why on earth they were being sent there.

Chapter 3: Action on the Maginot Line and a withdrawal

31 For example, Eric Linklater's account of the 51st Division in France records that on May 14th, "...in the Gordons' sector, the Germans fired 3,600 shells into a company front in half an hour" and the following day, another company of the Gordons was shelled for three hours. He also notes that on the 15th, the men in some of the furthest forward infantry positions were captured by the Germans. These kinds of attacks were beginning to happen all along the Saar Front and represented a major intensification of hostilities by the Germans.

Linklater E., *The Highland Division*. London: His Majesty's Stationery Office, 1942.

32 "Gimping up" is said to be a British military slang for dressing up smartly although that is not really how Ray uses the word here.

Partridge E., *A Dictionary of Slang and Unconventional English* (8th edition). Abingdon: Routledge; 1984 (first published, 1937).

33 Corruption of the French term, ligne de recueil, meaning roughly "handover line", or the place at which responsibility for operations is passed from one unit to another.

34 An order to "stand to" is an order to be in a state of readiness for action at any moment.

35 Note that Ray is not referring here to the large German town of Neunkirchen, which is in the Saar region but is situated more than thirty miles inside Germany. He is actually referring to the hamlet of Neunkirchen-lès-Bouzonville not much more than a mile away from the village of Colmen where Ray finds himself. Although Ray describes Neunkirchen as a "German village", it is actually (and was in 1940) situated immediately on the French side of the border. It was presumably in German hands during the incident that Ray describes here however.

36 A "loophole" is a small hole in a wall or other protective structure that allows just enough room for a weapon to be fired through it.

37 Ray does not mention – and maybe even several months later when he was writing the memoir, has not quite realised – the full significance of this "order

to withdraw" on May 15th. The order was for a general withdrawal of all French and British forces from the front line in the Saar region back to the safety of the Maginot Line fortifications. This was because the Germans had significantly stepped up their assault and the French commanders had realised that they would not be able to prevent German incursion into French territory. The French troops withdrew to the relative safety of the Maginot Line. The 51st Division mobilised for a return to northern France. A fuller explanation of these events is given in the introductory notes to the next chapter.

38 As it happens, the Kensington regimental history confirms that there was – briefly – a plan for the 51st Division to assist in the defence of Paris, An advance party from the division even set off for the capital to discuss the arrangements. They learned en route however that "...the defence of Paris by the division was cancelled". As usual the speculation among the rank and file about the Kensingtons' destination was otherwise incorrect.

Harpur B.V.M., Wood B.R., Evans J.J., Jacobson S. Cannon R. J., *The Kensingtons Second World War*. London: Regimental Old Comrades' Association; 1951 p. 27

Chapter 4: The Battle of Abbeville – and another withdrawal

39 The words of Captain Derek Lang (later, Lieutenant-General Sir Derek Lang), who was also captured at St Valery and subsequently wrote his own brilliant PoW escape memoir.

Lang D. *Return to St Valery*. London: Leo Cooper; 1974.

40 Gardner R., *Kensington to St Valery en Caux: Princess Louise's Kensington Regiment, France and England, Summer 1940*. Stroud: History Press; 2012.

41 Lang D., op. cit.

42 Angus Campbell cited in: Innes B., *St Valery: The Impossible Odds*. Edinburgh: Birlinn Limited; 2004. (Originally from Campbell's own book, Suathadh Ri Iomadh Rubha ["Touching On Many Points"], written in Gaelic and published by Gairm Publications of Glasgow in 1973).

43 Jim Charters was one of several 51st Division veterans interviewed by Sean Longden for his book *Dunkirk: The Men They Left Behind*.

Longden S. *Dunkirk: The Men They Left Behind*. London: Constable; 2008.

44 Shells (properly "mortar bombs") fired high into the air from guns on the ground and aimed to fall on close range targets.

45 A type of German aircraft, Stukas were dive-bombers designed to fly as low as 1500 feet (450 metres). They were equipped both to drop bombs and to fire machine guns (mounted under the wings) at targets on the ground.

46 The chocolate and cigarettes were a better find even than Ray thought. They have a part to play later in the story.

47 The Kensington Regiment's war diary supports Ray's observation of events and notes that D Company, "...undoubtedly helped lessen the severe casualties sustained [by the Camerons]".

48 This passing comment of Ray's seems perhaps to indicate that there was talk of evacuation from Dieppe. If that is the inference to be drawn, then that seems more likely to be rumour than fact. Dieppe was not a realistic option. Although not in

German hands at the time, there were significant concentrations of German forces between the 51st Division and the town.

49 See the introductory note to this chapter. HQ Company of the 1st Kensingtons along with "B" and "C" Companies had been allocated to Ark Force. Ark Force had been detached from the rest of the 51st Division and ordered south to protect the road to Le Havre.

Chapter 5: The fall of St Valery

50 General Fortune, in a signal to the War Office suggested 24,000, split roughly equally between French and British. Saul David gives 25,000 in Churchill's *Sacrifice of the Highland Division, France 1940* (London: Brassey's, 1994); Alistair Horne suggests 40,000 in *To Lose a Battle, France 1940* (London: Macmillan, 1969); and Martin Gilbert, 46,000 in *Second World War* (London: Phoenix Press; 2000).

51 From a letter written by Private Alexander McReady of the Black Watch (Royal Highlanders) quoted in: Linklater E., *The Highland Division*. London; His Majesty's Stationery Office, 1942.

52 Unpublished diary of Lieutenant Colonel H. R. Swinburn MC, Principal Staff Officer of the 51st Division, quoted in: David S., Churchill's *Sacrifice of the Highland Division, France 1940*. London: Brassey's, 1994.

53 Lang D. *Return to St Valery*. London: Leo Cooper; 1974.

54 Private Tom Copland, 1st Gordon Highlanders quoted in: David S., op cit.

55 McReady in Linklater, op cit.

56 Macdonald G., *A Cameron Can Never Yield*. Inverness: The Queen's Own Cameron Highlanders Regimental Association; 1999.

57 Lang, op cit.

58 Sergeant John Mackenzie, 2nd Seaforth Highlanders, quoted in: David S., op cit

59 Fred Coster, one of several 51st Division veterans interviewed for: Longden S. *Dunkirk: The Men They Left Behind*. London: Constable; 2008.

60 Gordon Barber in Longden S., ibid.

61 Official report of Admiral William James to the Admiralty June 13th, 1940.

62 Linklater, op cit.

63 Linklater, op cit.

64 Admiral William James, op cit.

65 Those evacuated from Veules St Roses included around fifteen men of the 1st Kensingtons. The majority of these were a number of members of D Company (thought to be thirteen) who had been deployed on the eastern side of St Valery and were perhaps simply nearer to Veules than St Valery at the time they were withdrawn. Another was an officer, Major de Chimay, who had been at St Valery earlier but had decided to try his luck elsewhere, making his own way along the beach to Veules. The final Kensington was Pte Walley who had lost his unit earlier in the fighting and had been travelling with an infantry battalion for the previous few days. It should also be noted that a small and intrepid number of the men trapped on the beach at St Valery managed to make their own way across the Channel in small boats they had commandeered. One particularly heroic group of seven soldiers included Pte Gratwood of the 1st Kensingtons. This group crossed

from St Valery to Ramsgate in two days and nights in a naval rowing boat. They had rowed six at a time in turn, with the seventh man resting. All the information in this end-note is summarised from the research of Gardner R.

Gardner R., *Kensington to St Valery en Caux: Princess Louise's Kensington Regiment, France and England, Summer 1940*. Stroud: History Press; 2012.

66 From a private letter written by Admiral James, one of a series of letters reflecting on wartime events published shortly after the war by James himself.
James, Admiral Sir William, *Portsmouth Letters*. London: Macmillan & Co.; 1946.

67 Linklater, op cit.

68 The story of one such group of evaders is told in: Moore W., *The Long Way Round*. London: Leo Cooper; 1986.

69 From the unpublished personal diary of Second Lieutenant Reginald Wood of A Company, 1st Battalion, Kensington Regiment, cited in Gardner.
Gardner, op cit.

70 The incident referred to by Ray in this jokey little aside crops up again towards the end of the memoir. Herne Hill, just outside Ilminster, is still a popular Somerset beauty spot.

71 As outlined in the introductory note to this chapter, the fighting to keep the Germans out of St Valery was desperate. Every single British and French soldier knew that if the Germans were able to enter the town in force before the expected evacuation, then all would be lost.

72 It is interesting to note that Ray was considering "escaping" before he had even been captured.

73 It is standard military practice, when defeat is inevitable and if circumstances allow, to damage equipment beyond repair. This is to prevent the enemy taking over the equipment and using it.

74 This was almost certainly incorrect information. It is believed that no vessels were able to reach the harbour at St Valery on June 11th (see introductory note to this chapter).

75 A Very light is a type of flare that is fired into the air from a pistol to provide temporary illumination over a wide area. In coloured form, Very lights can also be used for signalling purposes.

76 It is interesting that Ray writes that being at St Valery made him think of Dunkirk – but this may be a rhetorical touch. In his book, *Fo Sgail a Swastika: Under the Shadow of the Swastika* (Stornaway; Acair Ltd; 2000), Donald John Macdonald, formerly a private in the Cameron Highlanders and also captured at St Valery, observes that, "No-one [at St Valery] had any inkling or insight that most of the British army was already in England, having been evacuated at Dunkirk." This seems likely to be correct. The Dunkirk evacuation had only ended eight days before the 51st Division arrived at St Valery and there would have been no easy access to the latest news during that period.

77 Major General Sir Victor Morven Fortune KBE CB DSO DL was the Commander of the 51st Division, the man who had had to make the decision to surrender. Brief details of Maj Gen. Fortune's military career are given at the end of the book, in the list of soldiers named in Ray's memoir.

78 "Panzer" translates as "tank", so a "panzer division" is simply the equivalent of a British armoured division. The phrase is still used in that way in the modern

German army. However, during the Second World War the panzer divisions were the key to the tactic of "Blitzkrieg", which underpinned the overwhelming early successes of the German army. Panzer divisions had modern tanks, motorised infantry and a wide range of supporting weaponry. Their men were highly trained and they attacked with a speed and mobility previously unseen. Consequently, for British troops at the beginning of the war, the phrase "panzer division" came to carry fearsome connotations beyond its literal meaning – perhaps something like "crack troops".

79 Ray's understandable disgruntlement at the absence of the RAF from the skies over St Valery was shared by many others who were there. Similar complaints appear in other eye-witness accounts, not just of events at St Valery but also of events at Dunkirk. Pilots who had been shot down over northern France and forced to join the ground troops being evacuated reported being roundly abused on the beaches by soldiers who thought the RAF had not done enough to protect them (for examples see Patrick Bishop's book, *Fighter Boys*, published by Harper Collins in 2003). The explanation for the non-appearance of British planes at St Valery is given in the introductory note to this chapter

80 In his written report of the events at St Valery, Major A. A. De Chimay of the 1st Kensingtons, records that in the early morning of June 12th, "About 500 yards down the shore, we saw a small [presumably British] patrol boat about three miles out and Johnny Dodge decided to swim out to it. He had removed all his clothes and went out with a motor tyre inner tube ... In spite of lamp signals, the boat shortly altered course and obviously did not see Johnny Dodge. When I last saw him he was some 500 yards out and the tide was taking him to the west. I believe that being a good swimmer he eventually reached the coast somewhere west of St Valery." It should be noted that at the time of this exploit, Maj. Dodge was 46 years old.

Maj. A. A. De Chimay, cited in Gardner R., *Kensington to St Valery en Caux: Princess Louise's Kensington Regiment, France and England, Summer 1940*. Stroud: History Press; 2012.

81 According to his biography, on his return swim Maj. Dodge had to tread water for several hours waiting for the tide to turn. By the time he made it back to the beach the surrender had taken place. Maj. Dodge was still naked from his swim. A soldier threw a pair of trousers and a coat down to him from the cliffs but Maj. Dodge had no footwear. He decided to try and walk along the beach to Le Havre in the hope of rescue from there. In the night he bumped into a small group who had evaded capture at St Valery and were also hoping to make it to Le Havre. The group was however subsequently captured by Germans who discovered them hiding in a cave. The shingle had cut and bruised Maj. Dodge's bare feet so badly that he could barely walk, hence – presumably – his presence on the German truck where Ray saw him. The other men in the truck were likely also to have been wounded or possibly to have collapsed from fatigue on the march. There is more information about Maj. Dodge's extraordinary life in the list of "named soldiers" at the end of the book.

Carroll T., *The Dodger: The extraordinary story of Churchill's cousin and the Great Escape*. Edinburgh: Mainstream Publishing; 2012.

Chapter 6: "Gefangenenlager"

82 Estimates vary but Longden S. suggests this figure in his well researched book about British soldiers who missed out on evacuation.

Longden S. *Dunkirk: The Men They Left Behind*. London: Constable; 2008.

83 Two separate eye-witness accounts collected in Innes B, each suggest about a mile ("nearly one mile long" and "more than a mile long"). In his autobiographical account, Captain Derek Lang suggests four miles long. It is very likely that the column varied in length over the duration of the march anyway. From Ray's account it appears that sometimes other large groups of PoWs joined his column and sometimes the column was split up.

Innes B. *St Valery: The Impossible Odds*. Edinburgh: Birlinn Limited; 2004

Lang D. *Return to St Valery*. London: Leo Cooper; 1974.

84 Ray could not possibly have known this but just three weeks or so earlier, on May 27th, in one of the most infamous atrocities of the Second World War, soldiers of the SS Totenkopf ("Death's Head") Division had done precisely this. 99 men of the Royal Norfolk Regiment, captured during the retreat to Dunkirk, were lined up against a wall and machine gunned. Survivors of the initial assault were clubbed or bayoneted. Despite this, two men, privates William O'Callaghan and Albert Pooley, survived. Both were subsequently recaptured. Pte Pooley had been badly wounded and was repatriated. Pte O'Callaghan, who was also wounded but less seriously, spent the next five years in a PoW camp. In 1948, one of the German officers present at the killings was tried and found guilty of committing a war crime. He was executed.

85 Presumably malaria, which was not uncommon in British servicemen who had served in India, Africa or the Far East.

86 There was not a "revolution" but there had been intense and ill-tempered negotiations at the highest level of French government for several days. The Prime Minister, Paul Reynaud, wanted to find a way to fight on against the Germans (even if it meant organising that fight from French colonies in North Africa) . Others around him wanted to negotiate an armistice. Realising he was losing the argument, Reynaud resigned on June 15th. He was replaced by Philippe Pétain who promptly opened negotiations with Germany. An armistice was signed on June 22nd that gave Germany control over northern and western France, including Paris. Pétain and his government relocated to the city of Vichy. There, for the remainder of the war, the Pétain government administered the remaining 40% or so of France, essentially as a client state of Germany.

87 The Armistice between France and Germany was signed on June 22nd. Assuming Ray is correctly recalling where the PoW column was located when this news arrived, the column had travelled around 85 miles (140 kms) in 9 days or so. This is a much shorter average distance than the column was forced to cover later in the march. See the introductory note to this chapter for further information about distances.

88 It is suggested that around two million French soldiers were captured by the Germans between the invasion of May 10th and the armistice of June 22nd. This was an enormous number by any standards. From 1940 on there were almost constant negotiations between the Vichy Government of France and the German

authorities about the potential release of French PoWs. A number of different schemes for the repatriation of French prisoners were put in place as the war progressed. It is thought that these various arrangements allowed around one third of the original French prisoners to return to their homes before the end of the war. Around 120,000 French colonial soldiers from North Africa (largely from Algeria but also from Morocco and Tunisia) and French West Africa were among those captured in 1940. These prisoners were subject to harsher treatment in PoW camps than French nationals but nevertheless were also included in repatriation schemes.

Chapter 7: "La Citadelle"

89 A "fifth columnist" is one who has sympathy with the aims of an enemy and attempts to undermine the morale of his own side by subversive means.

90 The Siegfried Line (Westwall in German) was a 400 mile line of defensive fortifications inside the German border standing broadly parallel to the Maginot Line in France. It was effectively the Maginot Line in mirror image, built during the inter-war years to deter cross-border attacks by France.

91 This was not an isolated incident; other PoW memoirs also describe scraps of food being thrown to starving men for the "entertainment value".

92 This is presumably ersatz coffee. The German word "Ersatz" – literally "substitute" – has passed into English more generally to describe goods that pretend to be what they are not. This unpleasant-tasting ersatz coffee, made from roasted cereal grains or acorns, was obviously unforgettable – it crops up regularly in accounts of PoW life.

93 "Stormtroops" – in German, Sturmabteilung (abbreviated to SA), had originally risen to prominence in the 1930s as the paramilitary wing of the Nazi Party. By 1940 the organisation had begun to be assimilated into the regular German army and had lost the power and influence it once had. To some extent the role of the SA had been inherited by another paramilitary organisation, the Schutzstaffel (English: "Protection Squadron"), more familiarly known as the SS. The SS had also been absorbed into the regular army and SS troops were involved in the military action in northern France in 1940. The SS were known for being more reckless than the men of the regular army and were more likely to commit atrocities. It is possible that the soldier Ray describes having seen here is a member of the SS rather than the SA.

94 A similar incident in which armed guards attack local women handing out provisions to the passing PoWs is recounted in the official history of the Kensington Regiment in the Second World War: a young woman holding a baby among the civilians lining the road was attempting to hand a packet of cigarettes to a passing prisoner when "...she was seized by by two guards, thrown into the gutter, and the baby rolled screaming from her arms on to the cobbled road."

Harpur B.V.M., Wood B.R., Evans J.J., Jacobson S. Cannon R. J., *The Kensingtons Second World War.* London: Regimental Old Comrades' Association; 1951. p.19.

95 There are coalfields in the Pas-de-Calais, the area through which the column was passing at this time – so to see a miner was not unexpected. It must however, have been startling to hear that he was apparently British. Ray's comment does not give

much of a clue about what he thought might be the explanation. An ex-pat British miner seems unlikely but not impossible. Alternatively, a British escaper or evader in disguise? A military intelligence officer observing the treatment of the PoWs on the passing column?

96 Ray does not mention the location of his escape but in his de-briefing interview with MI9 after his return home, he reported that it happened near the small town of Wingles. Wingles is about 6 miles (10 kms) north of the city of Lens and 25 miles (40 kms) south of the Belgian border. It is about 12 miles (20 kms) from Béthune where Ray spent his last night in captivity.

The National Archives: Record no. WO 208/3300/115 (MI9 interview with Pte R. Bailey, 1940)

Chapter 8: Madame Benoit

97 Longden S. quotes wartime reports suggesting up to 5,000 British soldiers were in hiding in the Pas-de-Calais and western Belgium at this time although this does seem rather a high estimate.

Longden S. *Dunkirk: The Men They Left Behind*. London: Constable; 2008.

98 Website of the Imperial War Museum.

99 Aldershot was – and still is – a garrison town. The word is used here as shorthand for soldiers' bad language.

100 The Grimsby-based jam-making firm of Thomas Tickler was founded in the late 19th century. During the First World War, Tickler's held a supply contract with the British army and made the famous plum and apple jam, supplied in tins, that is ubiquitous in accounts of life in the trenches. There is almost nothing on the record about Tickler's supplying jam to the army in the Second World War. Presumably either they did still hold a contract – or perhaps, as these were the earliest months of the Second World War, the army was still supplying from old stock!

101 This was broadly correct of course – but it would be four long years before it happened.

Chapter 10: Adolf Hitler Bridge

102 He doesn't say so – but surely another reason for Ray's rage here is that Bedford lorries were built at the Vauxhall Works in Luton where he worked prior to being called up. It must have been galling indeed to see a vehicle that he might conceivably have helped to construct, dashing around the lanes of France painted up with swastikas. The lorry in question incidentally, was almost certainly formerly the property of the British Army. Huge numbers of British vehicles were left behind in France prior to the Dunkirk evacuation. Most were deliberately damaged by the British before they were abandoned but the Germans managed to put many of them back on the road.

103 In other words, at this point, Ray faces a straight choice between the two options for his journey. He can go straight to Tours, which will be a great deal quicker and – assuming Mme Benoit is correct about it being the easiest place to cross the border and that he can find his way easily enough – he will be in Vichy France a good deal sooner. Or he can make a significant detour to call on André and his family. There he could rest up for a while; take advice about how to travel to

the border and find out whether Tours is really the best place to attempt to cross. Undoubtedly also, he would receive practical help and moral support.

104 Small fighter planes were often "pegged" to the ground when not in use, to prevent them moving in windy weather.

Chapter 11: Vichy France via Cherbourg

105 Charles de Gaulle (1890 – 1970) was a distinguished soldier who had commanded troops in the Battle of France. In June 1940, he was appointed to a government post as Under-Secretary of State for National Defence and War with particular responsibility for liaison with Britain. De Gaulle opposed the armistice between France and Germany signed on June 22nd and with British support, was evacuated to London where he established the "Free France" government-in-exile and commanded the Free French Forces. De Gaulle remained the most important figure in French politics throughout the war.

106 Ray is referring here to the strip of German-occupied coastal territory that ran the entire length of France's Atlantic coast, all the way to the Spanish border. This strip had become German territory under the June armistice between Germany and France, and formed a kind of "extension" to the large area of northern France that Germany had occupied by force. Having possession of the Atlantic coast was of course vital to Hitler's military plans in terms of both Germany's projected future invasion of Britain and its need to defend against possible British attacks.

107 These must have been wine grapes, which have a thick skin, bitter tasting seeds and less sweet flesh than grapes grown for eating. Ray presumably did not know of this difference.

108 Reichswehr was a broad term meaning the German armed forces in general. By this time, the alternative term Wehrmacht was more commonly used.

Chapter 12: The "British" Consul

109 During the 1930s, Pierre Laval (1888 – 1945) had served twice as Prime Minister of France. After the armistice between France and Germany, Laval aligned himself with Philippe Pétain, Chief of State of the Vichy Regime. Under Pétain, Laval served in several senior positions. At the end of the war, he fled to Spain but was deported back to France. He was found guilty of collaboration with the enemy and on October 15th 1945, was executed by firing squad. Laval was one of eight prominent supporters of the Vichy government to be sentenced to death in the immediate post-war years but his execution was one of only three to be carried out.

110 Ray has been riding for some days along roads with an average elevation of 1500 – 1800 feet (around 450 – 550 metres). For comparison, this is rather higher than the highest point on the North Yorkshire Moors. It is not clear exactly where he is when he notes that he cycles past the highest point in the mountain range but we know he is between Ambert and Saint-Étienne. The mountain road between these two towns reaches a height of over 3,900 feet (almost 1,200 metres). 3,900 feet is higher than Mount Snowdon and close to the height of Ben Nevis. That would have been very tough going indeed on a hefty, 1940s, three-gear town bike.

111 In June 1940, when it became clear that France would fall, Italy had entered the war on the German side.

112 It was a condition of the armistice between Germany and France that any Allied soldiers discovered in Vichy France should be subject to arrest and detention by the French authorities.

113 Spain remained broadly "neutral" during the Second World War, although the Spanish dictator, General Franco, had ideological sympathies with Hitler and at times even considered actively joining the Axis powers. Additionally, Franco owed a debt to Germany – and to a lesser extent to Italy – for their material and political support during the Spanish Civil War. Consequently Spain adopted a hostile attitude to those small number of British escapers and evaders who made it to Spain after the fall of France. Any British soldier who became known to the authorities would be arrested and imprisoned. More detail about what happened to such men is given later in the book.

114 The Sûreté Nationale was, at this time, the criminal investigative branch of the French Police. Its role differed from that of the Gendarmerie, which focused broadly on law enforcement.

115 There is a description of Fort Saint-Jean and explanation of its role as an ad hoc internment camp for escaped British PoWs later in the book.

116 In his own autobiography, Rev. Donald Caskie had nothing but praise for the American consular official who had responsibility for the well-being and safety of British subjects in Marseille. Rev. Caskie names the official concerned as a Mr McFarlane and says of him that he was "kindly" and "generous"; a man for whom "nothing was too much to ask". Rev. Caskie adds that McFarlane carried out his responsibilities with "affectionate enthusiasm and a disregard for 'red tape'". Another escaped British PoW, Captain Charles Besley who also presented himself at the American Consulate at around this time, described meeting a British Officer, Major Dodds, who was acting as an "unofficial" British Vice-consul in Marseilles under the supervision of an official from the American Consulate (presumably Mr McFarlane). According to Cpt Besley, Major Dodds was officious, unhelpful and obstructive, and actively discouraged Cpt Besley from considering how to escape from Fort Saint-Jean. This is so remarkably similar to Ray's experience that it seems almost certain that Ray also met Major Dodds, rather than Mr Mcfarlane, especially as Ray doubts that the man he meets is American at all.

Caskie, Dr D. *The Tartan Pimpernel*. London: Oldbourne Book Company; 1957.

The National Archives: Record no. WO 373/60/491. (MI9 interview with Cpt C. Besley, 1940).

Chapter 13: Detective Inspector Gallibourne

117 Although swarms of locusts are not unknown in southern France, these insects are more likely to be cicadas (cigales in French), of which several species are common in the region and which often appear in very large numbers. Cicadas are traditionally considered by the local people to be bringers of good luck. This was unfortunately not so in Ray's case.

118 It is 105 miles (170 kilometres) from Marseilles to Monpellier and had taken Ray three days to cycle there (or nearly there). Given his state of exhaustion and

malnourishment and the other problems he had had to face, it must have been an huge ordeal. It is not surprising he felt such disappointment at having to give up – but his physical and psychological reserves in facing up to the journey back to Marseilles are to be marvelled at.

119 This inadvertent detour added around 12 miles (20 kilometres) to Ray's journey.

120 The German Armistice Commission (in German: Waffenstillstandskommission, abbreviated to WAKO) was, as Ray notes, the body charged with ensuring that the terms of the Franco-German armistice were observed in both occupied and unoccupied France. The Commission was formally established within the terms of agreement between the two governments with a brief to "regulate and supervise the carrying out of the armistice agreement". It was accountable to the German High Command and its headquarters were in Wiesbaden in Germany.

121 The "Sailors' Club" as Ray calls it was officially known as the British and American Seaman's Mission.

122 Reverend Donald Caskie (1902 – 1983) worked tirelessly to provide material comfort and emotional support to those British escapees who made it to Marseilles in 1940. For those who wished to try their luck in getting back to Britain he covertly supported what eventually became a well-organised, well-resourced escape network across the Pyrenees to Spain. There is more detailed biographical information about Rev. Caskie in the introductory note to the following chapter.

123 Ray gives no more information about Frank Humphries but cross-referencing information from Rev. Caskie's autobiography with shipping records from the period, strongly suggests that Frank had been aboard the Belgian/American merchant ship, *Ville de Namur*. The *Ville de Namur*, carrying livestock from New York to Liverpool via Bordeaux, was sunk by a German U-boat in the Bay of Biscay on June 19th, 1940. 54 of her crew of 79 survived. As a merchant seaman (as opposed to a military serviceman), Frank would have been able to stay long term at the Seaman's Mission if he wished, without having to submit to internment.

124 It was a requirement of the armistice agreement between France and Germany that Allied soldiers who were discovered in Vichy France should be arrested and detained. In practice, the French police, who were responsible for the enforcement of this agreement, seem – in Marseilles at least – to have taken as benign an approach to the rules as possible. Their idea seems to have been to persuade British escapers and evaders to accept internment on a quasi-voluntary basis. This included the freedom to come and go from the internment camp during certain hours of the day. This freedom operated on a "parole" system; that is to say on trust of good behaviour by the internees when they were at large in the city.

125 The historic main street in the old part of Marseilles near the Vieux Port.

126 After Italy's declaration of war on Britain and France on June 10th 1940, Italian aircraft launched a limited number of bombing raids on France. Attacks were made on Marseilles on the 17th and 21st-22nd of June, causing around 250 deaths. The state of war between Italy and France ended with the signing of an armistice on June 25th.

127 1924 adventure novel by P.C. Wren in which three British brothers enlist in the French Foreign Legion. Ray is most likely referring however, to the successful Hollywood movie based on the book. The movie starred Gary Cooper and had been released in the summer of 1939, just before the war began.

128 The French Foreign Legion (Légion étrangère) is a full-time, elite military force, originally established in the early 19th century, primarily to defend France's colonial interests. Although a branch of the French Army, the Foreign Legion is unique in that it recruits only foreign nationals. Despite its members coming from well over 100 different countries, the Foreign Legion is famous for fostering esprit de corps. Legionnaires swear allegiance not to France but to the Foreign Legion itself.

129 Traditionally, the French Foreign Legion has two mottoes. The first is expressed in Latin: Legio Patria Nostra ("The Legion is our homeland"). The second: Honneur et Fidélité ("Honour and Fidelity"), is expressed in French. This second motto differs in spirit from the motto of the regular French Army, Honneur et Patrie ("Honour and Fatherland").

Chapter 14: Life at Fort Saint-Jean

130 Fort Saint-Jean still stands. Since 2013, by the construction of a footbridge across the harbour, it has been incorporated into the Musée des Civilisations de l'Europe et de la Méditerranée.

131 The best way to understand the extraordinary wartime experience of Rev. Donald Caskie (later OBE), is to read his story in his own words. His autobiography, The Tartan Pimpernel, was published by Oldbourne in 1957.

132 The *Sidi-Bel-Abbès*, though built in Newcastle upon Tyne, was a French troopship. She was named after the Algerian city that was home to the training base of the French Foreign Legion. Later in the war, in 1943, the *Sidi-Bel-Abbès* was sunk by a U-boat while en route to Oran. 611 men, mostly Senegalese soldiers of the Free French Army, were lost in the attack, 520 more were saved by British escort ships.

133 The concentration camp, at Saint-Cyprien, was one of many such camps set up by the French Government in 1938 and 1939, to confine huge numbers of Spanish Republicans fleeing to France after their defeat in the Spanish Civil War (it is estimated that as many as half a million Spanish refugees may have crossed into France from northern Spain at this time). Most of these camps were sited close to the Franco-Spanish border. After the outbreak of the Second World War, the camps (which still housed enormous numbers of Spanish refugees) were used – often at the behest of the German authorities – to imprison many groups of "undesirable" foreigners. These groups included displaced Jews who had made their way to France from all over Europe; gypsies; communists and other anti-fascist activists; and very occasionally – as in this case – escaped British prisoners-of-war.

134 Île Ratonneau and Île d'If are two of a group of small islands situated just outside the Vieux Port at Marseilles. Both islands are fortified and formed part of the historic defences of the city.

135 Oran is an important port city on the north-west coast of Algeria about 125 miles (200 kilometres) from the Moroccan border. It is Algeria's second largest city after the capital, Algiers. Oran is 268 miles from Gibraltar by sea (431 kilometres / 233 nautical miles).

136 The regimental history reports that Freddie Ford escaped from the PoW column somewhere in the vicinity of Bethune. He got away from France by stealing a boat from Port Vendres, south of Perpignan, and sailing down the coast to Spain. His companion at Fort Saint-Jean and on the boat journey seems almost certain to

have been Pte William Miller of the East Surrey Regiment. Freddie and Ray were the only two PoWs from the Kensingtons to escape and make it back to Britain during the Second World War (but see endnotes to Chapter 5 for the story of Pte Gatwood's brave escape by boat from the beaches at St Valery).

Harpur B.V.M., Wood B.R., Evans J.J., Jacobson S. Cannon R. J., *The Kensingtons Second World War.* London: Regimental Old Comrades' Association; 1951.
WWII Escape and Evasion Information Exchange: www.conscript-heroes.com

137 After the signing of the armistice between France and Germany in June 1940, the British government was anxious that ships of the French fleet should not fall into the hands of the Germans and Italians. Around 40% of the French fleet, including the modern battle cruisers, *Dunkerque* and *Strasbourg*, was at the French military port of Mers el-Kabir just outside Oran in Algeria. During a tense and complex round of negotiations between British and French naval officials, France failed to give the British government the assurance it wanted that these ships would be placed beyond enemy reach (for example, by being sailed to neutral harbours in other parts of the world for the duration of the war). As a consequence, in a decision that remains one of the most controversial of the entire war, Churchill decided to order the destruction or disablement of the French ships at Mers el-Kabir. On July 3rd 1940, British Naval forces attacked the ships from the sea and air. The battleship *Bretagne* was sunk and five other French vessels were badly damaged. Almost 1300 French servicemen were killed. The incident caused great damage to Franco-British relations and ill-feeling towards the British lingered on among some sections of the French population for the rest of the war and beyond.

138 Almost unbelievably, it is possible to identify the two Scots protagonists in this story even though Ray himself does not mention their names. They were Gregor Macdonald and John McGlynn of the Cameron Highlanders. The experience is recounted by no less an authority than Gregor Macdonald himself in his book *A Cameron Can Never Yield* (The Queen's Own Cameron Highlanders Regimental Association, 1999). The story obviously passed into Marseilles-British folklore since Derek Lang, who was not in the city until sometime after Ray, also tells it in his book *Return to St Valery* (Leo Cooper, 1974). Lang had heard the tale at the Seaman's Mission from a third party. Derek Lang's version is consistent with Ray's; in both, the Germans cough up two francs. Interestingly in Macdonald's own account, the sum involved is a much more substantial twenty francs (ten francs plus a ten franc tip).

139 Earlier in this chapter Ray explained that some of the names he uses for his fellow internees are fictitious. This does not seem to apply to Charles de Clary Scott however (see "Named Soldiers" section for further details).

140 In the original manuscript, Ray names the port for which the General Chansey sailed as "Biferta", a place that seems not to exist. It is likely that he had misheard or misspelled the name of Bizerte, a port city in Tunisia, where there was an important French naval base.

Chapter 15: Joe Gugeleme – and a plan is made

141 During the Second World War, Scottish soldiers, particularly those serving with

Scottish regiments, were almost always nicknamed "Jock" by English soldiers. This nickname applied not only to individual Scotsmen but also to Scots collectively; a group of Scottish soldiers, even sometimes a entire Scottish regiment, might be referred to as "the Jocks". Jock Monaghan's real name was Hugh Monaghan. He served with the Gordon Highlanders. Like Ray, Jock had been captured at St Valery.

142 Ray's manuscript gives Jock's home town as "Stephenstone", a place name that does not seem to exist. It seems almost certain that he meant Stevenston, a small town on the Ayrshire coast, about thirty miles from Glasgow.

143 Interestingly, Sea Hawk, a 1940 Hollywood movie directed by Michael Curtiz, and starring Errol Flynn as the swashbuckling hero, was specifically conceived as a form of pro-British propaganda. It was intended to boost morale at home and rally support for a beleagured Britain among the American cinema audience. The film uses the Anglo-Spanish War (1585 – 1604) and specifically, the attempted attack on Britain by the Spanish Armada in 1588, as a broad parallel for the threat of Nazi invasion. The film includes a set piece speech by Queen Elizabeth I (Flora Robson) urging the defence of liberty against totalitarianism. It certainly seems to have had the desired effect on the audience of this Vichy cinema.

144 "Gugeleme" does not seem to be a known surname either in France or Corsica. This is however, the spelling that Ray uses on every occasion in the original manuscript that he writes Joe's name. It is possible that Ray is using a fictitious surname for Joe but that seems unlikely. He would surely have chosen an easily recognisable French surname rather than invent one from scratch. "Gugeleme" therefore looks like another misspelling of a foreign word by Ray. It seems a shame for the sake of Joe's place in the story but his correct surname must remain unknown.

145 It is just over 1,000 miles from Marseilles to Lisbon by the shortest route (approx 1700 kilometres).

146 This little notebook, around the size of a pocket diary, still exists. It was among the various odd items in the original auction lot.

147 Between Joe copying from the atlas, Ray copying from Joe's notes to the small notebook, and Ray copying first from the notebook to his draft manuscript and then again to the final manuscript, numerous spelling errors were made. Apart from the well known cities, practically all the place names in the route were misspelled. It took considerable time to sort it all out, especially as some of the way-marked places are small towns and villages – presumably chosen because Ray and Jock aimed to avoid main roads.

148 The border between France and Spain, and thus the necessity of traversing the Pyrenees, lies between Banyuls-sur-Mer and Portbou.

149 Unlikely as it sounds, this seems largely to have been true and was probably connected in some confused way with the "mad" plan to "pirate a full size steamship" to which Ray had referred a couple of paragraphs earlier. In his de-briefing interview with MI9 after his own escape and return to the UK, Cpt. Besley described an ambitious scheme to allow all the internees to get away from Fort Saint-Jean at the same time. He and another officer had been working secretly with the "Polish authorities" in Marseilles. It is not clear what these authorities were – perhaps a Catholic or Jewish relief agency of some kind? These authorities had

acquired a ship, the S.S. Storm, and were planning to evacuate 300 – 400 Poles from the city (again, it is not clear who these people were – perhaps refugees?). The organisers had agreed to smuggle up to 40 British PoWs in among the Poles, which would probably have meant all the men at Fort Saint-Jean. Unfortunately, despite prolonged negotiations, the ship was denied permission to sail by the port authorities and the plan had to be abandoned. If this audacious plan had worked out, it would surely have been one of the great British PoW escape stories of the war.

The National Archives: Record no. WO 373/60/491. (Cpt. C. Besley, de-briefing interview with MI9).

Chapter 16: The road to Perpignan

150 In mid-September 1940, Ramón Serrano Suñer, Minister of the Interior (and later Minister of Foreign Affairs) in the dictatorship government of General Franco, had visited Berlin to meet von Ribbentrop, the German Foreign Minister. Serrano Suñer's intention was to begin negotiating an agreement that would allow Spain to join the Axis Powers in the war. In the longer term however, the idea did not carry Franco's support and Spain remained – officially at least – a neutral country.

151 *Le Petit Marseillais* was a local daily newspaper of the period. It ceased publication in 1944.

152 As noted in the previous chapter, Ray used a small notebook to write down the planned route from Marseilles to Lisbon. During his and Jock's journey through the South of France and Spain, Ray also intermittently used the notebook to record their progress. The notebook was among the other miscellaneous items in the box containing the manuscripts originally bought at auction. The entries in the notebook are extremely brief – mostly just four or five lines for each one – but they are usually dated. Although Ray himself did not include these dates in writing his memoir, it seemed sensible to add them to the published version. All dates in this chapter and the next have therefore been inserted by the editor from that notebook.

153 In Vichy France at this time, alcohol sales in cafes and restaurants were prohibited on Tuesdays, Thursdays and Saturdays.

Chapter 17: "Frontier hoppers"

154 During the 1930s, the regular slogan of the Exide company which made batteries for cars and wireless sets, was that an Exide battery "still keeps going when the rest have stopped".

155 The few "farms" in this area are traditionally cultivated and maintained chestnut plantations in the forest. The timber from chestnut trees was used in the wine industry, both for making barrels and to supply stakes for use in vineyards.

156 Presumably Jock and Ray fear that the building may be a base for border guards.

157 At 4,174 feet (1,272 metres) the Puig de la Pourasse is roughly the same height as Ben Nevis. It lies only about five miles (eight kilometres) from Reynès as the crow flies but as we have seen, the journey is an arduous one involving climbs and descents – Ray and Jock will have covered many more than five miles to get there. In a straight line, it is less than a mile from the peak of Puig de la Pourasse to the

peak of Roc de France (Roc de Frausa in Catalan) but as Ray and Jock discovered, it is a challenging undertaking to get from the one to the other.

158 It is quite possible the elderly lady was speaking Spanish but in this region it was perhaps more likely Catalan.

159 The Roc de France is just over 4,750 feet (1,450 metres) high.

Chapter 18: The Spanish Eagle

160 As time went by and the number of refugees, displaced persons and escaped servicemen arriving in Spain increased, the Miranda camp was gradually expanded. It is believed that the Spanish authorites drew on German expertise for the construction of the camp's new buildings and the management of its inmates. By 1943 it is estimated that around 5,000 men of numerous nationalities were detained there.

161 Ryn, Z.J. (translated by Bałuk-Ulewiczowa, T.). "The concentration camp syndrome in Miranda de Ebro survivors (part 2)". Kraków: 2019;. Medical Review – Auschwitz. (Originally published in Polish as "KZ-syndrom u więźniów obozu koncentracyjnego Miranda de Ebro.", 1987.)

162 Undoubtedly this building was the isolated travellers' refuge and chapel, the Santuario de Nuestra Señora de las Salinas, situated at 3,500 feet (1,100 metres) in the foothills of the Pyrenees, a little way north of the village of Maçanet. The sanctuary was built in the 13th century. It is still in use.

163 Ramón Serrano Suñer, the Spanish Minister of the Interior had recently visited Berlin to discuss the possibility of Spain entering war as an ally of Germany. The idea had come to nothing, as Ray deduced. See endnote 150 for more detail on Suñer's mission to Berlin.

164 Here Ray is reflecting a widely held misconception of the period, that the Republican side in the Spanish Civil War was made up of communists and communist-sympathisers and that the Nationalists were proto-Fascists. In fact, both sides were coalitions representing a wide range of political affiliations – although the division was broadly between left and right.

165 The Falange Española Tradicionalista was the political party led by General Franco. It merged elements of fascism with other right wing ideologies and a belief in conservative, "traditional" Spanish values on social issues.

166 This is a particularly notable sentence in the context of Ray's original manuscript. It is the sole occasion in the entire text where Ray himself gives either a firm date for any particular event or a specific indication of the amount of time between two events. See the section "Editing the manuscript for publication" for information about how all the other dates have been added into the book.

167 Ray gives the name of the village as "Valemdetta" but no such place seems to exist. Vilamalla is the most likely possibility but the village might have also have been Valveralla. Both these villages lie between Figueres and Girona but along different routes.

Chapter 19: The road to Barcelona

168 To be "put where the dogs don't bite" is an archaic American expression meaning to be locked up. It's hard to imagine where Ray might have picked up such an

unusual phrase (from an American film possibly?) but it is another good example of his interest in words and language.

169 This is a sly reference to the policy of "appeasement" by Neville Chamberlain, UK Prime Minister between May 1937 and May 1940. In 1938 and 1939, Chamberlain had tried to avert the danger of major conflict in Europe, by accepting Hitler's demands for territory that he otherwise threatened to take by force.

170 The sudden appearance of the two things Ray needed most in the world – a stout pair of boots and fine umbrella – would indeed seem to have appeared, as he suggests, by divine intervention, as "gifts from heaven". He overlooks however, the rather inconvenient fact that he had just broken into a shed and stolen them.

Chapter 20: And so, home

171 This address is still present, written in pencil in Ray's notebook in this jovial, long-forgotten, Spanish policeman's handwriting.

172 Although Ray doesn't say so, it seems most likely that he disposed of his army-issue identity discs (his "dog tags") when he left the Benoits' house. He wouldn't have wanted his identity discs among his belongings in case he was ever searched. Their discovery would certainly have blown his cover as a *muet* Frenchman.

173 It is not entirely clear why Ray would have had to rush in through the embassy side gates if there had been police present. Perhaps the most likely explanation is that the Spanish police stationed at the embassy door would allow entry to the diplomatic staff but prevent access by anyone else, even if they were accompanied by a British official. Of course, once someone had slipped by the police and was on embassy premises they would be completely secure, so long as they did not leave again. It is hard to imagine what would be the feelings of an escaped PoW who had been on the road for weeks and suffered all kinds of dangers and privations, only to find himself apprehended by the Spanish authorities on the very doorstep of the British Embassy.

174 Conspicuous by its absence in Ray's account of his time at the embassy is any mention of a spot of bother that he got into while he was there and which is recorded in note form in his little notebook/diary of the time. It seems that he and one of the other privates fell out with the embassy's Military Attaché, one Lieutenant Colonel Drummond-Wolff. The details are not clear but it looks like the two young soldiers may have refused to undertake guard duty at the embassy on the grounds that they were not employed to do such a job. They were threatened by the Lieutentant Colonel with 28 days punishment on return to their units or even with being hauled before a court martial. What is interesting about this, is that despite his recent heroics, Ray does not seem to have become a more disciplined soldier.

175 In his debriefing after his return to the UK, Captain Charles Besley, who was also held at Figueres, reported that: "At Figueres, most of the British were in a small room where there was insufficient room to lie down. There was no sanitation and they were only allowed out twice during the day. I myself, with Cpl. Llewellyn-Jones and about 15 foreigners, were in a small alcove under the stairs, which was entirely open to the weather. We had nothing but the stone floor on which to sleep and no

blankets were supplied". He also described an incident in which two British sailors were savagely beaten by guards for an alleged escape attempt. The other British prisoners were held back at gunpoint while this happened. Despite the significant difficulties of Ray's own journey through Spain, he will surely have thought himself lucky to have avoided such experiences.

The National Archives: Record no. WO 373/60/491. (Cpt. C. Besley, de-briefing interview with MI9).

176 Spanish city on the Bay of Gibraltar.

177 MI9 (Section 9 of the British Directorate of Military Intelligence) was established in 1939 and remained in place throughout the Second World War. Its purpose was find ways of supporting escaped PoWs and military personnel – especially downed airmen – trying to evade capture in enemy territory. All PoWs who made it home were interviewed by MI9 so that lessons could be learned from their experiences.

178 Ray mentioned in Chapter 5 that he had skipped the lecture on what to do if taken prisoner of war, in order to take a girl for a walk in the countryside.

Afterword

179 Harpur B.V.M., Wood B.R., Evans J.J., Jacobson S. Cannon R. J., *The Kensingtons: Second World War*. London: Regimental Old Comrades' Association; 1951.

180 The National Archives. Record no. WO 169/10237 (War diary of the1st Battalion Princess Louise's Kensington Regiment July – December 1943).

181 The National Archives. Record no. WO 170/1407 (War diary of the1st Battalion Princess Louise's Kensington Regiment January – April 1944).

182 Harpur et al. Op cit.

Editing the manuscript

183 The website of the Imperial War Museum estimates that over the six years of the war, around 170,000 British and Commonwealth service personnel were held in PoW camps in Germany and German-occupied territory. Of those, around 1,200 escaped and made it home. In 1940, as one of the earliest escapers, Ray would have had no idea that the war would go on for so long or that over a thousand others would eventually repeat his feat. Of course, 1,200 is still only a tiny proportion (0.7%) of the total number captured. Every one of those escapes remains an achievement to be viewed with awe by those of us who will never be challenged to do the same.

184 Harpur B.V.M., Wood B.R., Evans J.J., Jacobson S. Cannon R. J., *The Kensingtons: Second World War*. London: Regimental Old Comrades' Association; 1951.

185 Gardner R., *Kensington to St Valery en Caux: Princess Louise's Kensington Regiment, France and England, Summer 1940*. Stroud: History Press; 2012.

Appendix 1: Soldiers named in Ray's memoir

186 Almost all of the information in this pen picture of Johnny Dodge comes from the biography of him published in 2012.

Carroll T., *The Dodger: The extraordinary story of Churchill's cousin and the*

Great Escape. Edinburgh: Mainstream Publishing; 2012.

187 The personal information about PSM Frost is drawn from the biographical note in Gardner R.

Gardner R., *Kensington to St Valery en Caux: Princess Louise's Kensington Regiment, France and England, Summer 1940*. Stroud: History Press; 2012.

188 The personal information about Pte Jim Pearce is drawn from the biographical note in Longden S.

Longden S. *Dunkirk: The Men They Left Behind*. London: Constable; 2008.

Acknowledgements

My thanks to my publisher Tartaruga Books. I am also enormously grateful to my old friend Jim Pollard without whose experience, guidance and professional expertise this book would not exist.

I acknowledge the assistance kindly given to me by Chris and Barbara Ayres. Their family history research supplied me with information about Raymond Bailey that I would certainly not have otherwise discovered. Chris and Barbara put me in touch with Raymond's closest living relative, Pamela Roy, who I particularly thank for talking to me about Raymond's family background.

I thank Sue Forber, Charlie Wilkins and Nina Möller for their long-time support for the idea of this book and for encouraging me to see the project through to the end. I thank all three also for their excellent proof-reading of the final drafts. Any errors that remain in the book are entirely mine.

Photo Credits

Cover Image	Imperial War Museum; RML 399
Title page	Photo by Harry Bailey. By family permission.
Page 9	David Wilkins
Page 15	War Archive/Alamy Stock Photo
Page 23	War Archive/Alamy Stock Photo
Page 83	*Sueddeutsche Zeitung* Photo/Alamy Stock Photo
Page 113	*Sueddeutsche Zeitung* Photo/Alamy Stock Photo
Page 223	*Sueddeutsche Zeitung* Photo/Alamy Stock Photo
Page 255	Unknown
Page 263	David Wilkins
Page 287	David Wilkins
Page 301	David Wilkins
Page 326	David Wilkins

About the editor

David Wilkins spent most of his working life in the charitable and public sectors. His work largely involved research and policy development in relation to social issues such as poverty, poor housing and public health. He also taught community work and health promotion at university. David retired from full-time work in 2015. He lives on the Isle of Portland in Dorset.

David has collected old diaries, manuscripts, letters, photo albums and other similar items for decades. He buys them wherever he finds them. Some of his most interesting discoveries are now in public collections. Old diaries and other personal accounts are often a particularly rich source of observation of their times. "Such sources can give us a tangible sense of their historical period," says David. "They connect us directly to other lives and other experiences."

Among David's ambitions for his retirement was to bring some of the personal stories he has discovered into the public domain. David's many years of research experience and of writing for publication in his professional life have proved invaluable in organising Raymond Bailey's original handwritten memoir into *Blighty or Bust*. David has set Raymond's thoroughly gripping and highly readable true story into its proper historical context.

Blighty or Bust is David's second such project. His first book, also based on a found memoir, *Schoolboy, Servant, GWR Apprentice*, was published in 2017 by the History Press.

looked from one side of the card to the other and I rembered the ink was just a slightly different colour on one side than the other. I wondered if he rumbled it but he didn't, my friends at Acheville had done their work well.

He looked at the photograph and then at me and without saying a word returned it and waved me to go. I did not need a second telling I had had my foot on a raised pedal for the past five minuits. I was off! I had outwitted the Riechwehr.

Two hundred yards or so further round the bend I arrived at the Vichy side of the demarcation line. Being slightly more advanced than the Germans they had gone to the trouble of erecting a small hut and throwing a barrier across the road.

A solitary French soldier was on duty,